T0322313

STRANGELAND

Also by Jon Sopel

*UnPresidented: Politics, pandemics and the race
that Trumped all others*

A Year at the Circus: Inside Trump's White House

*If Only They Didn't Speak English:
Notes from Trump's America*

Tony Blair – The Moderniser

STRANGELAND

HOW BRITAIN STOPPED MAKING SENSE

JON SOPEL

EBURY
PRESS

1

Ebury Press, an imprint of Ebury Publishing
One Embassy Gardens, 8 Viaduct Gdns,
Nine Elms, London SW11 7BW

Ebury Press is part of the Penguin Random House group of companies
whose addresses can be found at global.penguinrandomhouse.com

Penguin
Random House
UK

First published by Ebury Press in 2024
www.penguin.co.uk

A CIP catalogue record for this book is available from the British Library

ISBN 9781529938401

Printed and bound in Great Britain by Clays Ltd, Elcograf S.p.A.
The authorised representative in the EEA is Penguin Random House Ireland,
Morrison Chambers, 32 Nassau Street, Dublin D02 YH68.

Penguin Random House is committed to a sustainable future for our
business, our readers and our planet. This book is made from
Forest Stewardship Council® certified paper.

MIX
Paper | Supporting
responsible forestry
FSC
www.fsc.org   FSC® C018179

To Eliza and Jack Sopel

Two bundles of pure joy – annoyingly 10,000 miles away

CONTENTS

INTRODUCTION

As a visual metaphor for the Britain I came back to at the beginning of 2022 after eight years away, it was pretty perfect. Arguably the country's most famous landmark – which has graced a zillion postcards and features in any movie where scenes are filmed in London – was swaddled in plastic, held together by a complex lattice of scaffolding, with the clock at the top of the Elizabeth Tower unable to bong. Unable to lure Dick Whittington back. Big Ben, the Palace of Westminster's iconic timepiece, which ensured Parliament knew when to start business and told us when debates would end and votes begin, was out of action, the tower in danger of crumbling into the River Thames below.

This was a Britain that while I had been away had charted a new political and economic course for itself with the referendum to leave the European Union. At a time of rising economic protectionism, Britain voted to leave the biggest single market in the world – an act of self-harm that bewilders policymakers around the world, particularly in America, but which won the support of 52 per cent of British voters after a bitterly fought campaign.

Though the vote to leave the EU was six years earlier, 2022 would turn out to be the year when the political aftershocks of that decision would bring down the structures made unsteady by that June 2016 earthquake referendum – and it seemed to collapse in a pile of dusty masonry, twisted metal and broken glass. The sturdy political pillars of the UK would go through a rolling, rumbling, sometimes comedic convulsion. It would be the year of three prime ministers, four chancellors, a home secretary who lasted six days (six times longer than the education secretary who was there for just one). At the height of this absurd spectacle, another convulsion shook us to the core, when Queen Elizabeth II died, having served the nation with duty, dignity and discretion for 70 years. An audience with the new prime minister, Liz Truss, one day; gone 48 hours later.

With her death it felt that some other cherished bits of what it means to be British had seemingly gone as well. It just all started to feel a bit unrecognisable. Yes, Gary and *Match of the Day* were still there in the Saturday-night schedules and *Antiques Roadshow* was reassuringly still part of Sunday evening. The Royal Standard would in a seamless transfer of power fly again over Buckingham Palace, but down the road at the Palace of Westminster everything had stopped working – and Big Ben was its visual symbol. But this book is not about the fabric of Britain.

If it was, I might have a few things to say. It's probably best not to get me started, but we have gone from being a nation that was the first to industrialise, to pioneer the railways, electricity, the telephone and so much more, to a country whose infrastructure is falling to bits. Just look at the high-speed rail line that looks like it is never going to be completed. The billions and billions spent with compulsory purchases of homes and land; the noble desire that economic regeneration of the North West and North East would be high-speed lines running from Manchester and Leeds, meeting in Birmingham and then going into London. When the Sunak government pulled the plug on the project it looked as though it was going to go no further north than the West Midlands – and wouldn't actually make it all the way into London. The most expensive white elephant ever.

We've got more discussion about a bypass round or a tunnel underneath Stonehenge – I remember covering stories about that when I first went to work at BBC Radio Solent, 40 years ago. Best not to rush these things. Our shiny new multi-billion-pound aircraft carriers seem to break down every time they leave port, and are unable to take part in military exercises, while the army's latest drones apparently only work in good weather. Heathrow is still waiting for its Godot-like third runway. Hammersmith Bridge in London is closed five years after a temporary two-week shutdown for repairs – which have never happened. And whatever you do, don't fall into the River Thames below, because the levels of E. coli in the water are dangerously high from the privatised water companies pumping sewage into our rivers and seas. The effluent society.

We've become a nation where ambulances queue to offload patients at A & E, and where it's estimated 250 people each week are needlessly dying because of the long waits to be seen by an emergency doctor. It's become a country where schools had to close at the start of term because of the discovery that the cheap concrete used in construction years earlier was likely to bring ceilings down, but where the education secretary can't get back from abroad to deal with the crisis because the whole of the UK's air-traffic-control system has gone offline.

This book is, I suppose, about Britishness – the values that have guided us, the behaviour we have come to expect of our politicians, the way we do things, the way we conduct ourselves in this country – and it is written from the perspective of someone who has been out of the country for a few years and can't quite recognise what he has come back to. When I moved to the US in 2014, the coalition government had been going for four years, a bold and progressive move after the inconclusive 2010 election. The first time we had seen a proper coalition government since the wartime administration. Britain was still in its post-2012 London Olympics glow. Labour was trying to mount a fightback under Ed Miliband. David Cameron as prime minister and Nick Clegg his Liberal Democrat deputy had found a way to successfully share power and work together. Parts of it were technocratic, even if it was underpinned by the economics of Thatcherism where that chill word 'austerity' would assume ever more importance. In the US, where Barack Obama was midway through his second term, it seemed that dynastic politics was about to return with the election in 2016 looking like it was going to pit another member of the Bush family against another Clinton.

By 2022, all that had changed. The Boris Johnson government, in its determination to get Brexit done, was shaking the foundations of Westminster, riding roughshod over parliamentary rules and traditions (though he is not to be held responsible for Big Ben losing its voice). The rules his government introduced to cope with the unprecedented coronavirus pandemic were being dutifully obeyed everywhere around the country, except in Downing Street, where aides would go to Tesco to load up a wheeled suitcase with booze and then go back and party. When this all came to light, the prime minister dissembled – and the bonds of trust between the governing and the governed (never that strong at the best of times) frayed worryingly. The British sensibility to laugh at ourselves and roll our eyes became something different. There was anger; we suddenly became proponents of all manner of conspiracy theories. Identity politics turned poisonous. It felt as though we had seen the worst of what American politics and society could serve up and were saying, 'I'll have a double portion of that, please.'

And what a poisonous concoction America had produced. The Washington I left felt somehow powerless to cope with the bitter divisions that were tearing the country to pieces – and, yes, threatening to undermine US democracy itself. Being in the capital on 6 January 2021 when insurrectionists tried – and for a few hours succeeded – to stop the peaceful transfer of power to Joe Biden was shocking beyond belief. The Trump-supporting mob at Congress was seeking to stop the certification of his victory by any means, encouraged by the man still clinging on by his fingernails to power in the White House, who was unable to accept his defeat. It felt for a while that America was about to go through its second revolution: the first in 1776 to get rid of the British monarchy; the second in 2021 to get rid of democracy.

• • •

My posting to Washington as North America editor was my second stint as a foreign correspondent. I had spent four years living in Paris around the turn of the millennium, meaning that around a third of my BBC career had been spent abroad. Probably longer if you count all the trips that were just for a few days or weeks. The four years I spent in Paris from 1999 to 2003 were truly momentous. Yes, it was an interesting time in terms of Anglo-French relations. An aloof Jacques Chirac dealing with the ever-confident and, you felt, slightly grating Tony Blair. It was interesting for what was changing in France, and maybe a harbinger of other events to come. Namely the rise of the far right and the start of populism in Europe. In the 2002 French presidential election, something unthinkable happened. It wasn't a second round decided between the centre right and centre left, as it had always been in the history of the Fifth Republic. The far-right Front National led by Jean-Marie Le Pen beat the socialist standard bearer, the prime minister Lionel Jospin, leading to the 2002 election coming down to a contest of right versus far right. A far right which today is even more powerful. There were big domestic stories like the crash of Concorde as it took off from Charles de Gaulle airport. France proposed a ban on the import of British lamb following the outbreak of foot-and-mouth disease, which itself followed hot on the heels of our other unwanted agricultural export, mad cow disease.

But that is the normal bill of fare for a foreign correspondent: political upheaval, natural and unnatural disasters, the chafing of international relations. What shook the world profoundly when I was in Paris was 9/11 and the geopolitical jolt that it gave. That day I had been in Lille covering a court case to close the Sangatte refugee centre and stop the flow of illegal immigrants across the Channel (*plus ça change*), which was the lead item on *BBC News at One O'Clock*. I was to drive to Calais where I was to be the lead item on the *BBC News at Six O'Clock*. As we drove north, our producer in Paris rang, telling us to pull over at the nearest service station as something was unfolding in New York. At some French service station on the A25, we watched as the second plane flew into the Twin

Towers. Ours was the only other story on the news that evening, now coming right at the end of the bulletin. We continued on to Calais and edited our piece in a hotel, our eyes transfixed by the events in lower Manhattan.

In November of that year, I found myself packing my bags and body armour to fly from Paris to Delhi, from there to Dushanbe in Tajikistan, and then – after a complex journey involving bribes to a Russian general to cross a DMZ – into northern Afghanistan to move with the US- and UK-backed Northern Alliance on a front line as they sought to dislodge the Taliban from their rule. Then in early 2003, I would find myself heading to the Iraqi border as, once again, US forces, backed by British armour, were now trying to dislodge Saddam Hussein in what would become known as the 'war on terror'.

That summer, I moved back to the UK. But despite these seismic upheavals – the huge marches against Britain's involvement in Iraq, the dent to Tony Blair's seeming invincibility – the country felt much the same as when I had left. Blair was still prime minister, and he would go on to win another clear majority in the 2005 general election. Leaving Iraq to one side – and if you are one of those who believe Blair should have been put on trial at The Hague for war crimes for his involvement, I know that is a big ask – the country seemed to be humming along nicely. The most successful Labour prime minister in British history was doing what he'd promised and seemed to be delivering on his pledges. Perhaps the true impact on the political landscape was not the Conservative opposition to him, but the growing sense among a new breed of Tory politicians that they had to emulate what 'New Labour' had done. The much vaunted if rather elusive 'Third Way' seemed to be redefining politics, just as Margaret Thatcher had in the 1980s.

Ten years later, I was a foreign correspondent again. In 2014 I moved to an America that on the surface at least I thought I knew well. I had travelled to Washington on innumerable journeys, holidayed there – I'd ridden a Harley down the West Coast, for goodness' sake. But my sense of its geography still came largely from the music I grew up with. The Beach Boys, West Coast; Lou Reed and the Velvet Underground, New York; the Detroit of Motown and the Philadelphia sound of Harold Melvin & the Blue Notes. And even if I had only been to a tiny fraction of the places of Johnny Cash's 'I've Been Everywhere', I had a sense of this vast continent.

But when I actually turned the key on the sturdy, federal-style townhouse I would call home for the next eight years, I realised I didn't know America at all. It was a foreign country to me. Yes, I could make myself understood. There were no language barriers. But what I thought was merely an accent change by crossing the Atlantic – swapping a plum stuck in the mouth for a sometimes lazy drawl – I would soon discover was something much more profound. I tried to chronicle just how foreign a country it is in my first book on the US, *If Only They Didn't Speak English*.

Then, at the beginning of 2022, I returned to the UK – back to the city where I had grown up, London. The great thing about immersing yourself in the affairs of another country is not just that you are learning something new, but that it gives you fresh perspective on where you grew up. You have reference points. And Britain didn't feel like the country I left. Overwhelmingly, I was delighted to be back. Yes, I would miss the ludicrous buzz of being close to the testosterone-rich (well, maybe a bit less under Biden) power that Washington, DC, specialises in. And the job at its best – travelling on *Air Force One*, being part of a presidential motorcade, sitting and interviewing a serving president in the White House – takes some beating. But Washington is in essence a small, provincial city which just happens to be the epicentre of global power.

There is nothing provincial about London. It is noisy, exciting, diverse, varied, beautiful, gritty. Unlike Washington, however, it is no longer the epicentre of global power – though many act as though it still is. We are a country where the nations that make up its constituent parts are asking whether it really is that great to be part of the UK. And the centre of a sprawling Commonwealth whose members are re-evaluating its worth and asking tough questions about the legacy of empire.

So, what is the Britain I have come home to? In the US I was the outsider looking in – the time-honoured job of the foreign correspondent – with all the advantages and shortcomings that brings. This is the book of an insider who's been out but come back in. The return of a native, if you like. Returning to the UK in some ways has been disconcerting – or maybe discombobulating would be a better word. It is, after all, my home; it is where I grew up, a country I love and am proud of. But either it's changed, or I have. Maybe both.

It just feels like a strange land.

PART 1

CHAPTER 1

ANYTHING IS POSSIBLE (2016)

2016 was a decisive year in so many ways – and there are two obvious dates to symbolise this extraordinary 12 months. On 23 June, Britain voted to sever its 50-year-long marriage (which was rarely golden) with Europe in favour of 'taking back control'. And then in November, Donald Trump became America's 45th president.

But let's start with a third momentous date: 2 May.

That was the day Leicester City – *Leicester City*, for goodness' sake – won the English Premier League title; it was also the day when the Ohio governor, John Kasich, pulled out of the race for the Republican Party nomination – which meant that the property tycoon and US *Apprentice* host, Donald Trump, was, incredibly, the last man standing. A man who had never held any elective office, who had never served in the US armed forces –

some very convenient bone spurs greatly assisting his swerve of the draft – was the presumptive nominee for the GOP. The party of Lincoln, Eisenhower and Reagan was on its way to becoming the party of Trump.

I was doing a pre-recorded two-way for the *Today* programme that day, and Sarah Montague was the presenter in London. There was a slightly incredulous tone to her voice when she asked me, 'But surely Donald Trump won't become the next president?' I replied that Leicester City were 2,000–1 outsiders at the start of the season as they competed with 19 other teams for the league title; Donald Trump would now be in a straight head-to-head race with Hillary Clinton. Of course he could win, I said.

This turned out to be the year when anything could happen anywhere, and it invariably did. Over decades of reporting on politics, I had watched on numerous occasions when shiny insurgents would threaten to upend the fusty, established order with their new broom, and the alluring promise of sweeping away decades of failure. The excitement would mount – and then you would watch the British or American public go up to the edge, peer over the clifftop to the rocks and storm-tossed seas below, and sensibly take a few steps back – and politics would carry on in its conventional way.

Small, almost imperceptible political shifts were what we did, particularly on this side of the Atlantic. Who can forget the then Liberal Party leader David Steel's puffed-up, hubristic call in Llandudno in 1981 to 'go back to your constituencies and prepare for government'. This had come after some long-for-gotten Liberal by-election and local council wins. Labour was at war with itself and the Tories were at the height of their unpopularity with unemployment about to hit three million. The mould of British politics was being broken before our eyes; the two-party system would be confined to the non-recyclable wheelie-bin of history; Britain was about to realise its democratic potential. And then reality. Two years later Margaret Thatcher won the Conservatives a second term with – checks his notes – a majority of 144.

But in 2016, huge swathes of people walked up to the edge, clasped hands with the person next to them, closed their eyes and jumped. There had never been a year of so many Thelmas and Louises. Why? What had happened? And were the forces that drove this the same on both sides of the Atlantic?

The overlaps are obvious: many of those who had championed Brexit were big supporters of Trump, and vice versa. My abiding memory of the Republican Convention in 2016 in Cleveland, where Trump was crowned king, was walking outside the convention centre to see a circle of men and clouds of smoke rising. It's something you just don't see in the US. It was a knot of men, the 'bad boys' of Brexit, all puffing furiously on their cigarettes: Nigel Farage, Arron Banks and Andy Wigmore. And in so far as Trump supporters paid much attention to British politics, they would have probably approved of the forces driving Britain to leave the European Union.

Just after Trump won the Republican nomination that
year, he flew to the UK. Not unusual in itself: a swing through
the countries of key allies to show your seriousness about the
major foreign policy issues and geopolitical dilemmas is what
serious candidates do – Obama at the Brandenburg Gate, any
number of presidential candidates paying a courtesy visit to
the prime minister of the day in Downing Street – it's perfectly
normal. But Trump was less concerned about the globe than the
golf ball. He came to Scotland to visit two of his golf courses.
That was it.

But the day he came to the UK was significant. It was the
day after the Brexit vote, and I accompanied him on this trip. I
had been interviewing the former EU Commission president,
José Manuel Barroso, at a private event in New York the day
before – and the betting markets were saying it was 82 per cent
certain that Britain would remain inside the EU. Barroso was
relaxed and in a playful mood. Brexit was not going to happen,
he confidently told the audience of bankers and business executives. So when I took off from Newark, New Jersey, for the
flight to Glasgow, Britain was very much a part of the EU, David
Cameron was firmly installed in Downing Street and the pound
was rock solid against the dollar. None of those things was true
when we landed in a blustery Glasgow on 24 June, and drove to
one of Trump's golf courses. He, of course, flew in a Trump-
branded helicopter. (I sometimes wondered whether Trump had
a problem remembering his name, such was the number of

buildings and machines – and even golf tees – that bore his name in five huge letters.)

Trump's first port of call was his Turnberry golf course, which had been newly refurbished. There was a nuts news conference on the ninth hole – the famous lighthouse hole – where a piper marched him to the microphone, and he was flanked by three of his children, all looking as immaculately groomed as the greens and fairways themselves. One prankster went up to Trump to hand him a box of red golf balls with black Nazi insignias on them. 'Get him out of here,' Trump barked to the Scottish police officers. Rather less flashily, but noteworthy in her own way, was the comedian Janey Godley, who had caught the bus to be at the course so she could unfurl her hand-written sign, with the legend TRUMP IS A CUNT on it. She too was ushered away. Greenpeace protestors buzzed the golf course in a micro-light aircraft in a more serious breach of security.

The purpose of the news conference had nothing to do with the presidential election; it was a business trip. The line between Donald Trump's personal interests, business interests and political interests was so blurry as to be impossible to see. It was all one: brand Trump. Ostensibly, he was here in Scotland so that he could go into rhapsodic overdrive about just how wonderful his golf course was after a bit of remodelling and how luxurious the Turnberry hotel was after extensive refurbishment. He wanted more than anything for the golfing authorities to reinstate the course as one of those that would host The Open, the oldest and most prestigious tournament in the golfing world. To this day, that hasn't happened. But Trump is nothing if not an opportunist. And Brexit Britain was waking up to the crazy reality of what it had voted for the day before.

The Brexit vote had a galvanising effect on Trump. He had entered the presidential race a year or so earlier largely as a branding exercise. The entrepreneur-cum-TV host-cum-political wannabe could see no downside from months in the headlines. He thought he would get enough funding to see him through Iowa and New Hampshire, but would then fold to throw his weight behind Chris Christie, the then governor of New Jersey. But here we were in June 2016, just over four months out from the presidential election, and it was as if a question that had been rattling around his head had just been answered: *If boring, staid, risk-averse, set-in-its-ways, phlegmatic, keep-calm-and-carry-on Britain could take such a wild leap into the economic unknown, then surely swashbuckling, daring, entre-preneurial America might be willing to do just the same with a charmer like me.*

At the news conference, he was clear how important a moment this was for the UK – and him! 'I think really people see a big parallel. A lot of people are talking about that. Not only the United States but other countries. People want to take their country back. They want to have independence in a sense.' He claimed that he had long predicted the result, though evidence is scarce to back that up.

After a short visit to his other golfing property carved into the dunes outside Aberdeen, Trump flew back to the US, and the words playing on his tightly puckered lips were those of the man he so loathed and wanted to erase from the history books – the then president, Barack Obama. Maybe his slogan 'yes, we can' was going to be applicable to the Trump campaign too.

• • •

If there was a single uniting policy that linked Brexit with Trump's election victory, it was concern about immigration – no, maybe the better word is fear: fear there was an invasion underway, fear that 'we' were being swamped by 'them', fear that our identity was being erased, fear that our jobs were being taken, fear that unworthy foreigners were going to the front of the queue for housing and were overwhelming our public services.

Historically, there are important differences in American and British attitudes towards migration. The US proudly proclaims itself to be a nation of immigrants. The poem on the plinth of the Statue of Liberty in New York Harbor, where so many people hoping to make a better life for themselves would arrive to be processed on Ellis Island, said it all: 'Give me your tired, your poor, your huddled masses yearning to breathe free, the wretched refuse of your teeming shore.' And, staring kindly out to the ocean, Lady Liberty has been an enduring symbol for the best part of 150 years for those coming to start again in the United States of America – a beacon of hope, independence and freedom.

One of the great experiences of travelling extensively in the US, as I was lucky enough to do, is that not only do you recognise the extraordinary geographical diversity – it is more a continent than a country – but you see the different communities from state to state. America is a melting pot. When I spent periods in New York City I don't think I ever got a taxi driver from the same community twice. The whole world was in the city, driven by a single unifying idea that they were all Americans now in the land of the free and the home of the brave.

If you look at the names of people who come from North Dakota, every other person seems to have their roots in Norway. Like all patterns of migration, there were push and pull factors. Crop failures in the mid-nineteenth century in Norway and a series of agricultural disasters meant that thousands were in need and desperate. The push factor. The pull factor was that the US had introduced the Homestead Act in 1862, offering parcels of 160 acres of land to the adult head of a family for next to nothing in return for a commitment to farm the land for five years.

But go to other states and you'll find different ethnic groups in different places: the Irish in New York and Massachusetts, the Germans in Pennsylvania, the Japanese in the Pacific Northwest, the Hispanic communities in the states bordering Mexico – and more recently, the Somalis in Minnesota and the Ethiopians in Washington, DC.

Around the world, people of all nationalities, from countries at different stages of economic development, had looked at the US – with its equivalent of Willy Wonka's golden ticket, the fabled Green Card – with a sense of wonder. It was a dream. And it brought the brightest and best to the US. If you look at the list of directors of any of the Fortune 500 companies you will see the diversity of those in charge. They look very different from the boards of Mittelstand companies in Germany or, even more pronounced, the make-up of companies quoted on the Nikkei in Japan.

But in 2016, Donald Trump made clear that he didn't much like migration – particularly immigrants from across the southern border. In the opening remarks of his presidential campaign he declared that Mexicans were thieves, drug dealers and rapists. Remarks that he would double down on. Polite society in the US gasped. Newspaper leaders tutted a disapproving rebuke. Mainstream politicians disavowed his comments. But a lot of Americans – from all walks of life – lapped it up. Trump had tapped into concerns that the southern border had become too porous. There were too many people from Mexico and the Northern Triangle of Central America (Honduras, Guatemala and El Salvador) who'd crossed the Rio Grande illegally. They were not paying their taxes and should be sent packing. And thus one of Trump's most potent slogans of the 2016 campaign was born: build the wall.

After the Islamist-inspired terror attack in San Bernardino in December 2015, which left 14 people dead, Trump would extend his anti-immigration message to include all Muslims. He issued a statement that didn't pull any punches: he claimed that a significant segment of the Muslim population harboured 'great hatred towards Americans'. And he went on: 'Without looking at the various polling data, it is obvious to anybody the hatred is beyond comprehension … where this hatred comes from and why we will have to determine. Until we are able to determine and understand this problem and the dangerous threat it poses, our country cannot be the victims of horrendous attacks by people that believe only in Jihad, and have no sense of reason or respect for human life.' And then came the kicker – which he delightedly read out at a rally of supporters in South Carolina that evening:

'Donald J. Trump is calling for a total and complete shut-down of Muslims entering the United States until our country's representatives can figure out what the hell is going on.' The original statement didn't include the word 'hell'. That was added with a theatrical flourish at his rally. His audience erupted in applause and delight.

There was something else that gave this even greater resonance. The San Bernardino attack played into American fears that events thousands of miles away could very easily come to US soil – like they had on 9/11. And in 2015, there was that great tide of humanity on the move, trying to escape the civil war in Syria. For the most part the mainstream US media doesn't report much on the outside world – unless it involves American citizens, or the pictures are captivating. The Syrian exodus fitted the latter category. That the German chancellor, Angela Merkel, admitted more than a million refugees brought admiration from many. After all, Europe's last refugee crisis had been brought about by the country she now led following the Holocaust. Merkel was hailed for her moral and political courage by the UN refugee agency, the UNHCR.

Not so Donald Trump. He thought she'd taken total leave of her senses. And made no attempt to hide it. He called her policy 'insane' and a 'disaster'. He predicted there would be riots throughout Germany.

After he became president there was an excruciating coming together between the two in the Oval Office. In the business it's called a 'pool spray'. It's when the dozen or so journalists on pool duty that day (in other words you are working and filing for all news outlets, not just the one you are employed by) are ushered into the Oval Office to film the president and whoever the world leader in town is. The idea is to show rapport and bonhomie. Typically both leaders sit in armchairs, framed by the fireplace. Trump that day just showed disgust and disdain, lips pursed, hands between his knees, unwilling to shake hands with the German chancellor.

In the UK, as these seismic events were unfolding in Syria, Britain was preparing to go to the polls – the lead-up to which had seen Nigel Farage's anti-Europe and anti-migration party, UKIP, sweep the board in the 2014 European Parliament elections

– the first time in modern history that an election hadn't been won by either Labour or Conservatives. Mind you, European elections have nothing like the turnout that you get in a general election; the voting system is not first-past-the-post as you get in UK general elections; these elections are historically a chance to blow a raspberry at the ruling party at Westminster. There was little chance that UKIP in a general election would win more than a handful of seats.

Though he wasn't an MP (he had tried a number of times and failed), Nigel Farage was a massively influential figure in the events that would unfold. He is a sort of Pied Piper figure, where his blokeish, hail-fellow-well-met mien reached parts of the British electorate that conventional politicians failed to get close to. His mustard corduroys, tweed jackets and a politically incorrect Rothmans cigarette hanging from his mouth with a pint of ale in his hand made him an endearing 'everyman'. The reality of Farage as the quintessential 'ordinary geezer' does not bear close scrutiny. The son of a stockbroker, he attended the elite private school Dulwich College, where his flirtation with far-right politics began. And from there he went into the City too.

The author and broadcaster Michael Crick reported for Channel 4 on the concern that Dulwich College teachers had about the teenage Farage, quoting this correspondence between staff members at the school: 'Another colleague, who teaches the boy, described his publicly professed racist and neo-fascist views; and he cited a particular incident in which Farage was so offensive to a boy in his set, that he had to be removed from the lesson. This master stated his view that this behaviour was precisely why the boy should not be made a prefect. Yet another colleague described how, at a Combined Cadet Force (CCF) camp organised by the college, Farage and others had marched through a quiet Sussex village very late at night shouting Hitler-youth songs.'

When Nigel Farage was shown the correspondence, he admitted to being a 'troublemaker' at school who 'wound people up': 'Of course I said some ridiculous things, not necessarily racist things. It depends on how you define it.' He denied knowing any Hitler-youth songs 'in English or German'.

The fully formed Farage became a much subtler and more effective operator who, like Donald Trump, would get away with saying the kind of things eschewed by mainstream politicians. He was the master of the dog-whistle. And though in reality he was pretty much a one-man political party, his brilliance as a communicator and, yes, the resonance of his anti-European message put the fear of bejesus into the Conservative Party.

Such was the mood of panic UKIP induced at the top of the party that David Cameron, the leader of the coalition government, felt that he had to restate an earlier promise he'd made to his party that the British people would be given an in/out referendum on leaving the EU if – *if* – the Tories won an overall majority at the general election due in 2015. He thought it was a clever piece of political manoeuvring; canny internal party management. There was little expectation that Cameron's Tory Party would win an overall majority, so he was making a promise that in all likelihood he would never have to make good on. It would appease the Eurosceptic right-wing faction in his party in Parliament, a much more sizable number of the wider membership, and it would be a nod to the electorate as a whole that he got the message over why so many had voted for UKIP in the Euro elections. Cameron had gambled and won already. He'd seen off the referendum to change the voting system in 2011 by a whopping margin. And if not quite so emphatically, the Union had held together in the Scottish independence referendum in 2014. So, rolling the dice once more – this time on our relationship with the EU – seemed no big deal. He was on a gambler's lucky streak. What could possibly go wrong?

The task for the Eurosceptics – and indeed the Trump campaign in the US – was made somewhat easier by the chariness of many more liberal-minded politicians to talk about the issue of immigration. They were hoping it was a live rail they wouldn't need to grasp. Policymakers knew that as a society aged and got wealthier there were many jobs that were not going to be filled by the domestic population.

How many Britons are prepared to fruit-pick in East Anglia? How many Britons are willing to work in our care homes or take the lower-paid jobs in the NHS? On our building sites, how many of the workforce were born in the UK? Free movement within the EU did bring many, many people to these shores – but look what happened when so many went home after the 2016 vote and the transitional arrangements came to an end – there were serious labour shortages in all sorts of industries. But it would be a misnomer to think that all these people were bottom of the pile, uneducated drains on the welfare state, originating from the poorest countries within the EU.

In 2012, it was estimated that France's sixth biggest city was London. Yes, there were more French people living and working in the British capital than there were in Strasbourg, Nantes or Bordeaux. Labour laws and the tax regime made it much more attractive to come to the UK than set up business in France. It even became a campaign stop for presidential candidates. Just after the Brexit vote, Emmanuel Macron was touring France in his attempt to break the mould of the Fifth Republic – which had always either elected a president from the centre-right or the socialist left. The young banker was touring the country, selling his newly formed En Marche! party. And one of his biggest campaign stops in what would be his successful assault on the Élysée Palace? Addressing 3,000 supporters in Methodist Central Hall in Westminster. The 300,000 or so French citizens living in and around London were highly educated, young and ambitious. It was a huge gain for the British economy (and brought with it some excellent *boulangeries* too). Equally, anyone British who wanted to go and work in Europe could do so freely.

But a lot of well-meaning centrist politicians have tended to run a mile from talking about the economic benefits of migration. Immigration has always been seen as a problem in a way that was not – historically – the case in the US. Sure, at times there were worries in the US over the influx of Catholics from Italy and Ireland at the turn of the nineteenth century. And there was a good deal of concern about the influx of Jews in the 1930s when America was going through one of its isolationist periods. Overall though, America has been happy to acknowledge that it is a country built by foreigners. But the debate in Britain has been more awkward. Those same centrists would also shy away from talking about the frustrations immigration brings, for fear of being labelled racist or heartless. A surge in Polish migrants would invariably change the character of some towns and communities, which some local inhabitants found disconcerting. But few at Westminster wanted to discuss it. 'Don't poke the hornet's nest' seemed to be the factory default setting of many MPs. There is always going to be a group of voters who think there are too many of them over here, so best to talk about something else.

Worse still were the politicians who promised to do a lot about it and ended up doing next to nothing – the serial over-promisers and under-deliverers. Cameron's pledge when he became leader of the opposition to bring net migration – the difference between those entering the country and those leaving – down to the tens of thousands is a case in point. It was an easy slogan that proved impossible to deliver. And successive Conservative prime ministers (and boy, there have been a lot of them …) have made their own pledges along similar lines. By the time the Brexit vote happened, net migration had ballooned to a quarter of a million, a far cry from the Cameron pledge.*

But here's the thing: when you have politicians making half-hearted pledges that they don't keep then it is not much of a surprise when they are outflanked by consensus-breaking candidates who say that you've been offered semi-skimmed for years and it's made no difference, so why not come with us and we will give you the full-cream version. These are politicians who think that immigration is not a marginal issue at the bottom of a long list of voters' concerns – after economy, health, education, defence etc. – but is one that is front and centre.

The British Social Attitudes analysis of the Brexit vote found that concerns over immigration were the biggest driver of how people voted – and these people were older, more 'authoritarian', with a strong streak of social conservatism in them. They're also people who don't mind trudging to the polling station: they vote in higher numbers than young people. Drilling a little deeper into this survey, what you find is that there was a growing chasm between young people who had been educated to degree level, and the older generation who had left school after their O levels. And in that older cohort, anti-immigration views were found more in men than in women. The way it was

---

* By late 2023 – seven years after the vote to 'take back control' – net migration had climbed to a vertiginous three-quarters of a million.

characterised at the time, it was older white men that delivered Brexit – the male, pale and stale brigade.

Another massive difficulty with the EU referendum was that for years politicians had used Brussels as the whipping boy for all of Britain's failings, ills and shortcomings. Red tape? Blame Brussels. Inefficiency? It's all the fault of those bloated Eurocrats. Regulation? The interfering European Parliament. Indeed, every EU institution was maligned as a pernicious sovereignty stealer, chipping away at what it meant to be British.

In the mid-1990s, when I was a lobby correspondent at Westminster, I was tasked with trying to make the doings of the European Parliament more accessible and relevant to a British audience. I would set off on the Eurostar from Waterloo (as the departure point was then), feeling enthusiastic about the task ahead, only to arrive at the city of anonymous marble, steel and glass to find the whole place alienating. To the huge annoyance of the French, the *lingua franca* of the EU – and for that matter, the whole city of Brussels – was becoming English. The language of the EU may have been English, but to paraphrase the great Mr Spock from *Star Trek*, it's English, but not as we know it. Business was done in EU-speak – all derogations and qualified majorities. There was something slightly soul sapping about it.

But then again, as Otto von Bismarck famously observed, laws are like sausages – you don't want to see them being made.

And Britain's economic outlook was transformed by its membership of the EU. It was no longer the 'sick man' of Europe as it was widely seen in the 1960s and 1970s. Inflation was brought under control, and taken with the labour market reforms introduced by Margaret Thatcher when she was prime minister, Britain became a magnet for inward investment. That only grew when she took us into the newly created single market, which paved the way for the free movement of 'people, goods and services'.

At a stroke, all the tedious, time-consuming and costly paperwork that importers and exporters had to fill in when doing business with other European countries was gone. Japanese car makers were looking at Britain as the place to set up their factories because of the friction-free movement of parts and the finished product – the cars. Supply chains now worked on the basis of 'just in time', where if you were building a car you wouldn't have huge warehouses full of parts adjacent to the assembly line; you would bring the components in as and when they were needed, at the last minute. Britain's services sector was flourishing. And the financial services industry in the City of London had become a global powerhouse to rival New York, making a huge contribution to the GDP of the nation. Thatcher signed this agreement not because she was a Brussels-loving Europhile – she was anything but that – but because she identified it as being in Britain's best national interest to be part of it. And though it meant regulatory alignment – or to put it more simply, a level playing field (so if the British government wanted to subsidise a product or manufacturer to have a competitive advantage over, say, a French company, it wouldn't be able to) – this was a loss of parliamentary sovereignty worth paying.

Any treaty entered into with another country or group of countries is setting the rules for the road. Our membership of NATO is a loss of sovereignty in our ability to wage war (if that is something we would improbably choose to do unilaterally against another NATO member). But the benefits we gain from being part of the Western European defence umbrella are considered a small price to pay to have the heft of all those NATO nations – including the might of the US – behind us.

Yet how many British prime ministers spoke about the advantages of EU membership? How many have stood up in the Commons to speak about the benefits that we've derived? Edward Heath, sure. He led us into what was then the EEC. John Major had a torrid time getting the Maastricht Treaty through the Commons, but his polite, painstaking work in Brussels – a welcome change from the handbagging of Thatcher – won him important concessions and served to convince him that Britain had achieved a great deal from his weary partners. But he could hardly shout it from the hilltops while he was prime minister. That would risk increasing the torment inflicted on him by the group he called 'the bastards' in his own party. Only Tony Blair would consistently make the case *for* the EU and would be unabashed in his support for it. Politicians instead preferred to talk about their latest battle with Brussels, the skirmishes, the red lines, the unacceptable demands, the intolerable Eurocrats.

This had been Cameron's MO. Aside from his pledges to stop the flow of Europeans coming into the country, one of the first things he did when he became Tory leader was pull the Conservative Party out of the main centre-right group in the European Parliament, the EPP. That was the group to which Angela Merkel's Christian Democratic Union party belonged. But this caucus was far too pro-European for the Conservatives' liking: too integrationist, too federalist. Now cosseted with an oddball collection of far-right extremists in the European Parliament, the Tory leadership squandered huge influence in their bid to pacify an ever more uncompromising group on the right of the party at Westminster.

When the 2010 general election came and David Cameron found himself in coalition with the Europhile Liberal Democrats, he abandoned his first plan to hold an in/out referendum on membership of the EU. The Eurosceptics consistently held Cameron's poor old scorched feet to the flames. When Cameron vetoed a Eurozone rescue deal – to the utter fury and dismay of many in Europe – it was still not enough for his own militant tendency. The newspaper columnist and Conservative peer Danny Finkelstein memorably remarked that the Tory rebels could never take yes for an answer. For Cameron, it seemed, our relationship with the EU was less about what was best for Britain and much more about managing his restless and mutinous party.

The Labour Party didn't have a problem with party management on the issue of Europe – well, not until Jeremy Corbyn improbably became leader. The party was unapologetically pro-European. It had been through a conversion. Historically, Labour harboured serious doubts about the European project, thinking it was a rich man's club, doing down the workers. But that all changed in the 1980s and 1990s as the EU embraced a series of rules enhancing workers' rights and working conditions. The problem with Jeremy Corbyn was that of apparent arrested development. It seemed that all his views were shaped when he was 16 or 17 years old, and nothing was going to shift him from his CND-supporting, anti-American anti-Europeanism. He was totally at odds with his party, still thinking the EU was a capitalist cartel. And that was less than ideal in the referendum campaign. Yes, he did – sort of – campaign for remain, but you could tell his heart wasn't in it. That would prove costly.

From the Kinnock through to the Miliband era, the problem was not the MPs or the membership, it was the Eurosceptic press. Blair and Brown went to extraordinary lengths to cosy up to the Australian-born media mogul Rupert Murdoch – Blair once flying all the way to Australia to speak at a company meeting. (At least Blair was not in government then.) The charm offensive paid off. Murdoch's most powerful newspaper, the *Sun*, gave its backing to Labour and was full-throated in supporting Blair to win the 1997 general election. In government there would be no let-up of Keeping Rupert Happy. One of my more bizarre assignments was when I accompanied Gordon Brown on a tortuous journey from London to the snowy ski resort of Sun Valley, Idaho. Then Chancellor of the Exchequer, Brown travelled all this way so that he could speak to Murdoch executives. We flew from London to Seattle, Seattle to Salt Lake City, Salt Lake City to Boise, Idaho. And after the speech we flew straight back. This was a private event. No cameras, no footage. There was no governmental reason to be there; it was not an official meeting. But even still, the chancellor felt it was important enough to travel 6,000 miles there and 6,000 miles back just to reassure a newspaper owner. The British chancellor, a supplicant in the court of King Rupert.

Hostility to European ambitions from much of the right-wing press runs deep. When I was the BBC's Paris correspondent, I remember one tabloid front page with the headline 'Hop off you Frogs' – the details I can't remember, but it was the time of mad cow disease – or *la vache folle*, which sounded more like a nice old Belle Époque brasserie than a terrible disease afflicting hundreds of thousands of cattle – and a ban on the export of British beef. That was the front-page headline. But the banner at the top of the paper read 'Win an all-expenses trip to France for your family'. France was a country we loved to hate. Or was it the other way round? Was France really a country we hated to love, but did anyway?

When I read about the death of the former European Commission president Jacques Delors at the end of 2023, I was reminded of an escapade the *Sun* undertook. The headline was itself famous enough: 'Up Yours Delors'. But who remembers what had so enraged the sensibilities of the *Sun*'s editorial staff? It was in November 1990 and Delors had proposed the establishment of a single currency. A decade later it would become the euro, but then it was called the ECU – the European Currency Unit.

A council of war was called at the *Sun*'s Wapping HQ, and the editor, Kelvin MacKenzie, ordered an invasion of France. What that amounted to was two journalists being tasked with hiring a World War Two tank and driving it to Paris. Photographers would cover it all, and in a nod to the D-Day invasion itself, Page Three girls would be parachuted in – the redtop's very own 101st Airborne. The tank would be driven from Wapping by two of the journalists on the paper – my old friends George Pascoe-Watson and Patrick 'Paddy' Hennessy (now, more than 30 years on, chief of staff to the mayor of London, Sadiq Khan). They found a props supplier to the film industry who sourced a US tank and off they drove – to the utter bemusement of Parisians going about their daily lives. They were arrested when they tried to drape the *Sun* flags and Union Jacks over France's sacred memorial to its war dead, the Arc de Triomphe. Can you imagine the tabloid rage if French journalists had tried to pull a similar stunt at the Cenotaph?

And, lest we forget, the career of one Boris Johnson started as the *Daily Telegraph*'s Brussels correspondent. Brussels was full of dull but important stories. 'Sexy' was rarely a word that could be attached to being the purveyor of news copy from Belgium's capital. What Boris did was look at some mind-numbingly dull report, find some new, niche regulation buried in it – and use a grain of salt in the document to build a story that had a consistent theme: Brussels was planning a new assault on British sovereignty. These pieces, which invariably found their way onto the front page of the Euro-bashing *Daily Telegraph*, were in the main an 'inverted pyramid of piffle', to use a very Johnsonian phrase. Other journalists who were in Brussels at the time recall being rung up by their newsdesks in London following the latest Johnson 'exclusive', only to have to waste a morning following it up and discovering it bore no relation to reality. Never letting the facts get in the way of a good story is something that never left Johnson, even if his made-up quotes and dishonesty often led to him being fired from both journalistic and political positions. In the 2016 referendum he was happy to repeat the myth that one of his reasons for wanting to leave the EU was because of its attempt to ban bendy bananas. Bendy bananas? The whole story was bananas.

The Brexit campaign, as opposed to the years of internecine skirmishing within the Conservative Party that led up to it, was pretty unedifying. Arguably the key moment, the fulcrum on which the whole campaign swung, was the battle led by David Cameron and George Osborne to lure Boris Johnson to be part of 'Remain'. The outgoing London mayor would be the secret weapon, the front person for the campaign to stay in the EU. He had charisma, charm, a roguish quality that the British people seemed to love. More importantly, he was way more popular than the Conservative brand itself. Although this wasn't a referendum fought on party lines, it was going to be a Conservative prime minister spearheading it. So what a boon it would be to have the most popular, identifiable Tory alongside you. Yes, he'd written all sorts of nonsense about the EU over the years – but he was fundamentally a pro-European; his whole background was Europe. And, like Donald Trump in the US, Johnson could reach parts of the country – the bits of the electorate that had tuned out – that more conventional politicians struggled to engage. Cameron was right: Johnson was the one politician of his generation who could and would make a difference to how this referendum played out.

What we now know is that Boris Johnson sat in his house and wrote two versions of his *Daily Telegraph* column. One in which he argued why Britain should remain; the other why we should leave. But what it boiled down to was not some abstract economic calculus about future prosperity. Nor was it about the geopolitics of a strong and united Europe, or the historical importance of a Europe united after two world wars ravaged the continent in the twentieth century. These big, sweeping considerations, the *Weltanschauung* if you like, were secondary. The kernel of Boris's thinking was his place in the Conservative Party, and whether it would help or hinder his ambition to be PM.

The narrow, Boris-first reasoning was this: if he sided with the Leave campaign, then that would be the best way to position himself to succeed Cameron as Conservative Party leader. Whenever Johnson was asked about his leadership ambitions, he always reverted to metaphors of rugby: if the ball should fall loose from the back of the scrum, he might be there to pick it up. If Leave won, Johnson reasoned, Cameron would probably have to resign; if Remain won – but the Leave campaign had done well – then he would be perfectly positioned to play a big role in an administration that was trying to bring the country together after a fractious campaign. Make no mistake, any lofty ideas about Britain and Europe were of an entirely secondary order of importance compared to what was best for Alexander Boris de Pfeffel Johnson.

If it was just personal ambition on the part of Johnson, it might be just about acceptable. Let's not be too high-minded about all of this: there aren't many politicians who *don't* make the binary calculation of whether something will be good or bad for their own career as part of their assessment of the bigger picture. Selflessness is not necessarily the first hallmark of those seeking elected office. No, what is worse is that Johnson was partly driven by his desire to get one over on Cameron, dating back to their time together at Eton, then Oxford where both were members of the ghastly, braying Bullingdon club.

At Eton, Johnson was the King's scholar extraordinaire, but Cameron ended up getting a first at Oxford – to Johnson's 2:1. Johnson claims to have only a dim memory of Cameron (or Cameron Minor, as he referred to him) from their time at Eton, Britain's most elite private school. And reacting to his rival getting that first, he called Cameron a 'girly swot'. They both entered Parliament in 2001. And as the *Daily Mail* journalist Stephen Glover noted when Cameron became leader of the Conservative Party in 2005, Johnson 'was shocked to his foundations that the man whom he claimed to have outshone at Eton and Oxford could have leapt over him. It was as though a cosmic injustice had occurred.'

My old colleague from when I was a political correspondent at Westminster, Guto Harri, went on to work for Johnson as his communications director when he was mayor of London and, later, prime minister, and he tells this illuminating story.

Two years after Johnson had won the London mayoralty, it was Cameron's turn to face the British public in the 2010 election.

'Shouldn't you send Dave a text wishing him well?' asked Harri.

'Why?'

'Because you're old friends.'

'I don't see why I should wish him well.'

After Harri suggested that was rather ungracious, Johnson relented and sent this: 'Good luck Dave and don't worry, if you bog it up I'm standing by to fill the gap.'

Some might gently put forward the argument that a country as great as Great Britain deserved better than this.*

Once Johnson emerged onto his doorstep to tell reporters that he was backing Leave you felt the most enormous impetus had been given to those urging Britain to part company with the EU. He relished his appearances on the battle bus, telling people stories of bananas that had to be straightened and Hoovers that would no longer pick up dirt.

---

* While this book is about how Britain has changed since I have returned from the US, the Cameron/Johnson rivalry is an example of how *little* in this country has changed and how much it really needs to in this, the twenty-first century. If the Blair era brought us the slightly synthetic 'cool Britannia', at least you didn't feel that success depended on where you went to school. As I sit and write this, the four great offices of state are all held by men, all privately educated – one of whom went to Winchester College, another to Eton, and one who attended Charterhouse. If I were to go on, I might also point out that the heir to the throne and the Archbishop of Canterbury also attended Eton. A classless, meritocratic society this is not.

Those were the small untruths – the more tendentious claim (and that is being polite) was that the £350 million we paid into EU coffers each week as our price for membership would be rerouted to the NHS once Britain had left and 'taken back control'. But it was a nonsense. It took no account of the rebate that Margaret Thatcher had negotiated – and indeed, didn't take account of all the money that flowed back into the UK in EU grants. Wales, for example, was a net beneficiary of being part of the EU because of its weak economy and high levels of poverty.

The more pernicious lie – and it had racist overtones to it – was that if we stayed in the EU, Turkey, a Muslim country, was going to become the newest member with its 70 million-odd people able to come and live in Britain under free movement. This was advanced by Penny Mordaunt, who won such acclaim for her sword-carrying abilities during the coronation of King Charles. Back in 2016 she was the armed forces minister and was flashing her sword of untruth. She claimed that Britain would not have a veto on Turkey joining. That was a plain and simple lie. It requires unanimity for a country to be able to gain membership.

But if we're talking porkies, perhaps the biggest of them all was the claim made again and again that if we left the EU we would carry on trading with the continent just like before, as if nothing had changed. Some of the Brexiteer campaigners said we would stay in the single market, others that we would remain part of the customs union. No need to worry: Europe would be so desperate for our goods that they would let us carry on, just as before. That is not where we ended up. There was a delusional view that it would be like giving up your gym membership, but the gym would be so desperate to have you they would let you carry on using the facilities for free. If you pointed out that if the gym owners allowed us to do that, every other member would want the same, you were being a negative nelly.

For the most part though, the Leave campaign was much more positive than that of Remain. Leave, with Dominic Cummings's brilliant 'take back control' slogan, was about doing something to make life better: take back control of our laws, take back control of our borders, take back control of our economy etc. Whereas it felt as though Remain was all about painting a negative picture of how grim things would be if we pulled out. It was dubbed 'Project Fear': there be bogeymen out there and they be coming to get you.

The other shrewd part of their campaign was to travel light on detail. They had internalised the SNP campaign for Scottish independence and its shortcomings. The SNP, to give them their due, had come up with a detailed manifesto and costings for how the Scottish economy could exist outside of the rest of the UK. There was detailed analysis, for instance, on what the price of a barrel of oil needed to be. It meant that journalists could subject the costings to critical scrutiny. This is what you would expect a group to do when it is advocating such fundamental change.

Leave did none of that. *Keep it vague.* Keep saying 'it will be all right'. And make the point that anyone who says differently is just a merchant of doom, a 'remoaner'. What would the trading arrangements with the EU be? Let's cross that bridge when we come to it. What about trade with Northern Ireland when the Republic shares the same island – and the part of the Good Friday Agreement, which brought peace to the province, that specifically excludes hard borders between North and South? It will be fine. We'll have an oven-ready arrangement. Boris Johnson promised Unionist politicians there would be no border in the Irish Sea. That – like so many other things – turned out to be a lie.

That the issue of trade with Northern Ireland was batted away with a lazy waft of a Boris Johnson arm was one of the most striking features of the campaign. He promised frictionless movement of goods, but post-Brexit, Archie Norman, the chairman of Marks & Spencer, would point out that to get two lorries across the Irish Sea from England took a mind-boggling 700 pages of forms with 20 staff working for eight hours. It's like one of those annoying maths questions that I toiled with when I was at school. But at least with this one the answer is simple, and you really don't have to show your working out: if it takes 700 pages of form-filling, requiring 8 hours of work by 20 staff to get two lorries across the sea, and pre-Brexit it took no forms, no staff and no man-hours, which is quicker and better? But from the Brexiteers the philosophical insight of *The Best Exotic*

Marigold Hotel was the way to go: everything will be all right in the end, and if it's not all right, it's not the end.*

• • •

When explaining the events of 2016, it's perfectly true to say that the Brexit referendum was the result of the Conservatives winning an overall majority a year earlier, forcing Cameron to make good on his pre-election pledge. That explains the referendum, but to find an explanation for the result – for the disenchantment and resentment that so many voters felt towards the political establishment who were telling them to vote Remain – you have to go back a bit further.

The Cameron/Osborne years brought an economic policy summed up by one word: 'austerity'. Cameron, in a keynote

---

* Better still, when you're presented with charts and graphs and data which demonstrates how clearly the UK economy will suffer in terms of GDP from cutting itself off from the bloc where 50 per cent of your exports go, you play the card that Michael Gove memorably did during the campaign. 'People in this country have had enough of experts,' he declared. It is an astonishing statement to come from such a clever man. Just think about it for a moment. If you're on a flight and the captain comes on the Tannoy to tell you to take your seat immediately because of anticipated serious turbulence, do you roll your eyes and say, 'I'm sick of those bloody expert pilots who think they know how to fly a plane?' Or if an oncologist gives you a cancer diagnosis after blood tests and X-rays, do you fold your arms and say, 'Yeah, but what do you know?'

The populism in the Gove approach is something I will return to later. But what Gove was doing was deliberate. The problem the Leave campaign had was that nearly all serious economists, nearly all the leaders of FTSE 100 companies, nearly all the heads of the big banks thought that Brexit was an act of monumental self-harm.

speech while leader of the opposition in 2009, had said, 'the age of irresponsibility is giving way to the age of austerity', and he committed a new Conservative government to ending years of what he said was excessive government spending. When the coalition government was formed, there were cuts to welfare benefits, and the school building programme was pared back. Spending on the police, courts and prisons was cut. Over this long period, Britons saw the biggest cut in living standards since the Napoleonic Wars. These were cuts to the size of the state that George Osborne argued were essential. But there were many casualties of them. Child poverty grew massively as policies were skewed to throw money at the elderly (who vote) and against the young (who can't).

One of the explanations for the 2016 *événements* was the slow-burn effects – on both sides of the Atlantic – of the financial crash in 2008. Osborne's economic policy had been driven by what he saw as the need to put Britain's finances on an even keel after the profound shock that 2008 caused. It was a jolt that few if anyone had seen coming, and that in turn led to greater disenchantment and mistrust of those in authority who were trying to argue in 2016 that Brexit was a bad thing. The provocative statement made that year by Michael Gove, who was spearheading the Leave campaign, was that 'people have had enough of experts' – but that can be refashioned into a question. And it was memorably put by none other than Queen

Elizabeth when she went to the London School of Economics just after the credit crunch to open a new multimillion-pound academic wing. The Queen turned to Professor Luis Garicano, who was then director of research at the LSE's management department, and asked: 'If these things were so large, how come everyone missed them?' It was a brilliant question, which left a lot of extremely clever boffins opening and closing their mouths like goldfish at a synchronised bafflement competition.

There was the initial carnage wrought by the furring up of the entire banking system of credit. It was a period when we all had to go on a crash course into understanding the esoteric and massively lucrative world of banking and what went on behind the seemingly solid walls of our high street institutions. How many people had ever heard of synthetic collateralised debt obligations or credit default swaps, let alone the sub-prime mortgage market? And if asked to explain what those things meant, I suspect there are few outside the City of London who knew. But that wasn't the real problem. No, the real problem was far more shocking than that. There was hardly anyone in the City or on Wall Street who understood what the hell they were doing or what they were creating. All those pinstripe suits and Ferraris and no one with the faintest clue. It was like a children's game of pass the parcel, but rather than just passing it to the person sitting to your right, you added a few pounds of highly unstable Semtex before handing it to your neighbour

– and each player in this game did the same as the bomb got bigger and bigger.

It's estimated that around ten million Americans lost their homes when the banks foreclosed on all these people who were no longer able to pay their mortgages. Ten million! What is so egregious about this is so many of the people who had been lent vast sums of money had never been in a position to fund a mortgage. But credit was cheap, so you didn't do checks on affordability.

America grew ghost towns, and the repercussions echoed across the world, causing a recession and a crisis where the whole banking system and global financial system tottered precariously. In America, the visible symptom of that was the implosion at Lehman Brothers, the venerable Wall Street institution which went under. We watched on the news as the staff took their possessions away in cardboard boxes after it collapsed. In Britain, the mortgage lender Northern Rock had to be nationalised after the first bank run since the nineteenth century. Savers were seen queuing forlornly to get their money out before it collapsed. RBS was going the same way after growing at an unsustainable rate and exposing itself to huge amounts of rotten American debts. The government had to step in again to stop it from going under. Lloyds too needed help.

A decision was taken – almost certainly correctly – that these financial institutions were 'too big to fail'. They must be supported, whatever it takes. But of course, if that is the case, where is the moral hazard? How do you stop the reckless – and blind – gambling that took place within these institutions if there is no risk that they are ever going to be held to account? No one went to prison for their role in the world's most precipitate financial crisis in decades – all because they were too big to fail.

On the other side of the ledger, millions and millions of ordinary people and small business owners would discover that they had no such protection. They would lose their jobs, their homes, their businesses and their self-respect, and from the policymakers there was a shrug. If the banks were too big to fail, the ordinary Joes and Josephines were too small to bail.

And this wasn't just any ordinary recession. Sure, on both sides of the Atlantic recessions have come and gone. People have been laid off, homes have been repossessed – and then economic growth comes back and jobs are found and you go again. That's the economic cycle. But this recession came at the peak of globalisation and the burgeoning of the BRICS (Brazil, Russia, India, China and South Africa), not to mention the G20 economies. The steel mills that shuttered in the US in 2008 never reopened; the jobs went to other parts of the world – or to robots. This was repeated in textiles and all manner of other industries.

The combination of the long tail of the financial crash and the profound sense that there was a deeply unfair 'us' and 'them' when it came to how people were treated was a slow-burning fuse. So when Hillary Clinton ran her lacklustre campaign for the presidency, representing that most solid pillar of the American political establishment – former First Lady, former US senator, former secretary of state – people thought it represented more of the same. And when they looked at the scabrous, raucous, pugilistic alternative, Donald Trump, who was promising to take a wrecking ball to those solid pillars, the American people jumped. And those same forces could be seen at play in the EU referendum. The 'screw you' mood was undeniable. Cities like Sunderland – which had been reborn as a result of the massive inward investment from car-maker Nissan because of the single market – would now be in serious jeopardy as a result of leaving it. But they voted for Brexit. Farmers whose labours had been subsidised by the Common Agricultural Policy of Europe did the same. It was a new phenomenon. People were voting *against* their economic interests, in the seemingly blind hope that what would come along next could only be better, having taken back control. Well, that's what they'd been promised. It all sounded so alluringly simple: manufacturing would return, food prices would fall, immigration would be halted, economic growth would accelerate. Britain would be great again. America would be great again.

Like when the snake oil salesmen of old would roll into town and pitch their tent at the fair, offering to heal credulous citizens of their ills, there was no quick cure to be had. 2016 would turn out to be a year when enough of the electorate showed faith in the 'healer', even if the healer didn't really know what to do with the snake oil. The promise in Britain was that the referendum would be an end to the discussion, the end of the debilitating psychodrama, the full stop.

It was just the beginning.

CHAPTER 2

A SIMPLE PLAN (2019)

Three years later, in 2019, the rubber hit the road. It was a year when the easy campaign promises of 'taking back control' and 'making America great again' came up against the uncomfortable brick-wall reality of that horrible word 'implementation'. It was former New York governor Mario Cuomo's much-quoted phrase come to life: you campaign in poetry; you govern in prose.

In Washington, the year opened with the government shut. It is one of those arm-wrestle, I've-got-bigger-biceps-than-you moments that is a regular feature of US political life: a way of living that seems incomprehensibly ridiculous to the outside world. Donald Trump said he was prepared to shut down the US government, resulting in the laying off of hundreds of thousands of federal workers across the US, unless and until he got his way. He wanted $5 billion for the border wall with Mexico, a cornerstone of his election victory. This, despite his assurances on the campaign trail that Americans wouldn't have to fund it. He had rampaged around the country with his rousing message: 'We're going to build a wall … and who's going to pay for it?' At this point in the year-long panto, he and the whole audience would shout 'MEXICO!'

Of course, there was no way Mexico was ever going to write a cheque to Donald Trump for the construction of a border wall. If he wanted it built, he'd have to get Congress to approve the expenditure. And at the end of 2018, despite both houses being under Republican control, lawmakers refused. It was a rare rebuff to Trump, so without too much thought on the political fallout and likely trajectory of his decision, he went nuclear and shut the government down.*

Staff were told not to report to work unless they were involved in things like law enforcement, work involving national security or areas of safety like air traffic control. These staff work for nothing until the government shutdown is sorted and then they get payment retrospectively. But the longer the shutdown went on, the more the strains appeared. There were long delays if you wanted to catch a plane because of air traffic control being overstretched as more and more workers refused to work without pay – and remember in the US, with its vast

---

* Without getting into the dreary mechanics of this, every year 12 appropriation bills have to be passed to keep the various federal agencies solvent, and the financial settlement has to be signed off by the president. Without it, government stops and workers can't be paid – because without the necessary appropriations there is no money in the pot for salaries.

landmass, people board planes to travel like we get on buses and trains in the UK.

The 2019 government shutdown – which broke records for the length of time it endured – would end with a humiliating and demeaning climbdown by Trump. Made worse for him because it was the diminutive, sparrow-like figure of the new Democratic speaker of the House, Nancy Pelosi, sworn in at the beginning of 2019, who was seen to have won. Trump seethed at the optics of that.

Dramas like this oxygenate the cable news channels, which roll round the clock on Washington dysfunction, charting every twist and turn. But there was something else that was – perhaps surprisingly – attracting the attention of a highly insular, domestic-focused media. It was beginning to look like there was something almost as chaotically inexplicable happening on the other side of the pond.

With the US government shutdown, I found it quite difficult to get on the BBC bulletins. Who is that interested in the constitutional mechanics? And once you've explained that this is a likely ill-fated political manoeuvre on the part of the president, what else is there to say until it gets resolved? Sure, you can stand outside one of the majestic national parks and explain why they're no longer open to tourists, but how many people in the UK would be affected by that?

What kept me busy instead was appearing on US television to try to explain to an American audience what on earth was happening at Westminster, and why the mother of parliaments was in such a mother of a mess. Three years earlier in the US there was scarcely anyone outside of financial circles and the international think-tank world who had heard of Brexit, let alone paid it much attention – but because of the intertwined nature of the Brexit vote and Trump's victory, it now commanded considerable interest.

If the US was consumed by continuing resolutions, Britain had its own Kafkaesque nightmare of indicative votes. Well, Theresa May did. Having taken over from David Cameron as prime minister after his post-referendum resignation, it was down to May to make that vote reality. May wanted to achieve two simple things: do what was best for Britain's economic interests and our place in the world, and keep her party together to deliver a majority in Parliament. Simples.

It turned out to be a bit more complicated than the Brexit warriors had promised. The starting position of the ultras was to say we want all the benefits of being in the EU – access to the single market, free movement of goods and services – but none of the drawbacks, like anyone from the EU being able to come and work in the UK. Oh, and we won't be paying any membership fees.

I first voted in an election when Margaret Thatcher became prime minister in 1979. I was in Southampton, in my first year at university, and had campaigned for the Labour candidate, Bryan Gould. I still vividly remember walking back along The

Avenue to my halls of residence and running into a braying bunch of young Conservative activists who were wildly celebrating Maggie's victory. I was 19 then. By the time I was 48 in 2007 I had known just two other prime ministers – John Major and Tony Blair – so three PMs in the best part of three decades. And in the seven years since the beginning of 2016? There have been five, all Conservative. And one word explains it: Brexit.

The intractability of the issue, the political instability it produced, the rigidity and ideological fervour with which some approached it would convulse not just our politics but our constitutional arrangements in a way that was unprecedented in modern British history. The year 2019 was when the chickens started coming home to roost.

In the US, officials at the State Department, friends of the UK, policymakers and financiers thought it was an act of extraordinary self-harm, and one that would damage the special relationship. Henry Kissinger once memorably posed the question, 'If I want to speak to Europe, who do I call?' For decades, the answer to that was Britain. The British were the bridge that linked the US and Europe. When the White House couldn't understand the language that Europe was speaking, Whitehall was the translator. And it worked the other way round as well. When Europe was vexed about some new policy coming out of Washington, London was invariably the interlocutor despatched to find a way forward.

In fairness, Donald Trump loved Brexit, and so too did his ambassador in London, Woody Johnson – the billionaire heir to the Johnson & Johnson pharmaceutical company. I remember having breakfast with him at his residence, Winfield House, in Regent's Park and him waxing lyrical on how Brexit was going to be the start of a new Victorian age for the UK. It was all sunny uplands and endless opportunity.

Donald Trump thought the same. But he was utterly scathing about Theresa May's handling of it. The man who wrote (or had written for him) *The Art of the Deal* was for the all-guns-blazing approach to discussions with the EU. He said Britain should sue the EU and not negotiate until Brussels had surrendered. This from the man who had successfully negotiated his own government shutdown. On the eve of an awkward visit to London in 2018, Trump gave an interview to the *Sun* lambasting Theresa May's approach to Brexit, and adding for good measure that he thought Boris Johnson would make a fine British prime minister. When challenged about these quotes at a news conference, he said it was 'fake news'. A year later his position had not softened:

> I'm surprised at how badly it's all gone from the standpoint of a negotiation. I gave the prime minister my ideas on how to negotiate it and I think you would have been successful. She didn't listen to that and that's fine – she's got to do what she's got to do. I think it could have been

negotiated in a different manner, frankly. I hate to see everything being ripped apart right now.

Theresa May was in some ways the perfect choice to pick up the reins after the Brexit vote and Cameron's swift resignation. As home secretary she had largely kept out of the Brexit campaign. She certainly chose not to make herself the face of it in the way that Cameron, George Osborne and William Hague did. She supported Remain, but that support was tepid at best. She was a safe pair of hands – someone who had survived the agonies of being home secretary, the chalice with the most poison in it in British politics. The position of home secretary – one of the four great offices of state – has been the rock on which so many political careers have foundered. It is a sprawling department with responsibility for policing, national security, counterterrorism, prisons and immigration – so just think of all the catastrophes that could befall you: jail breaks, riots, illegal immigration, policing scandals. John Reid, who was home secretary in the Blair era, described the department as 'not fit for purpose'. But May navigated her way around it. She was hard-working, a details person.

She didn't have the easy charm – or swagger – of Cameron. But nor did she have the sense of entitlement of the old Etonian, which so many found grating. She was much more a product of Thatcher's meritocratic Britain than the self-satisfied hunting, fishing and shooting country squirearchy that Cameron seemed a throwback to.

The contest for the leadership was ugly. It looked like it would be May v Boris Johnson, until Michael Gove memorably knifed Johnson. Having offered to run the campaign for the former London mayor, Gove then had other ideas, saying of his Vote Leave co-chair: 'I came in the last few days, reluctantly and firmly, to the conclusion that while Boris has great attributes he was not capable of uniting that team and leading the party and the country in the way that I would have hoped.' Ouch.

At the chaotic news conference that followed, Johnson was left badly winded, and Nadine Dorries – whose love for Boris has often seemed to know no bounds – was in floods of tears, needing to be supported by her colleague Nadhim Zahawi. Gove, without missing a beat, announced that after this period of reflection he had concluded – shockingly – that he himself would be the perfect person to replace Cameron.

The Gove–Johnson relationship would have yet more twists and turns. It is rather tempting to cast them as the comic relief characters that you might find in one of Shakespeare's plays – the clown in *Othello*, the gravedigger in *Hamlet*, the fool in *Lear*. But in the years that followed, Gove and Johnson would provide much of the post-Brexit tragedy, with just occasional moments of hilarious absurdity.

With Britain in its purgatorial post-Brexit state, that was less than ideal. May's speech on entering Downing Street for the first time as prime minister was all about creating a nation where everyone feels valued; she said that she had a 'mission to make Britain a country that works for everyone'. But Britain had voted 52 per cent to 48 per cent for Brexit – and a sizable, well-organised, fervent, evangelical chunk of the Conservative Party at Westminster, and members around the country, were not much interested in the 48 per cent. They had won, and to the victor the spoils.

Among an influential group of Conservatives, the issue of Europe had become an article of almost religious zeal. There were no compromises they would consider. Their position was absolutist. They were well-organised and unbiddable. Britain was the greatest and we would rule the waves once more – but only after all the shackles with the European Union had been broken. These were the Conservative Party's jingoist jihadists.

Maybe no politician on earth or in history would have been able to square that circle of keeping the country united, delivering a Brexit that the Eurosceptic ultras demanded, and acting in Britain's long-term economic interests. To pull that off would require the foresight of an Abraham Lincoln, Mandela's generosity of spirit, the rhetorical might of Churchill, the determination of a Gandhi, the deal-making skill of an LBJ and the easy charm of a Blair. And decent, principled and honourable as I believe Theresa May to be, she was the vicar's daughter, she was Maidenhead woman: she wasn't superwoman.

I first got to know Theresa May after she entered Parliament as the MP for Maidenhead in 1997. I was the presenter of the London and the South East regional political programme, and this newly minted backbencher was always keen to appear. Actually, saying I 'got to know' her is overdoing it. There is something very unknowable about May. She is always scrupulously polite and immaculately turned out, but always guarded and often rather awkward. When I was North America editor and she was home secretary, I remember her coming to Washington and the ambassador throwing a reception for her. I was invited to stay for a whisky afterwards, and the two of us moved into the ambassador's study where there was a roaring log fire.

And we sat, with every conversational gambit I tried coming to nothing. She is not a person for small-talk; she is not someone who gossips – which, frankly, is the engine oil of Westminster: who's up, who's down, who's just done what to whom, who has got him or herself into the most mighty pickle. Of these matters she could not be less interested. I had just about enough humility to reflect on whether it was me that was the problem, and that she found me an insufferable bore – completely understandable, if so. But I have heard enough from her fellow ministers and others who've had a lot of contact with her that that is who she is.

She is also not fazed by silence. You know that slightly excruciating moment where you are at a dinner and the conversation dies; that moment when around the table you could hear a pin drop? An awkward embarrassed silence descends and no one quite knows how to restart the chat. Me? Well, I tend to start to babble. Words come spilling out, not necessarily linked to a cogent thought – but at least it's not that deathly silence. It's the TV presenter in me. There is a synapse that kicks in, telling me to 'fill, fill, fill'. But Theresa? She is happy to let the silence last.

Nicola Sturgeon, the former SNP leader, told me about a meeting she was invited to by Theresa May at Number 10. For a long period, the PM sat there in silence. And so Sturgeon started to fill the silence by doing all the talking. At the end of the meeting, she reflected that she had said way too much, and resolved that the next time they met, she would let the void expand if the same thing happened again. It did, and according to Sturgeon the silence was interminable. A former British diplomat told me how they had sat in the back of a car together in the gridlocked East Side of Manhattan during the United Nations General Assembly week and not a word was spoken.

One bit of Abraham Lincoln's playbook that she did try to borrow was forming a Cabinet of rivals, as the American president did after the Civil War in a bid to heal his nation's divides between north and south. Boris Johnson was rewarded with the Foreign Office, David Davis became Brexit secretary. There would be no place for Cameron's right-hand man, George Osborne. He was given a right old slapping down by her. She loathed the cocksure, affluent 'Notting Hill set', which Osborne was seen to epitomise. And she told him in no uncertain terms that he needed to get out and see the country a bit more, and understand better the lives of ordinary people.

Unfortunately for May, Osborne became editor of the London *Evening Standard* – giving him a megaphone with which to air his views of her. Or maybe a better metaphor would be a rather large club with which he could beat her over the head. Whichever you prefer, he used both. With alacrity. I think it's fair to say that there was a mutual antipathy. He would describe her premiership as a 'second-rate horror movie' and May as a 'dead woman walking'. Oh, and there was the comment made to friends that he wouldn't rest until she was 'chopped up in bags in my freezer'. Nice visual touch there. I should add that I have since sat at a breakfast where Osborne and May were at the same table. I can report they used their cutlery in the way that was meant – and not on each other.

The May premiership was torrid from beginning to end. In the press, the adjectives most frequently attached to her were 'beleaguered', 'hapless', and, from the less charitably minded, 'hopeless'. Conservative MPs were aware – of course – of her limitations. But she would be the cautious grown-up who would be able to keep the squabbling children on her backbenches vaguely in line.

In 2017 she called a general election, with the Tories comfortably ahead in the polls and predictions abounding that she would get the mandate that she wanted to deliver her 'My Way' Brexit deal. Forget the narrow majority bequeathed to her by David Cameron; she would ask the British people for the clear authority she sought. The right to govern decisively. This was a new side to the prime minister – no longer sensible-footwear Mrs May, this was stiletto-heels Theresa, gambling on a general election that did not need to happen. The woman who during the campaign gave us the confession that the naughtiest thing she'd ever done was run through a field of wheat was now in a smoky Las Vegas casino, blowing on the dice and hoping they came up with a double six.

Announcing the election, she said: 'The country is coming together but Westminster is not.' It was all so heady. There were projections suggesting the Tories could sweep to victory with 400 seats – and a majority well north of 100, while Labour would be annihilated, plunging below 200 – and if that happened, it would be condemning the party to its worst result since the 1920s. What wasn't to like? May would be the new Maggie. The year 2017 would be a rerun of 1983 and the post-Falklands War election.

Except the campaign shone a cruel light on all the limitations of Theresa May's political skills. For a start, she was testing the patience of the British people by subjecting them to weeks of relentless campaigning, party election broadcasts, unwanted door knocks and the whole hoopla that goes with a national plebiscite when it had only been two years since the last general election.

And then there was the party's manifesto. The signature policy amounted to telling people that they would have to pay far more for the costs of their own social care, including with any equity they may have built up in their homes. With the Conservative Party's legions of elderly homeowners, this proposal was a stonking stinker.

Labour branded it the 'dementia tax'. And outside Tory HQ you could smell the burning rubber and see black screech marks on the tarmac as they tried to perform a U-turn – while all the time pretending it was no such thing. 'Nothing's changed, nothing's changed,' Theresa May declared – convincing absolutely no one.

But the election changed *everything*. When you go into an unnecessary election with the sole aim of cashing in on some good poll numbers so you can return to Westminster with a bigger majority, and – oops – you end up going backwards and mislay your majority in a woeful campaign, no one is going to say, 'Well played, Theresa.' It had been an epic political miscalculation. She was forced into a deal with Unionist politicians in Northern Ireland to stay in power, while her backbenchers fumed and fulminated, with an ever-growing number agreeing with George Osborne – that she was indeed a dead woman walking.

Far from strengthening her hand in trying to unravel Brexit's Gordian knot, she was hobbled from the moment the new Parliament met. And when it falls to Cabinet ministers like Boris Johnson to make the clarion call to the party for unity and loyalty – as it did, and he did – you know you're in trouble. The woman whose slogan was 'strong and stable' had delivered the exact opposite, as she sought to strike an exit deal for the country with her European partners.

It would certainly be a lesson in political stamina.* Theresa May is nothing if not a trooper, and over the coming year she devoted herself to negotiating Britain's divorce settlement with the EU – a negotiation that would be long, arduous, tortuous and fractious. When it was finally agreed, it showed the extent to which compromises would have to be made to avoid a chaotic departure.

First though, she would have to win over the Cabinet.

In July 2018 she sat down with her most senior ministers at an all-day meeting in Chequers, the prime minister's country house in Buckinghamshire. This was the sell: the proposals would give the UK an independent trade policy, with the ability to set its own non-EU tariffs and to reach separate trade deals. The European Court of Justice would end its role in UK affairs.

---

* When I was a young correspondent watching from the House of Commons press gallery, I would regularly witness some brutal mauling being handed out to a minister. Michael White, then the political editor of the *Guardian*, once said something along the lines of what fun it is to see it happen, like being in the Colosseum in Rome where a Christian is about to be savaged by the lion, and it's all for our delectation. But spare a thought for the Christian in this analogy. How did Theresa May manage to get out of bed each morning when she knew the piles of ordure that would be flying her way the moment she left the Downing Street flat? I know it is fashionable to be cynical about politics and politicians – what is it that the American writer H.L. Mencken said? Something about the relationship between a journalist and a politician being the same as that between a dog and a lamp-post. I admire the politicians who are prepared to serve their communities and country – because I know I sure as hell wouldn't want to do it myself.

And there would be an end to annual payments to the EU budget except for 'appropriate contributions for joint action in specific areas'.

It sounded like Brexit, but was it Brexit enough? Well, no. The Chequers agreement made clear that the UK would 'maintain a common rule book for all goods' with the EU after Brexit. And that a treaty would be signed committing the UK to 'continued harmonisation' with EU rules – avoiding friction at the UK–EU border, including Northern Ireland. In other words, Britain would be locked in a customs union with the EU for several more years while it negotiated a more permanent, but vaguely defined, free trade deal with its most important trading partner. Outside the EU, Britain would be having to take edicts from Brussels, but have no role in deciding them: a rule-taker, not a rule-maker. And it wasn't so much that the hundred-page document was full of holes, but there were a helluva lot of questions that weren't answered or skirted over.

No doubt about it – this was a soft Brexit. Some might even say squidgy. But it was May's quiet determination to walk that 52–48 per cent tightrope – to honour the Brexit vote and the need to leave the European Union, to limit damage to Britain's economic interests, to be cognisant that a very large minority didn't want Brexit at all.

The marathon session ended with the apparent agreement of the whole Cabinet – a notable triumph for Theresa May and the small, tight team around her. But it wasn't to last. Once again, the Conservative Party's perpetual Euro-psychodrama was about to enter a new and destructive phase. The free-wheeling Brexit secretary, David Davis, was first out. Prior to his departure, he was memorably photographed in a meeting, across a desk from his European counterpart, Michel Barnier. It was a picture worth a thousand words. On Davis's side, there he sat – with no papers; on the other the serious-minded tech-nocrat, Barnier, with a mountain of bulging files. It was the amateur versus the professional; the wishful thinker that Brexit was a doddle, against the man who understood the migraine-| inducing complexity of it all. Yes, Davis would later explain, they had all their files stored digitally – but the old saying in politics is that if you're having to explain, you're losing.

With the Chequers deal, the former SAS reservist (as he is wont to tell people) decided he was out. Who dares whines, I guess. His decision on Sunday night to announce his departure from government caused a serious headache. No, not for Theresa May (well it probably did, in fairness), but for the person who saw himself as the natural leader of the Eurosceptic wing of the party. Yes, our foreign secretary, Boris Johnson, was in serious danger of being outmanoeuvred by the Brexit secretary.

So the next day Johnson quit too. He explained his delay thus:

The government now has a song to sing. The trouble is that I have practised the words over the weekend and find that they stick in the throat. We must have collective responsibility. Since I cannot in all conscience champion these proposals, I have sadly concluded that I must go.

He talked in his resignation letter about how Britain was 'headed for the status of colony – and many will struggle to see the economic or political advantages of that particular arrangement'. And he warned that the dream of Brexit 'is dying, suffocated by needless self-doubt'. And in terms that Donald Trump had used to berate her negotiating style, the outgoing foreign secretary complained in much more Johnsonian terms that 'it is as though we are sending our vanguard into battle with the white flags fluttering above them'. Though Trump would never manage the same rhetorical flourish, the message was identical – it was almost as if the two platinum blonds an Atlantic Ocean apart were conferring ...

In Theresa May's reply to Johnson's missive you could almost run your hand along her risen hackles. 'I am sorry – and a little surprised – to receive it after the productive discussions we had at Chequers on Friday, and the comprehensive and detailed proposal which we agreed as a Cabinet.' As discussed, May is not prone to the performative or the demonstrative, but her 'and a little surprised' is withering. I'm sure if you put it into Google Translate it would come out as 'you unprincipled, careerist bastard'.

She had taken on the mission impossible, but instead of the tape self-destructing, it was she who was going up in smoke –

and it would turn out to be a long, slow, painful political death, as Britain seemed to have become ungovernable.

The Withdrawal Agreement from the European Union, when it was finally agreed in November 2018 after 16 months of negotiation, amounted to some 585 pages, dealing with all the mind-boggling complexity that was thrown up by the seemingly simple proposition of 'vote leave'. Understandably, millions of those who had voted for this simple offering had no conception of triggering Article 50 or Northern Ireland backstops, they just wanted it done, and couldn't – frankly – understand why something they had been promised would be so simple was turning into such an epic head-scratcher. And so the leaders of Brexit, who of course knew all along of the complexity involved, changed their tune. The problem was not Brexit, but an establishment that didn't want to deliver on it. This, despite the millions of man-hours spent by civil servants over this period trying to turn 'take back control' into practical solutions.

It was probably a relief to have Johnson out of the Cabinet in many ways. But for Conservatives increasingly disillusioned by May, there was now a king across the water. A king who desperately wanted to have that crown placed on his dishevelled mop of hair. And he was fast out of the blocks, criticising what had been agreed.

Then came the inevitable. A vote of confidence in Theresa May a month later. Enough letters had been sent to the chairman of the Conservative backbench 1922 Committee, Sir Graham

Brady, to trigger a contest. Of the 317 Tory MPs able to vote, 200 backed her – so 63 per cent of the parliamentary party. In football, when your side wins even though you know in your heart it didn't deserve to, you think to yourself that a win is a win is a win – and it's three more points. Politics ain't like that. She had won, but she was on borrowed time.

The House of Commons chamber was more of a torture chamber for Theresa May, as her attempts to get the Withdrawal Agreement passed would need the approval of MPs. Her date with destiny was 15 January 2019. The blood, sweat and tears; the resignations and rebuffs; the line-by-line negotiation of the future relationship with the EU; the threats, cajoling and arm-twisting would come to a dramatic head.

A sitting government has enormous power over its back-benchers. The chief whip – the person charged with enforcing discipline – can offer carrots to those who behave well: the promise of ministerial office and all that goes with it. They can deliver little treats for a constituency MP – a new health clinic here, a town bypass there, the siting of a government office creating new jobs. And then there are the sticks: the threat that if you vote against the government there will be no career advancement, and the ultimate threat, when it's a big vote, that the PM might call a general election and you might lose your seat. Against that there is always a hard core of irreconcilables – the has-beens and never-will-bes. But the whips' office should never be underestimated.

All of which makes the events of 15 January even more remarkable. May didn't just lose, she went down in the most ignominious of defeats. The house voted 202 for her deal, 432 against. It was the biggest government defeat since universal suffrage; it was a calamity that made Ramsay MacDonald's mauling of 1924 – hitherto the biggest defeat suffered by a government – look like a moderate success story.

However tempting it is to make it so, the narrative here is not just about Theresa May. Yes, this happened on her watch; yes, to quote the post-war US president Harry Truman, the buck stopped with her. But given the passions, and given the increasingly bitter divisions in the country, there was no easy win to be had. Outside the Palace of Westminster, the place was a cauldron. Rival groups of Remainers and Brexiteers had gathered for this critical vote. Brexit had injected poison into the political bloodstream.

What Theresa May said in the wake of the defeat was telling. She noted: 'The house has spoken, and the government will listen … It is clear that the house does not support this deal, but tonight's vote tells us nothing about what it does support.' There was no majority for anything.

Having survived a confidence vote from within her own party, May said she would welcome a vote of confidence in the government. In other words, a motion put down by Labour, which if it was carried would force a general election. The Tory rebels who so wanted to be rid of May made clear PDQ that they would not back a Labour move that would trigger a general election and another date with destiny for the country – and a bitterly divided Conservative Party.

That vote took place the next day, 16 January, and the government survived – but by a narrow majority. May said she would reach out to other party leaders in Britain to see where common ground could be found. But even something as sensible sounding as that caused the temperature to rise within the Cabinet.

Several ministers, including Amber Rudd, Philip Hammond and Greg Clark, had been urging her to pursue a cross-party solution. But Brexit-supporting Cabinet ministers – like Andrea Leadsom and Penny Mordaunt – wanted instead revisions to the Irish backstop – or failing that, to prepare Britain for a 'managed no-deal' departure – an oxymoron if ever there was one.

That the idea of Britain leaving the EU with a no-deal Brexit could get serious purchase seemed to encapsulate the madness that had gripped certain sections of the political class and media. A no-deal Brexit would have meant Britain going onto 'World Trade Organisation' rules. We would have been a country without a trade deal with another country, resulting in tariffs being imposed on *all* British exports going to the EU. And without an agreement on food and safety standards, say, the EU could turn round and say, 'We don't want any of your produce.' It would have been devastating – but previously sane people were saying it was better than a

Withdrawal Agreement that kept Britain yoked – even temporarily – to the EU.

With a lack of good options, Theresa May decided she would give her Withdrawal Agreement one more heave. Well, two actually. So the government went again. Like the 'meaningful' vote of 15 January, the second attempt by the prime minister two months later to pass the Withdrawal Agreement foundered – this time only crashing by 149 votes.

I was being asked to appear a lot on US television at this time to try to explain the 'indicative votes' and 'meaningful votes' and 'Business of the House motions'. I had spent ten years in Westminster as a lobby correspondent and sort of thought I knew my way around the arcane bits of Commons procedure – but I was flapping a bit. 'Jon, tell us what's happening in 10 Downing today?' (For some reason Americans tend to refer to the PM's residence without adding the 'Street'. I have no idea why.) And while I could give a compelling overview of the arguments, the machinery was something else.

Normally the business of the Commons is set by the leader of the house – the government's chief business manager. But now, after a highly unusual vote, the ordinary Joes from the backbenches seized control of the agenda (lunatics taking over the asylum?), so MPs could vote not just on government proposals for sorting the impasse – they could also come up with their own ingenious ways to break the deadlock. Again, there was no majority to be had.

There would be one more attempt, but with a seductive twist for recalcitrant Conservative MPs. With the third vote that came at the end of March, Theresa May offered up an unusual and compelling sacrifice: herself. If Tory MPs would just back her wretched proposal, she would quit. Ride off into the sunset. Leave it to someone else to sort. The vote also left out some other bits that her Tory tormentors hated – but still it wasn't enough. Down she went again. When a government source after this unprecedented vote was asked what it all meant, he replied, 'Last person out, turn off the lights.'

Theresa May would declare the next day that Britain was in a grave position – and that was not hyperbolic. The markets were jittery, the pound was tanking on the foreign exchanges – particularly as part of her agreement with other EU leaders meant Britain was due to leave the EU in a couple of weeks' time. A no-deal Brexit was looking ever more likely. The situation was dire.

All this time I was in Washington, and I would sit in my little glass box of an office and watch the various bits of BBC output feeling at once a million miles away from everything and yet deeply affected by it. And as our salaries were paid in sterling and converted to US dollars, when the pound sank, so did our monthly salary. I would wander from my little glass box to the office next door where the bureau chief, Paul, sat and we would look at each other bewildered at what was happening at home. It was when Trump officials started asking me solicitously about the madness of what was going on in the UK that I knew we were in serious trouble.

Some inside the Cabinet thought that maybe the only way to find a way through this was to offer the British people a second referendum. It was an approach that many Remainers actively campaigned for. But that always seemed to me a ridiculous idea. For a start, it would have massively increased the sense of mistrust in and alienation from the political establishment. You would be telling those who had – for better or worse – voted for Brexit that they had got the answer wrong, and they needed to try again.

There is also the Winchester parable. In 1997, I was working in Westminster but living in Winchester. On the day of the general election, when Labour swept to power, I happened to speak to Alastair Campbell, then Tony Blair's communications director. I said that my wife and her best friend hadn't yet voted and were undecided between Labour and Lib Dem. Without hesitation, Campbell said that Labour had no chance in Winchester, so they ought to vote for the Lib Dem candidate, which they did. Mark Oaten, the Liberal Democrat, after several recounts, won the seat with a majority of two. The parable is not the power of voting, although of course it does make a difference. No, the parable is in what happened next. Gerry Malone, who had lost the previously safe Conservative seat, took it to the High Court. He won the case, and the election in Winchester was refought. This time, Oaten turned a majority of 2 into a majority of 21,000. The British sense of fair play had been offended in Winchester by Malone's actions. It seemed to me that a second referendum would have produced a similar effect.

There was the possibility of a general election, or another Commons vote – but May was blocked by the speaker, John Bercow, who refused to allow a vote on something that MPs had already rejected. She tried to get the Labour leader, Jeremy Corbyn, on board with a variety of inducements, but those talks came to nothing. Britain, with its long history of compromise and political deal-making, was in a different place in 2019. If there was an agreement to be found that would unlock this, Theresa May wasn't the person to find it.

Given her calamitous general election decision in 2017, given the votes of no confidence and the crushing Commons defeats, given the antipathy of so many of her backbenchers and her lack of retail skills, maybe the remarkable thing is not that she failed, but that she managed to stay in the saddle as long as she did. Either way, it was now completely over.

Theresa May had earned the nickname 'the Maybot' because of her rather robotic, dry, slightly emotionless language. It was coined by the *Guardian* sketch writer John Crace. But in Downing Street on 24 May, behind the same podium from which she had spoken three years earlier about healing divisions in the UK, it was a very different Theresa May that the world saw. Dressed in a red suit, she was the epitome of calm until she reached the end, and then her voice cracked and her face crumpled. 'I will shortly leave the job that it has been the honour of my life to hold – the second female prime minister but certainly not the last. I do so with no ill-will, but with enormous and enduring gratitude to have had the opportunity to serve the country I love.' It was gracious and in keeping with the woman that Britain had never really got to know. But it was also mad. The country had gone over the edge, and she'd gone with it.

In her first few months in office, her mantra was 'Brexit means Brexit'. And she reiterated in her departure from Downing Street that she still believed that. But what did it mean? Like a student trying to translate complex hieroglyphics, making sense of it eluded her. She knew what she *wanted* it to mean, but in the end not a single person in Parliament seemed to agree with her translation. It would be for someone else to try.

And there was one someone who was out of the traps like a hypersonic missile. Boris Johnson, who had played such a decisive role in bringing down first David Cameron and now Theresa May, thought this time – for sure – the crown was his for the taking. Johnson, who quickly became the bookies' favourite, set out his stall. But unlike many in the souks and bazaars around the world, there would be no haggling over the price. Under his leadership, Brexit would happen in the autumn, no ifs or buts. 'We will leave the EU on 31 October, deal or no deal.' The message was addressed to the country – but his real audience was the 300 or so MPs in Parliament, and the 100,000 or so Tory members in the country who would be picking Britain's next prime minister. 'Take it or leave it, Europe. There'll be a new sheriff in town if I win,' he seemed to be saying.

Theresa May had played by the rules and lost. The conclusion of Boris Johnson seemed to be – not for the first time, and most definitely not for the last – who needs rules?

• • •

Throughout all this I was in Washington, and it was during the leadership contest that I got a flavour of what a Boris Johnson premiership would be like. Our ambassador in DC was Sir Kim Darroch. A private telegram he'd written assessing the state of the Trump administration had been leaked. Predictably, the thin-skinned president gave Darroch a kicking. But the advice coming from the White House was that the storm would pass, and that Darroch should hunker down. He had the full backing of the Foreign Office, and the outgoing PM, Theresa May. After all, if an ambassador is not going to write candidly about what he sees and understands about the governance of the country he or she is in, then what's the point of having an ambassador?

What did for Darroch was not the mauling from Trump, but a single knife wound to the chest from Boris. In one of the Tory leadership debates, Johnson was asked six times whether our ambassador in Washington had his support. On six occasions, he refused to give it. There was shock and fury across Whitehall. Johnson was the runaway favourite to become our next prime minister. By refusing to back the ambassador, he had in effect sacked him – and Darroch had no option but to quit.

It was a pretty tawdry episode all round: the leak in the first place, the Trump reaction to it – but worst of all was the deliberate ambivalence of the man who would be our next prime minister. And once Darroch had resigned, Johnson showed another less than admirable aspect of his personality. He was busy going around, lavishing praise on Darroch saying what a brilliant diplomat he was. According to one source, he also tried to speak repeatedly to the soon-to-be quitting ambassador to tell him it was all a terrible misunderstanding and that the media had misinterpreted what he said in the leadership debate. Darroch wouldn't take his calls.

In the great sweep of everything else that was going on, this is a minor incident – but it speaks to a lot more. Let's face it – what Johnson did was entirely driven by his desire to stay in the good books of Trump. This devil-may-care attitude to norms of behaviour and his proper obligations might have helped Johnson then, but it would be a harbinger of the problems that would come later. But Johnson never thought about what would come later. This was the here and now, and he would need the US president as an ally as the path to Brexit became rockier. And Darroch was sacrificed so there were no impediments. But what does it say about Britain's weakness, post-Brexit, that the British PM has to sacrifice an ambassador simply because he had been doing his job? As a former foreign secretary, David Miliband, would point out, Johnson's desire to stay in the good graces of the White House was a manifestation of weakness: 'In today's global village, when you pull away from your neighbours [the EU] everyone can take advantage.'

The great myth in all this was that because Trump had supported Brexit he was going to give the UK a fabulous trade deal. But what leverage did Britain have now that it had left the EU? In the end there was no trade deal. It just wasn't a priority for Trump. And so the question remains: what did the sacrifice of Darroch achieve other than to make our ambassadors around the world feel that the new PM would not have their backs?

Johnson won the leadership contest handsomely, seeing off his rival, Jeremy Hunt, with more or less twice the number of votes of the Tory Party membership. That he won was no big surprise – and one of the first to congratulate him was the US president. Donald Trump noted that 'a really good man is going to be the prime minister of the UK now', and Johnson would 'get it done', referring to Brexit. The president added the sort of Trumpian endorsement that Johnson probably didn't want given the unpopularity of the US president in Britain: 'They call him "Britain Trump" and people are saying that's a good thing.'

On the day of his victory, Johnson promised that he would 'deliver Brexit, unite the country and defeat Jeremy Corbyn'. Two out of the three he would deliver on – and in quick succession. Uniting the country though? Forget it. He would become one of the most divisive and polarising prime ministers in modern British history. It wasn't just about policy though. On policy, Thatcher was a deeply polarising figure, but few questioned her integrity, sincerity or probity. With Johnson, *everything* about his conduct as prime minister and first lord of the treasury was under scrutiny. You would have to go back 100 years to the period of the Liberal prime minister Lloyd George to find anyone close to Johnson for poor behaviour. Stanley Baldwin, who would go on to become Conservative prime minister in those inter-war years, said of Lloyd George, 'He had a morally disintegrating effect on all whom he had to deal with.' Of Donald Trump in the White House and Boris Johnson in Downing Street the same could arguably be said.

By the time Boris Johnson had got his feet under the desk in the Georgian Tardis that is Downing Street it was the summer recess, when MPs go off to escape the madness of Westminster. And it had been the most bonkers period. Brexit issues, though, were still unresolved and would have to be tackled once MPs returned to Westminster. Except Johnson and the new leader of the house, Jacob Rees-Mogg – fellow Etonian and MP for the mid-nineteenth century – had cooked up a cunning plan. They wanted MPs *not* to come back; have an extra five weeks of holidays, kids – and that will save all that messy debate over Europe.

The mechanism by which they attempted to do this was proroguing Parliament. What happens is the PM goes to the sovereign and says Parliament doesn't need to come back until the opening of the new session, which is marked by the Queen's Speech where the legislative agenda is set out. It is normally a matter of a few days between the end of one parliamentary session and the start of the new – the prorogation. But Johnson wanted it to last for weeks.

The speaker, John Bercow, whose job is to uphold the sovereignty of Parliament from a power-grabbing executive, was scathing when he found out about the plan. 'I have had no contact from the government, but if the reports that it is seeking to prorogue Parliament are confirmed, this move represents a constitutional outrage,' he said. 'However it is dressed up, it is blindingly obvious that the purpose of prorogation now would be to stop Parliament debating Brexit.'

A legal challenge was mounted that went all the way to the UK Supreme Court. And the unanimous, jaw-dropping verdict of the 11 justices was delivered by the president, Lady Hale. She said: 'The decision to advise Her Majesty to prorogue Parliament was unlawful because it had the effect of frustrating or preventing the ability of Parliament to carry out its constitutional functions without reasonable justification.' The most senior member of the judiciary said that the advice the PM had given to the Queen was unlawful. This was legal and political dynamite. The unperturbable and languid Rees-Mogg apparently told his fellow ministers at the Cabinet meeting which followed – without irony – that it was a constitutional coup that had been mounted by the courts.

Johnson was not deterred – and his tactics would become much more aggressive. In early September there was a Commons vote on something that sounded tedious and procedural: it was about whether it was only the government that had the right to propose new laws. A group of senior Tories wanted to make a no-deal Brexit impossible by legislating against it. The government went nuclear.

There were 21 Tories who voted against Johnson to bring about a government defeat. But far from this being the end of it, it was just the start. The chief whip, on Johnson's instruction, removed the whip from all of them. They were no longer Conservative MPs. Out went the father of the house, Kenneth Clarke; gone was Winston Churchill's grandson, Sir Nicholas Soames. Theresa May's chancellor, Philip Hammond, was gone. Cabinet minister David Gauke and former attorney general Dominic Grieve were ousted. Likewise, leadership contender Rory Stewart. And the list went on. These weren't nobodies whose careers were being ended. These were the big beasts of the party.

It felt like a purge. Forget the Tory Party being a broad church. It was fit in, or fuck off. One practical effect of this mass expulsion was that Johnson now led a minority government, even with the votes of the DUP, so he moved to call a general election – and this would be another vote that he would lose – three times. The coalition had introduced the Fixed Term Parliaments Act, and that required the government of the day to secure a two-thirds majority before it would be able to call a general election.

On the fourth attempt, Johnson got his way: there would be a general election on 12 December 2019. After the vote, he said, 'There is only one way to get Brexit done in the face of this unrelenting parliamentary obstructionism, this endless, wilful, fingers-crossed, "not me, guv" refusal to deliver on the mandate of the people, and that is to refresh this Parliament and give the people a choice.' Those three words – get Brexit done – were the beginning, middle and end of the Tory offering to the British people. After so much dysfunction, political paralysis, incompetence and hand-wringing, it seemed the British people just wanted the pain and torment to end.

It would be a dramatic end to a dramatic year. I watched the results come in in the ballroom of the British Embassy in Washington, where a big screen had been set up for the general election watch party, with the wonderful Andy Warhol silk-screen print of Elizabeth II over the fireplace looking down on us. Boris Johnson was going to achieve far more than 15 minutes of fame, as he swept to victory securing for the Conservatives their biggest majority since Margaret Thatcher in 1987. I had never known a political night like it. When Blair won big in 1997 you could see it coming from a long way out. The Tories had been in government for 18 years. It was clearly over. Johnson on that night in December was winning in places that just seemed totally unimaginable. Labour's red wall had crumbled;

the industrial heartlands – for which, historically, read Labour heartlands – had gone blue. Many of them for the first time ever. Even Tony Blair's old seat of Sedgefield in the solidly Labour North East, where they used to weigh the Labour vote rather than count it, went Tory – and so did dozens of others. You just had to wipe your eyes in disbelief. To the American friends I was watching this with, I had to say just imagine Oklahoma going Democrat or New York voting Republican.

Just after seven o'clock the next morning in London, Johnson declared that Brexit was now the 'irrefutable, irresistible, unarguable decision of the British people' and he made a vow to those who had 'lent' their vote to the Tories in those historic Labour-voting mining and industrial regions: 'I will not let you down.'

For the Boris Johnson fan-club this was proof positive that he was the great man of destiny, just like his hero Winston Churchill. That he was the man to set Britain on a different, resurgent path. And he had the Midas touch too, as the master reader of the mood of the British people. There is no doubt that he had won the Conservatives a hugely impressive victory; one that substantially – overwhelmingly – redrew the political map of England. It is broadly a fair analysis to give him all the credit, so long as you exclude one thing: Jeremy Corbyn.

With Corbyn as Labour leader they had someone who was – arguably – totally unelectable as prime minister. He had been mired in a ghastly antisemitism row, which the then Labour leadership showed itself to be utterly incapable of dealing with. A human rights watchdog would later find that Labour was responsible for 'unlawful' discrimination and harassment of Jews during the four and a half years of Corbyn's leadership. What a stain on Labour's reputation. Corbyn, who sees himself as a paragon of virtue where racism is concerned, would go on to claim that the report dramatically overstated the problem.

Corbyn was way to the left of any previous Labour leader, and his was the politics of protest. I was a lobby correspondent in the 1990s when he was part of a small handful of hard-left MPs. He never wanted any part in the modernisation of the party. Kinnock's red rose socialism? Forget it. Blair's New Labour? Yuck. Corbyn would regularly turn up at the tiny BBC office in the Commons, just off the press gallery, with a news release pronouncing solidarity with this or that cause, and asking whether we'd like to interview him. I can't remember an occasion when the answer was 'yes'. And away he'd skulk. The idea that one day he would become leader was beyond imagination.

He went into the 2019 election with spending commitments that were like the ones you make in your head when you have your EuroMillions lottery ticket in front of you, in the moments before none of your numbers coming up in the draw. We would all get free broadband. Why, I'm not sure, as there are millions of Britons happily paying for their broadband, just like they do their electricity and gas. But there would be renationalisation of parts of the energy sector – without shareholders being paid the full value of the companies.

On the critical question of Europe, Corbyn was offering a second referendum, but his ambivalence towards that issue was well-established. He tried to speak the language of Remain – but the words sat uncomfortably in his mouth. And it was equally telling that after the poisoning by the Russian FSB of former KGB man Sergei Skripal in Salisbury – a chemical weapons attack on British soil, no less – Corbyn couldn't bring himself to condemn Moscow. The one thing you could never accuse Corbyn of was being inauthentic. But when the centre of political gravity in Britain is in an entirely different place, it's going to be difficult to lead Labour to victory in a general election.

As it was, he led Labour to its most calamitous election defeat since 1935.

Johnson was now established as one of the truly significant figures of modern British political history. He was one of the principal reasons that Brexit happened, and weeks after his election victory, Britain did leave the EU. He had in the most basic sense made good on the campaign pledge to 'get Brexit done'. But his claim that there was an 'oven-ready Brexit' that would lead the country to a post-European nirvana turned out to be utter nonsense. His antics and demeanour led to a new word gaining currency in the English language – 'boosterism'. The Collins dictionary defines it as 'the practice of enthusiastically praising something in order to persuade other people that it is very good even if it is not'. Johnson and Brexit in a nutshell.

It had fallen to him to lead Britain out of the EU and to make good on Brexit. With that overwhelming mandate from the British people, a Labour Party in tatters and the Liberal Democrats an insignificant rump, Conservatives thought this would be the start of a long and uninterrupted Johnsonian age; at the end of 2019, his dominance of the political landscape was total. Funny how quickly things can change.

CHAPTER 3

IT CAN'T HAPPEN HERE (2021)

January 6th was the most shocking day of my journalistic career. It was the day when Congress should have certified Biden's victory. When I went live on *BBC News at Ten* that night the mob was still in control of Congress – and Joe Biden's victory had most certainly not been certified. Lawmakers were still cowering in their offices hiding behind makeshift barricades – with desks, cupboards and filing cabinets pushed against doors to stop the rioters getting in. One section of the mob was hunting for the Democrat speaker of the House, Nancy Pelosi; another was chanting 'hang Mike Pence' – the vice president who'd followed the Constitution rather than the wishes of Donald Trump. The Capitol Police who maintain order at the two houses of Congress had been totally overwhelmed. I said that evening it felt that US democracy was in a precarious position. I was very conscious that, dramatic though this was, I should not be OTT. When something as self-evidently dramatic as that is unfolding you don't need to gild the lily.

What we have learnt since then is that it was far, far worse; far more precarious than anyone realised at the time. It left me with an uncomfortable feeling, the sort of feeling you have when you hear that a friend's home has been broken into, and you start wondering how safe your house is. After American democracy's near miss, it would be almost negligent not to ask questions about the robustness of your own democracy.

Arguably you would have to go back 150 years to the US Civil War to find anything as momentous and so full of portent for the United States. Of course, in terms of lives lost, January 6th was nothing compared to the scarring horror of 9/11, or indeed Pearl Harbor, America's other day of infamy, as Franklin D. Roosevelt would frame the attack by the Japanese on the American navy in Hawaii on 7 December 1941. The January 6th riot at the Capitol, in terms of physical casualties, was no more than your average mass shooting incident, which occurs daily in the US – the Gun Violence Archive counted 656 mass shooting incidents in 2023 alone. There were only a handful of deaths at the Capitol. But this was different.

Why Pearl Harbor and 9/11 hold such a grip on the American imagination is that they both in their own ways showed that the US – for all its undoubted military might – is not totally inoculated from what is happening in the outside world. The US is blessed to have friendly nations to the north and south – Canada and Mexico – and to have thousands of miles of water going east and west thanks to the Atlantic and Pacific oceans. You also have a land of abundance – the oil riches of Texas and Oklahoma, and more recently the fracking potential in the Dakotas, the fruit belt of California and Florida, the coal mines of West Virginia and Pennsylvania, and the bread basket of the Midwest meant there was – and still is to some extent – a self-sufficiency that other countries could only dream about. The uniqueness of this geography allows Americans often to think they have perfect insulation from the argumentative, quarrelsome, dangerous, sectarian rest of the world. Yes, bad things may happen *there*, but – praise the Lord – they don't happen *here* in the peaceful US of A. It is a common mindset.

This helps explain another recurrent tension in American history and thinking: isolationism, that understandable desire to pull up the drawbridge and shut yourself off from all the unpleasantness in the world. If you think like that, you recoil from the suggestion that the US should be the global policeman, bringing peace to the world's trouble spots, committing US men and hardware to far-flung places that your average American has never heard of. I remember being in Washington as President Clinton sought to give the country's citizens a lesson on the historical importance of the Balkans. 'We're going to roll down the map,' he told the American people before going into his explanation on why the break-up of Yugoslavia and the events of Sarajevo or Pristina were of direct concern to someone in Duluth, Minnesota, or Peoria, Illinois. (It didn't work.)

Other presidents since World War Two also tried, to varying degrees of success. Dwight Eisenhower and Korea, Lyndon B. Johnson with Vietnam, George H.W. Bush and his son, George W. Bush, over Iraq. The endless conflict in Afghanistan ended abruptly (and some might argue ignominiously) under Joe Biden, who then found himself ramping-up involvement in Ukraine. From Asia Pacific to Europe, from the Middle East to Africa and across to Latin America, there aren't many places on the globe where American servicemen and -women have not been entangled.

It is the life of being the world's pre-eminent superpower. It is the recognition that it is in American interests to be active players in this unstable globe – because if they aren't, the unstable world will wash up on their shores. Pearl Harbor and 9/11 were jolting reminders of why the drawbridge strategy has obvious limitations. Not doing anything is as much a policy choice as getting involved.

That is why January 6th was so important. This was not America at war with the outside world but at war with itself. Historians I am sure will say it is ludicrous for me to go back to the American Civil War for the nearest parallel, but I can't think what else compares. So let me make the argument (and also acknowledge the limitations of my case). Only a few people died on January 6th against the 600,000 plus who died in the terrible and brutal battles between the Union and Confederate armies. There was no secession. No issue like slavery at stake. So, in that sense, January 6th might just be dismissed as a curious blip.

But in other ways it was worse. This was an insurrection, a coup attempt that was eventually defeated – and it was based on a lie. Yes, a plain and downright untruth – nurtured, perpetuated and weaponised by a president who just didn't have the emotional capacity to accept that he had lost the 2020 election; that he was a loser. Not only that, Trump was egged on by some bad people in his inner circle who were beneficiaries of the executive power a president is able to deploy. For a whole basketful of dubious motivations they were happy to encourage him to cling to office. There was a slew of spineless Republican lawmakers shamefully – and some shamelessly – indulging this baseless fantasy of a 'stolen election', and there were lawyers who would willingly bear false witness to stay in Donald Trump's good graces. The bonds that kept a nation together were stretched to breaking point.

At least of the Civil War you can say there was a proper *casus belli* – the Southern states with their powerful white plantation owners were terrified that their economic wellbeing – and US economic growth – would be seriously jeopardised by Abraham Lincoln's moves to abolish slavery. Repellent though the argument may be to twenty-first-century sensibilities, the concerns of the Confederate Generals Robert E. Lee and Stonewall Jackson were real.

But what of their pale imitations on January 6th? What was their *casus belli*? For the anti-abolitionists of the nineteenth century and their highly able generals we had on January 6th a ragbag bunch of neo-fascist white supremacists like the Oath Keepers and the all-male, right-wing, misogynist Proud Boys. And then there was one other group hellbent on mayhem, and that was QAnon – the conspiracy theorists that seemed to think that more or less everyone in Washington was part of some paedophile ring, with the exception of Donald Trump who would vanquish these sexual deviants. It wasn't confined to the District of Columbia, to be fair. Oprah Winfrey, the Dalai Lama, Pope Francis and Tom Hanks were apparently all in on it. They were all satanic child molesters who then went on to eat their victims.

So far-fetched was some of this stuff that QAnon was the almost comedic end of it – who can forget the 'QAnon Shaman' running amok in Congress with his bare tattooed chest, fur hat with horns coming out of it and full warpaint on his face, while carrying a spear? Jacob Chansley cut an extraordinary figure as he sought to whip up the crowd outside Congress, with his seditious talk of meting out justice to Mike Pence, who had 'betrayed' Trump with his decision to certify Joe Biden's election victory. Chansley was imprisoned for his role in the January 6th riots. But for all the menace and fiery rhetoric that he represented on the day, he was the picture of meekness itself in court. 'I have no excuse,' he said. 'No excuses whatsoever. My behaviour is indefensible.'

My former BBC colleague Gabriel Gatehouse chronicled brilliantly the rise of QAnon, and how it moved from being this quirky handful of apparent whack jobs who would turn up at Trump rallies holding up the letter Q – the supposed codeword of someone in the deep state who was going to blow the lid off the Satan-worshipping paedos – to something more sinister with a considerable grip on public opinion. They were promising a day of reckoning: the coming storm. And Donald Trump did nothing to distance himself from them. If they wanted to support him – then fine.

After Biden took office, they kept on predicting a 'second coming' – when the Democrat pretender would be swept away and Donald Trump would be rightly restored – the date shifting as each new deadline for 'the storm' passed. The fertile imaginations of QAnon don't rest though: a new theory is that Biden was actually the murderer of JFK in 1963. (You'll have to stay with me for this.) The young Biden apparently looks like Lee Harvey Oswald, who carried out the murder. Never mind that every American saw Lee Harvey Oswald murdered by Jack Ruby in the basement of Dallas Police HQ as he was about to appear in court. It's the JFK assassination theory no one had seen coming. The 35th president of the US murdered by the 46th. Now that's what you call a plot twist.

An alarming number of Americans are buying into this garbage. A survey at the start of 2024 by the Public Religion Research Institute and the Brookings Institution found that roughly a quarter of the US population shared the views of QAnon. That puts the cult on a similar footing as the major religions in America. Worse still, according to this survey almost as many thought that 'true American patriots may have to resort to violence in order to save our country'. Not surprisingly, half of those thought the 2020 election was stolen. These are scary numbers. So QAnon is not quite the joke that we would like it to be.

I was surrounded by a mob of Trump supporters the day after the riot. By now the Capitol Police and the National Guard had reasserted control, and the whole of the area around Congress had been cordoned off with razor wire and heavy metal fencing. I was going live from as near as you could get to the Capitol on *BBC News at Six*, which Sophie Raworth was presenting in London. The crowd started to jeer and heckle me – so much so that Sophie had to apologise for the distracting noise – but the jeers and catcalling turned into a chant. One or two voices at first, then a chorus of 'You lost, go home. You lost, go home.' I carried on, and was trying to figure out what their chant meant. Did they think because I was BBC, I had to be liberal and was therefore a Biden supporter? And, of course, in their eyes he had lost the election. It was the only thing that made any sense. So I asked one of the scary-looking middle-aged guys what on earth the chant meant. He looked at me with fury, jabbed me in the chest and said just one thing: '1776'. As sledges go, that one takes some beating.

More potent, better organised and equipped were the Proud Boys and the Oath Keepers. It is tempting to think that what unfolded on January 6th was a simple case of Donald Trump addressing a crowd at the Ellipse. He fires them up with his rhetoric of fighting like hell to protect the country. And they all go and march on the Capitol after he'd finished speaking. Sure, many did. The mood that frigid morning was ugly and unlike anything I had experienced in my years of covering Trump. When I used to approach Trump supporters with my cameraman and microphone, yes, I was called fake news – but it was done in jokey terms. Not today. Today there was no jest, just fury. The mood was ugly, edgy – and two of the people I interviewed that lunchtime – dressed in paramilitary clothing, wearing lightweight body armour – would be filmed in the Capitol building and later charged with criminal offences. They had come looking for trouble and sure enough, they found it.

But these right-wing militias had arrived in Washington with a plan. We now know that the leaders of the Proud Boys and the Oath Keepers had met the night before to plan their assault. They were heavily armed, there was a chain of command and orders were given. They turned up at the Capitol in their khaki fatigues and Kevlar helmets. The Oath Keepers were nearly all ex-military. And their leader, Stewart Rhodes, would later be found guilty of seditious conspiracy and sentenced to 18 years in jail. His trial would hear hair-raising evidence of the extent of the planned coup.

One witness described how a hotel room in Arlington, Virginia – just across the Potomac river from Washington – had become the Oath Keepers' extraordinary arsenal. 'I had not seen that many weapons in one location since I was in the military,' said Terry Cummings, a relative newcomer to the organisation, who had been called to give evidence in Rhodes's trial. This was to be the base for the Oath Keepers QRF – quick reaction force. The planning had started just after the November election and the declaration of Joe Biden as the victor.

Rhodes and his co-defendants were communicating via the encrypted app Signal. The messages were flying between him and the group's regional leaders organising and activating the plan for January 6th. Many were urging Trump to invoke the Insurrection Act, which Rhodes argued would license the group to use force to prevent Congress from certifying the 2020 election results. One of the co-conspirators, Brian Ulrich, had written: 'Trump acts now maybe a few hundred radicals die trying to burn down cities. Trump sits on his hands, Biden wins, millions die resisting the death of the 1st and 2nd amendment.' These people were planning for a violent apocalypse.

In the many court cases that followed, one message from one person kept on coming up in evidence. It was the tweet from Donald Trump on 19 December 2020, urging his supporters to descend on Washington on January 6th, when Congress was meant to be going through the purely ceremonial job of confirming Biden's victory. The outgoing president wrote about the 'big protest' – and finished thus: 'Be there, will be wild.' These people made sure it was.

Inevitably, in the aftermath of January 6th – in the court cases that followed (hundreds have been prosecuted for their role in the violence) and in the congressional investigation that unfolded – much focus has been on the militias. It's obvious. If you're doing January 6th the movie, you're going to focus on these anti-government militia leaders with their weapons and ammunition belts, and the handcuffs with which they were going to perform citizen's arrests on the Nancy Pelosis of this world. And they were at the heart of the mayhem, as they bulldozed their way past the police and ran amok along the marble corridors of the Capitol. Pictorially they were where the action was. But it is the politics of what unfolded that is more important.

What this dreadful day represents in all its technicolour hideousness is how fragile our democracy is – whether in the US or the UK. It revealed fundamental weaknesses in our democratic structures and arrangements, and how easily they can be exploited by bad actors. The guardrails that are meant to keep our democracy safe were found to be far more brittle than we realised.

After the most brutal battle of the Civil War in Gettysburg, Pennsylvania, Abraham Lincoln went there to mark the dedication of the town as a national cemetery in 1863. It was there that he gave one of the most famous – and short-est – speeches in American political history. After the riot at the Capitol, 158 years on from Lincoln's speech, it was not fantastical to wonder whether government of the people, by the people and for the people was indeed about to perish.

Of course, there have been contentious elections before. The one where arguably an election was stolen was the 1960 contest between John F. Kennedy and Richard Nixon. Nixon might go on to become America's most controversial president and be forced to resign over the Watergate break-in. But in 1960 he was the victim. The powerful mayor of Chicago, Richard Daley, seemed to mysteriously magic up over 8,000 votes for Kennedy that allowed him to carry the state. But Nixon accepted defeat graciously. Later, in 2000, Bush v Gore looked like it would be the most contentious election in American history.

Until Trump. We shouldn't have been surprised. Even after his victory four years earlier he wouldn't – couldn't – accept that Hillary Clinton had polled three million more votes than he did. What she hadn't done was win the only battle that matters and that is the race for 270 electoral college votes. Nevertheless, the suggestion that more people across America preferred Clinton to him was an affront to Trump. He ordered one of his most trusted cheerleaders to lead a commission of inquiry to unearth widespread fraud that would explain his loss of the popular vote. It led to nothing. Trump still refused to accept defeat.

On polling day in 2020 there was a rare moment of near self-reflection on the part of Donald Trump in his attitude towards the election result. He had gone to visit his campaign headquarters, just outside Washington, DC, and predicted it was going to be a great night. 'Winning is easy,' he tells reporters. 'Losing is never easy,' he went. 'Not for me it's not.'

Let us be clear, though: Donald Trump DID lose in November 2020. To understand what happened on January 6th we need to consider the day itself, the lead-up to it, and its aftermath. Anyone who has done the most basic study of US politics knows that there is a written constitution, and there are three co-equal branches of government – the executive, the legislature and the judiciary. These are the checks and balances that the Founding Fathers of the US drew up in the late eighteenth century, and which had served America well. So why at the beginning of 2021 did they seem so perilously fragile?

After the results were declared in the 50 states there were legal challenges – some 60 of them – by Trump and his supporters. And in all of them the courts found nothing improper or dismissed the cases as vexatious. Some of the litigation was heard by judges that Donald Trump himself had appointed. The attorney general, William Barr, asked the FBI to look into allegations that there may have been fraud, and Barr – who hitherto had been slavishly loyal to the president, told Trump that there was no evidence of wrongdoing. Within the Department of Homeland Security, an election security coordinator had been appointed by Trump to look out for interference in the November poll. He too found nothing untoward. In each of the 50 states, the most senior official after the governor, the secretary of state, has to certify the results, and only does so after he or she is satisfied that the election has been conducted properly. Every secretary of state said they were happy. There was an attempt by some Trump loyalists to take a case to the Supreme Court to get them to intervene. The nine justices – six of whom are conservatives, three of which had been appointed by Trump – were having no part in it.

This may have been Trump's lawyers trying to game the system, but that is what lawyers are paid to do – find an angle, a crack where you might be able to prise something open. It may not have been pretty, but it wasn't unconstitutional. It was testing the Constitution.

Other things that happened were very much on the wrong side of the line. Perhaps the most notorious was Trump's call to the secretary of state in the key swing state of Georgia. Brad Raffensperger is a Republican who had backed Trump for the presidency. He also follows election rules. And unfortunately for Donald Trump, when the votes were tallied, he had lost the state to Biden by 11,779 votes – so all the electoral college votes of that state would go to Biden. Trump rang him, and in an hour-long call tried to strong-arm him. The call was recorded and released to the press by the Georgia authorities – a punchy move given Trump's vindictiveness. At one point the president says:

'What I want to do is this. I just want to find, uh, 11,780 votes, which is one more than we have, because we won the state.' He also suggested that Raffensperger might have committed a criminal offence by *not* overturning the result in his favour. It is a fascinating call for it shows so many aspects of Trump's personality. At times self-pitying, at others menacing and overbearing – but all the time there is just a hint of desperation in his voice as he refuses to come to terms with the sheer impossibility that he lost. The call took place on 2 January 2021. The inauguration of Joe Biden was less than three weeks away.

There are similar stories from other states where Trump was hoping to win but didn't. But let us just stick with Georgia, the 'peach state' where things were far from peachy. Allegations were also made about the voting machines being used, and whether they were – somehow – switching votes for Trump, to count for Biden. This view was memorably advanced by Trump's praetorian guard of lawyers at one of the most chaotic and surreal news conferences I have ever witnessed. It was the one where Rudy Giuliani's hair dye started to melt under the heat of the camera lights, and he had brown streaks running down his face.

One of the most fearsome attorneys at this presser was Sidney Powell. Despite having no background in election law, she was one of the most outspoken on the theory about the Dominion voting machines. It was a conspiracy involving the Chinese, Hugo Chávez (who had died many years before), and, of course, George Soros. No conspiracy theory from the right is complete without his name cropping up. She argued that the machines' software had been tampered with, arrant nonsense that was picked up by Rupert Murdoch's Fox News with alacrity. This would cost them dear.

Powell herself would plead guilty to a misdemeanour offence in a case brought by the district attorney of Fulton County in Georgia (Fulton County is – essentially – the Atlanta area). She was initially charged with much more serious offences of racketeering and conspiracy to commit election fraud, but accepted a lesser charge in return for giving evidence in the other cases that arise – mainly – from Donald Trump's call to Raffensperger.

The other person who has found his reputation trashed by his association with Donald Trump is Rudy Giuliani, he of the leaky hair dye. Giuliani – once known as America's mayor for his heroic role in New York post 9/11 – is now a laughing stock, an almost pitiable figure were it not for the ignominious role he has played in his own demise. Leave aside the massively embarrassing cameo he played in a Sacha Baron Cohen film, in which he was seen undoing his trousers and lying back on a bed in the hope that an actress playing the part of Borat's daughter was going to tend to his desires. If that was sleazy, what he did in Georgia was downright malevolent.

He accused two election workers in Georgia, Wandrea Moss and her mother, Ruby Freeman, of 'ballot stuffing'. After the polls had closed in Georgia, Giuliani shared a video from an absentee ballot counting centre in Fulton County. He alleged that this showed the two women were cheating and scanning ballots multiple times to benefit Joe Biden. As an attorney to the Trump campaign, media personality, and former New York mayor, Giuliani has a massive social media following – and he used it to whip up a storm against these two hitherto anonymous African American women.

They faced death threats and endless racial smears. A year-long investigation by the secretary of state's office found the allegations to be baseless and without foundation. A hand recount found that the numbers tallied. What Giuliani had alleged was totally false and bogus. He was sued for defamation and eventually acknowledged that his statements about the two women were false. A jury heard that the two women feared for their lives after what Giuliani had done. Giuliani was ordered to pay the two women a staggering $148 million in damages. Soon after the case, Giuliani filed for bankruptcy.

A third member of the Trump legal team, Jenna Ellis, faced a similar fall from grace. She too was prominent at the Giuliani hair dye event at Republican National Committee HQ, she too was involved in the Georgia lies, and she too now has a criminal conviction after pleading guilty in October 2023 to one felony count of aiding and abetting false statements in writing. She's also been publicly censured by the Colorado Supreme Court – her home state – for recklessly making ten public misrepresentations, which she admitted to, including the claim that Trump won the 2020 election and that it had been stolen from him.

Why did these well-known lawyers lie through their teeth about the election? Why make up stories about election workers that bring about your financial downfall; why go along with something you know not to be true? Who knows what psychological factors were at play – were they frightened of Trump? Did they just want to please? Or maybe they had made a calculation that he would get away with it, and they would too, boosting their chances of preferment in the next Trump administration if the coup attempt were successful.

These are just the obvious characters. They are the people you would build the movie or the play around. There are the goodies – the Brad Raffenspergers and Mike Pences who despite being Trump supporters felt their first loyalty was to the Constitution; the William Barrs who told Trump he was wrong and suffered the consequences (in Barr's case, being promptly fired as attorney general). And then there are the baddies – the grifters who became the face of the Trump legal team, even though they now admit they were telling a pack of lies; and the paramilitary leaders who led their men into battle.

There are others whose role in the events of January 6th are less direct. Steve Bannon entered the White House with Donald Trump as his chief of strategy having masterminded the Trump election campaign in its final stages. Indeed, it would be easy to paint Bannon as the puppet master and Trump the puppet. He is a white nationalist – he describes himself as a populist nationalist – with strong anarchic tendencies; he came into the White

House seemingly wanting to burn everything to the ground. I interviewed him in 2019 in New Mexico on the border with Mexico, where he was involved in fundraising to build more of the wall that would keep illegal immigrants out.*

He is a complex man. On camera he is a straight-down-the-line, out-and-out populist. He is nothing but full-throated in his support of Trump and what he is trying to do to make America great again. But off camera? He is much more nuanced. He is well read, has a strong sense of history, loves the BBC and the *Guardian* (whose politics he hates). But none of that would ever come across in his public utterances. That would be bad for the image. After the interview I took a torrent of abuse for putting a 'fascist-enabler' on camera. At the time I defended the integrity of the interview because I believe we need to hear from people whose views we might not agree with – particularly someone as influential as him. But over time I have come to a slightly different view. What's the point of putting on camera someone who espouses views that are so different from what they express in private? It's just a con on the public. It feels that well-intentioned broadcasters like the BBC are playing by a set of rules that populist politicians have long since ripped up.

A leaked recording unearthed by *Mother Jones* magazine has Bannon telling associates on 31 October 2020 (so only a few days before the election) that President Trump had a plan to

---

* It later emerged there was massive fraud in the fundraising, which led to Bannon being charged. Trump pardoned him before he left office.

declare victory on election night – even if he was losing. Trump knew the slow counting of Democratic-leaning postal votes meant the early returns would show leads for him in key swing states. His 'strategy' would be to use this as a reason to make the assertion that he had won, while claiming that the inevitable shifts in vote totals towards Joe Biden would be the result of fraud. 'What Trump's gonna do is just declare victory. Right? He's gonna declare victory. But that doesn't mean he's a winner,' Bannon told people while laughing. 'He's just gonna say he's a winner.' Which of course is *exactly* what happened when Trump addressed supporters at the White House on election night.

Bannon also seemed to know exactly how the day was going to unfold on January 6th. The congressional investigation found that the day before the riot, Bannon spoke by phone to Trump twice. After the first conversation, the former Trump aide announced on his podcast, *The War Room*, that 'all hell was going to break loose'. The subpoena for Bannon to appear before the committee was ignored, and he was held to be in contempt of Congress. He would later be sentenced to four months in prison for this defiance.

On the day itself, as chaos was unfolding, as the all too flimsy barricades of the Capitol were being breeched and the anorexically thin blue line dissolved, just down Pennsylvania Avenue in the White House, Trump was holed up in the private dining room. The one alteration he'd made to its historic fixtures and fittings was to install a giant plasma TV screen across one wall. And from there he sat and purred with delight at what he was witnessing. One White House press secretary said he was 'gleeful'. The rioters were people who'd taken him at his word and gone and fought like hell. Nero would have approved.

Testimony given at the January 6th inquiry revealed that Donald Trump was being implored to get involved – by his daughter Ivanka, the House minority leader Kevin McCarthy, his general counsel, senators and friends. The phone of his chief of staff, Mark Meadows, was burning red hot as the situation was spiralling out of control. But the White House call logs show that during this period, Trump refused to speak to anyone. At the Capitol it was violent mayhem; in the rest of the White House, it was pandemonium. But in the private dining room, where Donald Trump sat alone watching Fox News's wall-to-wall coverage, it was a hive of inactivity.

No calls were made to the National Guard; there was no contact with the FBI; he made no inquiries to defence chiefs or homeland security officials. He was liking what he saw too much. The inquiry heard evidence that the Pentagon called the White House to coordinate a response to the worsening situation in Congress. But the message came back that 'he doesn't want anything done'. About an hour into the riot, Trump did tweet out condemnation of his vice president, Mike Pence, for letting him down. This coincided with various members of Pence's Secret Service detail ringing their families to say their farewells, as it seemed as though they were about to be lynched by the mob that was closing in on the secure location Pence had been rushed away to. A makeshift gallows had been built specially for the VP.

Over three hours would elapse between him finishing his speech at the Ellipse and him intervening to call off the dogs. The video that was released had the feel of a hostage video. You could just tell Donald Trump hated having to read it out loud. And the tone fell a long way short of condemnatory:

> I know your pain. I know you're hurt. We had an election that was stolen from us. It was a landslide election, and everyone knows it, especially the other side, but you have to go home now. We have to have peace. We have to have law and order. We have to respect our great people in law and order. We don't want anybody hurt. It's a very tough period of time. There's never been a time like this where such a thing happened, where they could take it away from all of us, from me, from you, from our country. This was a fraudulent election, but we can't play into the hands of these people. We have to have peace. So, go home. We love you. You're very special. You've seen what happens. You see the way others are treated that are so bad and so evil. I know how you feel. But go home and go home at peace.

The myth of a stolen election was perpetuated, with no evidence ever presented to a court or official body to justify the claim.

The mob that had just attacked police officers and officials, who had defiled and vandalised the sacred heart of US democracy, were now very special people.

When certification of Joe Biden's victory did eventually take place later that day, 147 Republican members of the House of Representatives (three quarters of the Republican party) voted *against* certification. Nothing like this had ever happened before. It was as though a whole generation of Republican lawmakers had been born without spines.

During this period various news organisations tried to get on-the-record statements from these people to explain why they had taken this decision. Invariably, answer came there none. When Emily Maitlis and I were doing the *Americast* podcast we managed to get one Republican onto the show to explain why he'd voted not to certify Biden's victory. His weasel words were that a lot of the voters in his district thought the election *had* been stolen and he had a duty to represent their views. But did *he* think that there had been a fraud so great that it would have affected the outcome of the election? He wouldn't say.

That is not leadership. It is abject cowardice. And it can be explained like this. If you're elected to Congress, your term is two years before you're up for re-election. And what you live in mortal fear of, as a Republican congressman or -woman, is not being beaten by a Democrat opponent – most of the election districts are so gerrymandered that the chances of them flipping from one party to another are relatively slim. Instead what sends a shiver down your spine is having to fight a Republican opponent in a primary challenge. So keeping your supporters happy is an important consideration, ever more so in the era of MAGA and Trump.

Of the 147 wobbling jellies, maybe a handful genuinely believed the election was stolen; the rest just didn't want to incur the wrath of Trump. Like in a mafia operation, you stay in line, or punishment comes your way. That punishment takes two forms. The warning shot is when Trump goes after you on social media for being a RINO (Republican in name only) or worse. That will get picked up by all the media in your district, and your voters will quickly be aware that you have displeased the king. If that doesn't bring you into line, then the equivalent of being sent to swim with the fishes wearing concrete boots is Trump backing a primary challenger to unseat you from your district.

Let's look at the evidence for this. When the Democrat-run House set up the January 6th inquiry, not surprisingly there weren't a whole lot of Republicans who wanted to serve on it. But two principled members of the GOP did. One was Liz Cheney, the Wyoming congresswoman and daughter of former vice president Dick Cheney. She is an out-and-out conservative with firm views on all the hot-button issues like abortion and gun control. But she was unsparing in her criticism of Donald Trump on January 6th. So too was Adam Kinzinger, an Illinois congressman, who was a military veteran having served in

Afghanistan and Iraq. Neither is now in Congress. They went against Trump and paid the price.

Others over the years sought to highlight egregious behaviour on the part of the president, and for all of them it was a thoroughly unpleasant experience. Consider the official who brought to public attention Trump's attempt to strong-arm the then unknown Ukrainian leader, Volodymyr Zelensky, into dishing dirt on Joe Biden's son, Hunter, in return for aid that Congress had already approved for Ukraine. In other words, making agreed US foreign policy conditional and dependent on a foreign leader damaging a political opponent. The head of European affairs on the National Security Council, Lieutenant Colonel Alexander Vindman, was on the call when Trump made these demands, and made an official complaint. It led to the president's first impeachment – and Vindman was treated appallingly. Very few wanted to be in Donald Trump's crosshairs.

So in the frenzy of the post-election period a whole series of White House officials resigned and just slipped away. Ivanka, the most trusted of the Trump children, who along with her husband, Jared Kushner, had been given outsize roles in the administration, quietly left for Florida. No word of criticism, but no word of support for the patriarch either – maybe in Trumpland silence speaks volumes. And there were others too who saw wrongdoing, but felt it more expedient just to go quietly into the night.

It would be wrong to think that January 6th came out of nowhere. Past was prelude. In 2016 Trump had made clear that he might only accept the result of the election if it was to his liking. As Covid gripped America and upended the election year, many more mail-in ballots were sent out than usual. And based on nothing – because no votes had yet been cast – Trump started making allegations of widespread fraud and vote rigging. Week in, week out in the run-up to the 2020 election, and in the aftermath of it, Trump set about undermining confidence in the very pillars of US democracy: the fairness of the voting system – it was rigged; the freedom of the press – we were fake news; the independence of the judiciary – they're crony Democrat judges; the forces of law and order – the FBI and intelligence services weren't to be trusted as they were Trump haters. And if ever any Trump legislation was rejected, he would go after the feebleness of the lawmakers in Congress. Chip, chip, chip. Keep weakening those pillars so that the only person you can believe and trust in is Donald Trump.

Going right back to the start of the Trump presidency, the almighty clash between the head of the FBI, James Comey, and the president set the tone. The black spot was marked on his forehead when he reported to Trump about Russian interference in the presidential election. Trump didn't want to hear it. He railed against the notion. He wanted to believe the words of Vladimir Putin over his own intelligence chiefs. Across government departments and agencies this became a real concern.

There were strong elements of Martin Niemöller's warning about the Nazis – first they came after the voting system, but I did not speak out; then they went for the judiciary, but I am not a judge, so I did not speak out … Lawmakers and officials were afraid to speak out or pusillanimously acquiescing, while bad actors, slimy sycophants and ne'er-do-wells sought preferment with the demagogue. And before you know it, your robust constitution, with its much vaunted three co-equal branches of government, is looking decidedly shaky.

• • •

It is tempting to look at January 6th and comfort ourselves with the idea that it was the high-water mark: the moment after which the flood waters subsided and the danger passed. But if you look at what has happened since the events of January 6th it is instructive of how quickly people can forget. When the former Liberal Democrat Paddy Ashdown was dealing with the Bosnia crisis in the 1990s he came up with a vivid metaphor to describe the state of play after the cessation of hostilities. He said it was like a lemonade bottle that had been roughly shaken up. With the lid screwed tightly on, it looked as though it was fine – but remove the cap and the liquid would go everywhere. Post January 6th, the US felt like that. Domestic terrorism was now seen as the biggest threat, and the various security agencies were tasked with keeping the lid on.

In the days after the riot, many around Trump realised it had been a disaster for him and the MAGA brand. A second video was produced. This time the rioters were condemned, and Trump conceded that the election was over. But Trump only recorded this under extreme pressure from his own Cabinet. There were threats to invoke the 25th Amendment and remove Trump from office on the grounds of being unfit to serve. But where had that Cabinet been in the weeks leading up to the insurgency?

There was a new tone too in Congress, where smashed windows were still being repaired and offices restored after their sacking by the mob. Kevin McCarthy, the Republican leader, finally found his voice. 'The president bears responsibility for Wednesday's attack on Congress by mob rioters,' McCarthy said on the House floor. 'He should have immediately denounced the mob when he saw what was unfolding. These facts require immediate action by President Trump.' Tough talk indeed.

Except McCarthy had a bigger ambition. He wanted to succeed Nancy Pelosi as speaker of the House – the third most senior position in the US Constitution. And though Trump was weakened, he still enjoyed absurd levels of support. So a few weeks after McCarthy told Trump to take responsibility, he got on a plane to Mar-a-Lago, the beachside members' club in Palm Beach, Florida, where the ex-president was now holed up. In the post-match photo of the two of them, Trump is beaming one of his biggest smiles and McCarthy is looking pale and sheepish.

He had surrendered, crawling and grovelling his way back into Trump's good books. Gone was the language that Trump must bear responsibility for the events that unfolded. Instead, everyone had to accept their share of blame. The joint statement was all about how a united GOP was going to win back the House in the midterm elections. And McCarthy said that was his reason for going.*

In the Senate with the Republican leader Mitch McConnell, it was a similar story. He breathed fire about Trump, said he'd disgraced himself and the presidency – but delayed scheduling Trump's second impeachment trial so that it wouldn't result in him being disbarred from holding office in the future. So even after January 6th, though Trump might have been damaged goods, no one dared to take him on. They all wanted to see the XL Bully brought to heel, but no one was prepared to be the person to try to grab the snarling animal by the collar.

---

* A more hilarious and astonishing explanation has been provided by Liz Cheney, who was part of McCarthy's inner circle until she voted for Trump's second impeachment and played a part in the House January 6th inquiry. In her book *Oath and Honor*, she goes after the 'enablers and collaborators' who were willing to violate their oath to the Constitution out of political expediency and loyalty to Donald Trump. And she recounts this story of when she heard McCarthy was planning to embark on a secret mission to Palm Beach to see him:

'Mar-a-Lago? What the hell, Kevin?' Cheney asked, according to the book.

'They're really worried,' McCarthy said. 'Trump's not eating, so they asked me to come see him.'

'What? You went to Mar-a-Lago because Trump's not eating?' Cheney fired back.

'Yeah, he's really depressed,' McCarthy said.

What saved America on January 6th from total crisis were the actions of those few good men and women who either said 'no' to Trump and his lieutenants, or who had stayed in the room to curb the president's wilder demands. One of the most remarkable things I was told at the start of his presidency was about an agreement that had been struck by a handful of senior officials – mostly former generals – that there could never be a time when all of them were out of Washington at the same time. Their reasoning? There always had to be a grown-up in the room to rein Trump in.

By 2021, these people had largely disappeared, to be replaced by low-grade officials who knew that whatever the question, the only acceptable response was 'Yes, Mr President.' This was the chaotic, last throw of the dice by a man clinging to power by whatever desperate means. He wanted to insert people in the key government departments – like the Pentagon, like the Justice Department – who would somehow thwart Biden from taking over. Arcane, tendentious legal theories were dreamt up that would justify the move.

One of the hallmarks of the Trump presidency was that whatever the plan there was invariably chaos in the implementation. And arguably that played an important part in explaining why the coup attempt failed. There were just about enough grown-ups left in the key places who were able to block the wilder wishes of Trump.

But if you play that 'what if' game you can see how the outcome might have been very different. What if he had been better organised? What if he had ensured that he had the vital levers of power under his control, the right people in the right places? What if the Brad Raffenspergers and William Barrs of the world had given Trump the answers he wanted to hear? What if Mike Pence had been browbeaten into accepting the subversive plan not to certify the election, and instead declare Trump the winner? Sure, constitutional provisions would kick in, and any move of that nature would have ended up before the Supreme Court, the most conservative Supreme Court in decades. Would they owe him fealty? Thankfully it didn't come to that.

The danger did not pass after January 6th, and it still has not passed. Unlike 2016, when Donald Trump was completely unprepared for high office and had no clue who he should appoint to fill the thousands of jobs in his gift to run the machinery of government, this time he knows what to do.

In the years he has been out of office, there has been more discipline and more focus; there is greater clarity of thought. And a lot of thinking and a lot of work has gone into a blueprint for Donald Trump's return to power. There are some radical proposals – to wind back environment commitments and the like. But that is not what stands out.

No, what is striking – and terrifying – in Project 2025, a piece of work led by the right-wing Heritage Foundation and supported by a number of other deeply conservative think-tanks, is the massive extension of power it would give the president. And in a carefully produced video in which Donald

Trump reads studiously off the teleprompter and does not riff, he goes through what this would mean. He would be able to order the Justice Department to pursue his enemies and those who had shown him disloyalty in the past. The Insurrection Act would be resurrected, allowing the military to play a role in law enforcement under the direction of the president. Project 2025's director, Paul Dans, a former Trump administration official, said in September 2023 that Project 2025 is 'systematically preparing to march into office and bring a new army, aligned, trained, and essentially weaponised conservatives ready to do battle against the deep state'. For deep state, read independent-minded public officials. Tens of thousands of civil servants would be fired and replaced by conservatives fully aligned to the president's agenda, ready to do Trump's bidding.

This maximalist interpretation of an old idea – the unitary executive theory, which according to some interpretations of Article Two of the Constitution gives the president absolute control over the executive branch of government – is the intellectual underpinning to justify vengeance and score-settling; it would allow Trump to go after anyone who showed resistance in the past or who might in the future cavil at his absolute authority.

If Trump had had those sorts of powers on January 6th, it most certainly would have been a different story. Project 2025 is Trump identifying the weaknesses of his January 2021 manoeuvring, and making sure that if there was the need for another showdown with those who would deny him, he would have the muscle to win, and win emphatically.

There is another assertion that Donald Trump has sought to make, particularly as his legal woes piled up: he has been charged in four different indictments – over business fraud in the Stormy Daniels hush money case, election interference in Georgia, the events of January 6th, and refusing to hand back classified documents he had squirrelled away in Mar-a-Lago. No president has ever faced criminal charges before; Trump by the end of 2023 had 91. So from his legal team an assertion: Donald Trump had absolute immunity from prosecution for what he did when he was president. The argument made was that if he hadn't faced impeachment for it, he could not be prosecuted. He was above the law.

It is Donald Trump as Louis XIV. *L'état, c'est moi.* For Sun King of the seventeenth century, read sunbed king of the twenty-first. The argument got short shrift when in early 2024 the case ended up in the DC appeals court where three federal judges handed down a withering verdict on the Trump assertion. It was a major blow to Trump, but the Supreme Court waded in, partially upholding his claim that a president does indeed have immunity if he was giving instructions in relation to his role as head of state. An important chunk of the electorate is still with him, and each time he faces a setback, his supporters believe more firmly that it is the work of some kind of deep-state witch-hunt to bring him down.

Three years on from the January 6th attacks there was a poll in the *Washington Post* that was simultaneously astonishing and yet so predictable. It found that 25 per cent of those questioned believed that the riots that day had been instigated – yes, *instigated* – by the FBI. The principal law enforcement agency in the US had fomented the riots. There is no evidence of it, and no obvious reason why they would have. But I guess it was conveniently exculpatory for the rioters. 'It wasn't me wot dun it, it was those evil FBI officers wot made me.'

If you examine the proposition for just a moment, what possible gain was there? The basic position of MAGA loyalists is that the FBI is a Trump-hating organisation (even though James Comey's re-opening of the investigation into Hillary Clinton's use of a private email server just days before the 2016 election was arguably the biggest single factor that helped Trump win). So the logic would have to go that the feds agitated for a riot as a means of discrediting Trump. But, as discussed, it was the president who told everyone to come to Washington on January 6th, and who promised his supporters it was going to be wild. It was Donald Trump who told supporters to 'fight like hell'. It was Trump who told Republican lawmakers not to certify the election victory. Maybe one should be optimistic – 75 per cent of Americans don't believe that to be the case. But 25 per cent of Americans is 80 million people. And that is a lot of people.

This poll came out in January 2024. Around this time Donald Trump developed a new and topical line in his speeches. Trump started comparing those who had been found guilty of rioting, attempted insurrection, unlawful entry and criminal damage at the Capitol on January 6th with those Israelis – women, babies, grandparents and everyone in between – who were brutally ripped from their homes by the terrorist group Hamas on 7 October 2023. He started referring to those who, via due process and the application of the law of the land, had been found guilty of criminal offences and sentenced by a jury of their peers to a time in prison – as 'hostages'. In Donald Trump's mind, the rioters who attacked policemen and smashed up the Capitol were no different from the kibbutzniks or concertgoers who were kidnapped by Hamas and held in tunnels under Gaza. It is a pretty grotesque comparison.

But the comparison serves his purposes. For all that the US with its brilliant, codified constitution and Britain with its series of precedents, laws and rules have served both nations well, they depend on one thing above all: that elected leaders will play by the rules. If you lose an election, you accept it, nurse your wounds and try again if you have the support. But what happens if you end up with a president – or a prime minister – who doesn't accept there are constraints on what he can do, who chafes at any leash, who rejects behavioural norms? Who claims to have won an election he lost? And most pertinently, can convince a substantial chunk of the electorate that they're doing nothing wrong? Then your democracy is in serious trouble.

January 6th was – and choose your metaphor as you like – the canary in the coalmine, the dashboard where every warning sign is flashing red, the pressure cooker where the valve is about to blow. The most central tenet of living in a democratic society is that after a free and fair election there should be the peaceful transfer of power. It's non-negotiable. That didn't happen on January 6th. And as I reported on all this from Washington – the day, the aftermath, the second impeachment of Trump – and then the capitulation of so many of his Republican critics, I couldn't help but peer across the Atlantic and wonder whether the same could happen in Britain.

PART 2

CHAPTER 4

GOOD CHAP

By the summer of 2021 I had been North America editor for seven years. My wife, Linda, had had to move back from Washington just before Covid struck to take care of her elderly mother. And after three books, endless reports and countless articles, I felt it was time for me too. Editorially, the circus had left town – and there is nothing worse than being a foreign correspondent, a long way from home, kicking your heels because interest in the story you are there to cover is draining away. If my family had been there with me, it might have been fun sticking around in Washington with plenty of time for fun road trips to tick off the ten or so states that I had yet to visit.

The preceding seven years had been an astonishing, all-consuming whirlwind of news. There had been the tail end of Obama. The 2016 election, clashes with Donald Trump, two of the three impeachments in American history, resignations, sackings and bloodbaths, the reshaping of the Supreme Court, Covid chaos (and Trump getting carted off to hospital with it), presidential debates, Biden's election victory, Trump's attempts – both lawful and unlawful – to overturn the result, January 6th – January 6th! – and its aftermath, Biden installed … it was non bloody stop.

But then came cold turkey. The move from Trump to Biden was akin to going from a daily crack pipe and 80g of Oxycontin thrown in for good measure to half a pint of watery lemonade shandy once a week. Sitting alone in my apartment, with none of the editors overly interested in what I had to offer, was hard. For the first few weeks, yes, there was a slight novelty value. But then it grew boring.

It was time to work out what I was going to do when I came back.

There is nothing quite so marvellous as being appointed a foreign correspondent for the BBC, the pre-eminent broadcasting organisation in the world. But re-entry tends to be more fraught. For me, it wasn't an option to go anywhere else but back to London. Washington is the top of the tree as far as foreign postings go – whether in the diplomatic world or the journalistic one. And then aged 62, I wanted to come back to London, which is my hometown. I wanted to get a season ticket for White Hart Lane (desperate, I know), Tottenham being the club that I had supported since I was a kid. I missed the theatre, the restaurants – the unique buzz of the greatest and most diverse capital in the world.

Washington is a fine city, but it is provincial. There is an elegance to it – but it is (say it quietly) a little bit dull. It is a city that is early to rise and early to bed. When I had to take a flight from Reagan National – the airport in DC for internal flights in the US – I would drive along the Potomac at 4.30 in the morning, and the army of joggers would be out there; the personal trainers would be putting their victims through painful stretches and lunges on or across park benches. Middle-aged Lycra louts would be racing their lightweight bikes round the national monuments. It was like one giant, early-morning, city-wide advert for Lululemon, Nike and AirPods.

These same people would be showered by 6.30 and in the office by seven. But the corollary of that was that by nine each evening they would be tucked up in bed with a herbal infusion. Dear friends of ours were always suggesting we meet for the early-bird special dinner, where you sit down at 5.30. We became adept at finding excuses why that wouldn't, couldn't and shouldn't work. Washington is a city more dedicated to work than fun; to fitness rather than fatness. And that makes it a very different city from much of the rest of the US.

Some loose conversations with bosses in London had started to take place – and some ideas were floated about what I might do post-Washington – there were some presenting roles discussed, a senior posting as international editor that would be London-based but would involve a lot of foreign travel. It was slightly problematic in that it would step on other people's feet – and the thought of endless turf battles was not attractive. Been there, done it, got the badge. But then I got a call that did take me aback. I was told that Laura Kuenssberg would, in the coming months, announce that she was stepping down as political editor, and the BBC would like me to succeed her. I was sworn to secrecy, as Laura wasn't ready to announce her move just yet.

The job is probably the biggest in British broadcasting, and I was being offered it. Well, sort of. There would have to be a board (the BBC term for a job interview), and the post would probably have to be advertised externally if there were no diversity candidates from within the organisation. But I was also told that no one else was getting a call like this, and I was assured by the person ringing me that he wasn't acting unilaterally; there was buy-in from the very top. It was mine if I wanted it.

It was immensely flattering. I had become a political correspondent for the BBC in 1989 and the political editor then was the late, great John Cole who had chronicled the Thatcher years so adroitly. And look at those who've followed – Robin Oakley, Andrew Marr, Nick Robinson and Laura – all brilliant journalists. So to be approached about such an important job – one of the 'crown jewels' posts within the BBC – was huge. And surprising given my age and background.

Nevertheless, although it was still likely to be months away – possibly not until the beginning of 2022 – there was a path back for me from the US to London – or SW1 to be more precise. I sought to embrace the idea of a role that would put me at the heart of the nation's debate about its politics. And I thought that I might tell the story quite well. In the phone call I had I was told that the BBC wanted me to cover British politics in the way I had covered Trump. By that I think what was meant was acerbically, uncompromisingly and with an arched eyebrow.

But the more deeply I thought about it, the more gnawing questions and doubts I had in my mind. There was one person outside my immediate family who I took into my confidence about it. He is someone who has spent years working at the intersection of politics, PR and government, and his assessment was terse and to the point: 'I wouldn't wish that job on my worst enemy.'

It had been a very long time since I had been a 'lobby correspondent' – 23 years to be precise – before many of the young breed of 'SpAds', or special advisors, had even been born. There was something that filled me with close to dread at the thought of being shouted at by this or that one, telling me that I had got the line wrong on what the government/opposition was doing. The more I thought about it, the more I thought I was the wrong person for the job.

Partly this was because I'd be at the centre of a very different kind of British politics than was there before I left.* The ways of doing business in our parliamentary democracy had evolved over the years – the way the Commons does business these days has changed a huge amount from when I first went to work at Westminster. Then, it was run along the lines of a gentlemen's club – the barristers and doctors, company directors and consultants would earn their real money in the morning, and the house wouldn't start work until the afternoon and would sit late into the night. What could have been less family friendly?

The Commons remains as adversarial as it was when Churchill refused to countenance changing the layout of the chamber after it was destroyed by the Nazi incendiary bombs that hit the Palace of Westminster in May 1941. It would be rebuilt with steeply raked rows of seats, the two sides facing each other, and red lines in the carpet on either side – two sword lengths apart, to signify that all disputes must be settled by argument and not by force. The nineteenth-century Gothic

---

* The clincher came, though, when I had a long conversation with Tim Davie, the director general, about it. He was nothing but encouraging – though he did start the conversation with the words 'Do you really want to do this?' To which of course I replied 'yes', when what I wanted to say was 'no'. He told me that he wanted me to do the job just as I had been reporting the US. And I thought to myself, *that is the last thing you want.* Look at what had happened to Emily after saying it was clear that Dominic Cummings had broken the Covid lockdown rules. The BBC doesn't want to be in an endless brawl with the government over coverage. And I didn't much fancy being at the centre of one.

revivalist architect was Augustus Pugin, and the atmosphere in the chamber was pugilistic. Under Churchill's orders, the bearpit adversarialism must not be disrupted. There would be no hemicycles with deputies fanning out. In his black robes would be the speaker, a Member of Parliament who enjoyed the confidence of all sides and who would set aside his or her party allegiance – presiding over its business to ensure that the government of the day, of whichever political hue, would not ride roughshod over the legislature. Announcements from ministers must be made in the Commons chamber so that there could be scrutiny by the opposition and backbench MPs.

The place ran on process and precedent. You would not call another Member of Parliament a liar – because after all they were 'honourable' members; you might get away with calling someone a 'stranger to the truth', but not a liar. This is from the UK Parliament website: 'Words to which objection has been taken by the Speaker over the years include blackguard, coward, git, guttersnipe, hooligan, rat, swine, stoolpigeon and traitor.' But that meant – equally – it was incumbent upon MPs and ministers to be honest and tell the truth.

The scandals in the 1990s involving a number of Conservative MPs being paid by outside companies or organisations to ask questions in Parliament without ever declaring their interest (and the financial reward that came with it) shocked the public, putting these principles to the test. Compared to what we've seen more recently, a brown envelope full of used fifties, the odd gold watch or a couple of nights at the Ritz in Paris seem almost charmingly naïve. They owed more to Private Walker in *Dad's Army* – always able to lay his hands on some nice pork sausages or half a dozen eggs. Nevertheless, the hue and cry was sufficient for the then prime minister, John Major, to order the establishment of the Committee on Standards in Public Life, whose remit was to advise on correct ethical behaviour – not just of MPs, but those who hold positions of trust – like teachers, workers in local government, quangos and the like. Its first chairman was Lord Nolan, and he set out seven principles – that those who are in public life should display selflessness, integrity, leadership, objectivity, openness, honesty and accountability. Here was – at last – a set of rules against which politicians – and others – could be judged.

Those rules would face further scrutiny in 2009 with the MPs' expenses scandal, where more systemic abuses were exposed. Indeed, it felt as though more or less every MP in the House of Commons was on the make. The place filled with Private Walkers – or Del Boys and Rodneys from *Only Fools and Horses*.

The rules relating to lobbying and the transparency around it were deemed to be 'poor'. There needed, too, to be stricter guidelines concerning the conduct of ministers and senior civil servants. There would be more policing to stop the system being abused. The Ministerial Code, which used to exist as a private internal circular given to those in government, first became public in 1992. It would go through a series of iterations. There would be an independent advisor on ministerial interests.

For MPs there would now be a Parliamentary commissioner for standards, a non-partisan public servant whose job would be to examine breaches of the House of Commons Code of Conduct. His or her conclusions would then be passed to the House of Commons Committee on Standards, consisting of seven MPs and seven lay people. They would then make their recommendation to Parliament on what sort of punishment should be meted out to an errant MP. The quirks and foibles of the gentlemen's club needed to give way to the standards of a modern-day public company with accountability and transparency, though some vestiges of the past would stubbornly remain.

When I was a political correspondent in the 1990s, I used to simultaneously despair and marvel at the opulent, imperial grandeur of the State Opening of Parliament. It was a wonderful colourful and theatrical spectacle: the Household Cavalry clippety-clopping down Whitehall, clanking along, all shining brass and bright tunics; the gold coach carrying the sovereign making the tight turn into the Palace of Westminster, with plenty of sand laid on the road – and all done perfectly to time. To the second, you knew when the coach would arrive at the Sovereign's Entrance under the Victoria Tower. And there would be all sorts of exotic-sounding people who would seem more at home in a Harry Potter book than in a modern parliament. There's someone called the Gold Stick in Waiting – not to be confused with Black Rod. There's the Lord Great Chamberlain, the Earl Marshal, the Comptroller and Vice Chamberlain of the household, and then in all their finery would be the lords spiritual and temporal as well as the diplomats to the Court of St James in national costume.

As theatre, marvellous. As a sign of a modern-day democracy, absurd. If we can get all this ceremonial to run like the most expensive Swiss precision timepiece, why can't we get our trains to run on time or the M25 to move more freely?

Still, our parliamentary democracy has largely worked. We have been lucky enough to live our lives in a country with political stability and the rule of law, where the political system has – more or less – delivered what the people want. And where – by and large – MPs work hard for the constituencies they represent. In governmental terms there are ministers of the Crown, tasked with delivering on the ruling party's manifesto, aided by a civil service that is strictly neutral and which will serve the government of the day, regardless of its political stripe.

Is our political system perfect? Nothing like. Could it be improved and modernised? Most certainly. Is the talent pool of MPs as good or as richly varied as it might be? Nowhere near. But an executive answerable to Parliament, a prime minister who is the first among equals of his Cabinet, a lower house where legislation is debated before going off to the revising chamber, and a set of rules that would give an ethical underpinning to the behaviour of our elected representatives has worked well – and stably – for centuries.

Yet by the time I returned to Britain in 2022, it didn't look or feel anything like that – which was ironic, because one of the cornerstones of the Brexit debate was about asserting the primacy of the British Parliament above all else. The neutered, shackled, hobbled, poor thing it had become after 50 years of being undermined by Brussels would be cast into history. Parliament would be sovereign once again – muscular, virile, unfettered: the only place able to make and unmake laws.

Well, that was the theory – but something had been lost. If Bagehot and Dicey were the great constitutional experts of the Victorian era, Peter Hennessy is probably the foremost expert of the recently passed Elizabethan age. His books, his erudition, his calmness – and his generosity – have been a massive help to political practitioners and theorists alike. He is that fusion between academia and journalism, which means he can offer brilliant insight while able to turn a catchy phrase. He also maintains an affection for our rather shambling, somewhat rickety way of doing things in Britain with our uncodified constitution. A few decades ago, this most eminent historian of the post-war era came up with a novel description of our constitutional arrangements. He called it the 'good chap' theory of government. What could be more quintessentially British than that?

The basic tenet of the 'good chap' theory is that the letter of our constitutional law – our precedents and body of jurisprudence – is less important than whether the players understand the spirit of what was intended; that they can be trusted to do the right thing. In other words, they are gentlemen, not rogues. Or, to use a very nineteenth-century word, scoundrels.

And has there ever been a scoundrel like Boris Johnson to hold the office of prime minister? On virtually every front you care to look at, or every metric you measure him by, you will find a sometimes-casual disregard, and a frequent wilful connivance, to flout the norms of behaviour and to cock a snook at the rules – whether it be in his candour with Parliament, public appointments or in being transparent about his own behaviour. The charge sheet is long.

Matthew Parris, the former Conservative MP and one-time colleague of Boris Johnson when they worked on the *Spectator* together, summed Johnson up thus in a column for *The Times*:

> There's a pattern to Boris's life, and it isn't the lust for office, or for applause, or for susceptible women, that mark out this pattern in red warning ink. It's the casual dishonesty, the cruelty, the betrayal; and, beneath the betrayal, the emptiness of *real* ambition: the ambition to do anything useful with office once it is attained.

That was written in 2016, long before Johnson had secured the premiership. It was a shrewd foretaste and predictor of what was to come.

For much of the time that I was in the US, I resisted the temptation to compare Johnson to Trump. It seemed to me lazy, reductive even. Johnson is much better educated, more erudite. Trump wasn't wont to quote Cincinnatus – he probably thought it was just an energy company in Ohio. While Trump thought that climate change was a Chinese hoax, Johnson took it seriously and led global attempts to make progress on it at the Cop26 climate change conference in Glasgow. And in social outlook, Johnson is much more liberal than Trump. It seemed once Johnson's initial instinct to be a Covid denier had gone – and after his near-death experience – Britain seemed to be a lot more serious-minded about dealing with the pandemic than the chaos in the US, with Trump's endless flailing around.*

---

* I remember reading a story when I was in Washington about Johnson. He had been kicked out by his wife and was dating the woman who would become the third Mrs Johnson, Carrie Symonds. He had parked his car outside her flat in south London on a yellow line, and had forgotten about it. Weeks it was left there. The windscreen was plastered with parking tickets and bird poo in roughly equal measure. In the British press it was a very typical Boris Johnson story: it played to his chaotic and shambolic life, but was ever so slightly endearing too. It got me thinking about the differences between these two blond men whose fates seemed so intertwined. There were some obvious dissimilarities: Trump never had a hair out of place – there is probably a Trump-dedicated hole in the ozone layer from all the lacquer he's used to keep that barnet in place; Johnson – quite deliberately cultivated – never has a hair *in* place.

Over this one small episode, it seemed to me the difference between Trump and Johnson was clear. Trump would have known damned well he was parked illegally and would have been calculating how he was going to avoid paying the fines; Johnson, by contrast, would have been oblivious in that lackadaisical, dishevelled way of his – and would ultimately have borrowed the money from someone else and eventually paid off what he owed the council. Or better still, got the gullible friend with deep pockets to pay.

As time went on, though, and I understood more how Johnson operated, as his behaviour was exposed to sunlight and his untruths were found out, I came to revise that opinion: they were similar in so many ways.

They both had an insatiable thirst for publicity; they loved being the centre of attention. Both had a certain charisma – they knew that in any room full of people, *they* would be the centre of attention. There was also a shameless, don't give a damn attitude if one of their stories or claims unravelled. Both had – at best – a tenuous relationship with the truth. Johnson was fired from his first job on *The Times* for making up quotes. He was fired by Michael Howard when he was leader of the Conservative Party for not telling the truth. There was a regular pattern.

And friendships? Who is Trump genuinely close to? Who are Johnson's great pals? It is striking, looking at their respective careers, just how many people who were seen as their greatest ally/right-hand man one minute were chewed up and spat out the next. Entering the orbit of either and emerging unscathed, reputation intact, was a feat that few managed to execute successfully. A *New Yorker* cartoon captured it perfectly: it depicted a conveyor belt where you are initially welcomed with your red MAGA hat on into the West Wing, then leave a little later with a knife sticking out of your back. Johnson was less confrontational, more British maybe, but how many emerged from the Boris Downing Street with their reputation enhanced?

There was a magic – or maybe it is alchemy – that they also shared. Neither was really treated like a politician. The normal rules of political gravity didn't apply to them. They were those rare – slightly outsiderish – beasts who convinced the public that they were different, and shouldn't be held to the same standards by which we judge our politicians. Indeed, both had come to public attention as non-politicians: Trump as the entrepreneur – full of dash and brash – who went on to host *The Apprentice*; Johnson as the chat-show, quiz-show king. Donald Trump was heard boasting on a tape of how he could grab women 'by the pussy' in the run-up to the 2016 election, which would have spelt curtains for any conventional politician. And being caught paying off a porn-star just before the election? Trump shrugged these off and his supporters gave him an indulgent and forgiving smile. Even the fact that Trump had five children from three different marriages. Just imagine how the projection of that would change if, say, Barack Obama had had five children from three different women. And with Johnson? We literally didn't know how many children he'd had and with whom. It was a question he refused to answer. I can't think of many senior politicians who'd be able to get away with that.

The phrase used of Trump was that voters took him seriously but not literally, while sneering journalists – who consistently underestimated his appeal – took him literally but not seriously. The same could be said of Boris Johnson, who came to the attention of the British public first as a journalist-cum-entertainer. His appearances on *Have I Got News for You*, or on chat shows with the great Barry Humphries, cemented his place in the nation's affections as this rather exotic, amiable clown. He came across as self-deprecating, funny and clever.

The ability to make people laugh – and to get people laughing *with* you – is a big part of the Johnson schtick. In September 2021, Johnson came to Washington. At the time there was a cold fury in the White House over his threatened Brexit moves, which could have jeopardised the Good Friday Agreement. There was also general disbelief in the White House that Britain – of all countries – might have been about to break international law by ripping up its treaty obligations with the EU over the whole Ireland question. Relations had soured. And yet he came to the ambassador's residence in DC, and Britain had just agreed a deal which would allow British lamb to go back on sale in the US, after being banned 30 years earlier as a result of mad cow disease. Not a big deal, as not that much lamb is eaten in the US, but it was a small victory.

A number of rather disdainful senior White House staffers were present, and for some reason I was the only British journalist there. The special relationship was not feeling very special. Whether it was something that had been scripted or ad-libbed on the spot, I don't know – but Johnson started riffing on what the newspaper headlines might be: 'Wham-bam, thank you lamb', 'Shama lamb a ding dong' and the like. It was very funny, irresistible and – grudgingly – he had everyone laughing. He'd charmed his audience. A buffoon, maybe. But a clever one and a funny one. And when he saw me, he greeted me like a long-lost friend – even though we had never been more than acquaintances. (Despite myself, I felt a little glow of warmth.)

Johnson is unlike any British politician I have known and his charm has its dark side. There's a saying attributed to Aristotle but used as the guiding principle of the Jesuit movement: 'Give me the child until he is seven and I will show you the man.' It is clear that Johnson as a child at Eton had all the character traits that would mark out the adult, filled-out, fully formed version. A letter was unearthed by Andrew Gimson, who wrote a perceptive biography of Johnson, *Boris: The Adventures of Boris Johnson*. Johnson was older than seven when it was written; he was a teenager – but the point still stands. It is from Martin Hammond, Johnson's housemaster and classics teacher and was written to Johnson's father, Stanley:

> Boris really has adopted a disgracefully cavalier attitude to his classical studies. It is a question of priorities, which most of his colleagues have no difficulty in sorting out. Boris sometimes seems affronted when criticised for what amounts to a gross failure of responsibility (and surprised at the same time that he was not appointed Captain of the School for next half). I think he honestly believes that

it is churlish of us not to regard him as an exception, one who should be free of the network of obligation which binds everyone else.

That last sentence in particular is laser guided for what we would see in his – ultimately – ill-fated premiership. Like the Greek tragedies that he would be much better at quoting than me, the thing that gave Johnson his greatest strength would also be his undoing. That he should be at liberty to do whatever he likes, 'free of the network of obligation which binds everyone else', would give him the brazenness and imperturbability to propel him to the greatest prize in British politics. And it would bring him down just as abruptly.

At the end of 2019, though, having secured the Conservatives their biggest general election victory in decades, Johnson was apparently walking on water. And he wasn't going to face much opposition or criticism from within the Conservative Party when he seemed to have single-handedly revivified the Tory brand. That so many Conservatives from northern and Midlands constituencies – areas that had previously been Labour – were able to place their well-upholstered buttocks on the green leather benches was almost entirely thanks to him. He was the lord and master of all he surveyed. And he behaved accordingly.

But then, only a few weeks after winning the election, the pandemic arrived. It would set the Johnson premiership on an entirely different trajectory from any that he could have possibly imagined. Leaders around the world were scrambling. What would it mean? What was the worst-case scenario? How could we keep our population safe? Was this – literally – the end of the world? In March 2020, when the world started shutting down, it was far from clear what the answers were to those questions. It was the severest of tests for the very best, most politically agile, technocratic and scientifically astute leaders, let alone for a chaotic one like Johnson.

It would be easy to reach for the Claudius quotation in *Hamlet*, 'When sorrows come, they come not single spies but in battalions.' It's true that battalions did eventually drive Johnson from office, but it was a series of separate events, over a stretched 18-month timescale that – when put together – painted a coherent picture; a pattern of behaviour in which each scandal or demarche had common, recurrent features with similar patterns of behaviour. Yes, they were about Johnson and his proclivity to do whatever felt expedient at any given moment, but they were also about how vulnerable our parliamentary system could be to the 'bad chap' exercise of government.

The first taste of what was to come cannot be separated from its peak-Covid backdrop. It was when Boris Johnson's chief of staff, Dominic Cummings – arguably the Rasputin to Johnson's Tsar Nicholas II – drove from his home in Islington, north London, to County Durham at the height of the Covid lockdown. April 2020 was a time when Britons had been ordered to stay at home, with all non-essential travel prohibited. Yet, while experiencing mild symptoms of the disease, he had taken his wife and four-year-old son on a 264-mile trip to where his parents had an estate with a number of properties on it.

That was bad enough, and difficult to explain with a straight face. But what emerged next was beyond parody. He was spotted on the banks of the river by Barnard Castle – 30 miles from where he was staying in County Durham. It appeared to be at a lovely picnic spot, an outing which any other spring would have been glorious – but was egregious in 2020. It also just happened to be his wife's birthday. A more flagrant breach of the Covid lockdown rules it was hard to imagine, but the explanation that came from Cummings next was chutzpah on anabolic steroids: he had gone on the 60-mile round trip to Barnard Castle to test his eyesight before attempting the drive back to London.

It was risible. The British public could see through it clearly – with 20:20 vision, and without the need to get in the car to be quite sure. But Cummings was Johnson's chief aide; he was the substance behind the bluster, so he must be protected. The orders went out from Number 10: protect Cummings. The wagons were circled.

Cummings went out into a socially distanced Downing Street garden to answer reporters' questions. He told them he had 'behaved reasonably and legally', and when asked about how his behaviour would be perceived, he said, 'Who cares about good looks? It's a question of doing the right thing. It's not about what you guys think.'

It might have been shrewder of Johnson to have dispensed with Cummings altogether and thrown him under the bus there and then. Johnson would later discover that hell hath no fury like a Cummings scorned. But whether out of loyalty (I don't quite buy that) or Johnson's belief that he couldn't achieve what he wanted in government without him (much more plausible), Cummings stayed on – even though this was proving costly to the government. Johnson might have amassed the power as prime minister, but it felt as though the dispensing of it in policy – and people – was down to Cummings. He would be the brains to get Brexit done (still hanging precariously); he was the one who wanted to reshape government and root out civil service dead wood. It was him who wanted flame-throwers and original thinkers rather than pen-pushers and process merchants. He ordered ministers around and told them who they could have as their special advisors. When Cummings went into Number 10, it wasn't a case of the PM saying, 'This is what I want you to do.' It was Cummings saying, 'This is what I'm going to do, and if you don't like it, I'm not coming.'

But the sense of public outrage over Barnard Castle was great. For the first time there was muttering on the normally pliant and obedient Conservative backbenches; ministers were being made to look ridiculous with their tortured and strangled syntax to justify Cummings's behaviour, the press was having a field day and the opposition parties, which had been in national-emergency, speak-with-one-voice mode, now turned on the government for the sheer hypocrisy of it. Johnson's approval rating slumped, but not by so much that he thought a reset in the chaotic way he governed was required.

As it happens, Cummings would be gone by the autumn, in a departure which spoke to the dysfunction at the heart of the administration. It was inevitable. Ultimately, Johnson was only ever going to show true loyalty to Johnson; Cummings, who David Cameron once described as a 'career psychopath', was brilliant, mercurial – and impossible. Danny Finkelstein, the sometime Conservative advisor and sometime newspaper columnist, wrote:

> When Johnson hired Cummings to be his chief adviser, he must surely have noticed the regularity with which his relationships with his bosses had broken down ... what is it in the career of Johnson that made Cummings think that his strengths lay in getting processes right, taking hard decisions and saying no to people?

Powerful advisors have always brought jealousies and rivalries. During Harold Wilson's time in office, the presence of Marcia Falkender caused resentment (and fear). When Thatcher was PM, it was her economic advisor, Sir Alan Walters, who was seen as far too powerful a figure by the chancellor, Nigel Lawson, which in turn led to a mighty showdown. Alastair Campbell was a very public face of the Blair government, but when he became the centre of the debate over the dossier justifying the invasion of Iraq, it was clear he would have to go. So the idea that an advisor like Cummings provoked disquiet was nothing new in British politics. What was unexpected was where the battle lines were drawn.

The critical fight was not between Cummings and Johnson. Nor was it between Cummings and other ministers whose noses had been put out of joint by his abrasive style. No, it was between Cummings and Carrie Symonds, who was now married to Johnson. She thought that he and the communications chief, Lee Cain, were toxic. Symonds, who had been a Conservative Party press officer, told her husband he had to go. And Johnson – who hates confrontation and just wants to please the last person he has spoken to – eventually agreed. Cummings would later take aim at both of them:

> While it's true that I think Carrie has been a dreadful influence, and it was incredibly foolish of her to start a briefing war with me and others, it's also only fair to point out that he lies to her all the time about stuff and she's often operating on duff information herself. This is obviously an incredibly toxic combination.

'Lies' would be a word that came up again and again in this period. Cummings left Downing Street with a box of his possessions like one of those Wall Street bankers at Lehman Brothers after the financial crisis. But he was not going to disappear quietly into the sunset. There was brief talk that with Cummings and Johnson's press secretary, Lee Cain, gone there could be a reset of the Downing Street operation, a fresh start, a chance to get that fabled Downing Street machine purring instead of spluttering. It would be short-lived.

• • •

As one Dominic Cummings-shaped calamity walked out, the next mini-crisis blew in, just days later, and it concerned the then home secretary, Priti Patel. Of course, all governments are beset by unsettling events and squalls that come at them out of the blue. The 'events, dear boy, events' that Harold Macmillan used to talk about. What was so consistent about the dramas of the Johnson years was that the way *he* behaved and reacted invariably became more of a talking point than the original 'sin'.

With Priti Patel, the charge was that she had bullied her civil servants in the Home Office. A report was ordered into the claims. Deliciously, it would come out at the end of the national anti-bullying week. Sir Alex Allan, the prime minister's independent advisor on the Ministerial Code, conducted the investigation. I had first met Sir Alex when he was working as the principal private secretary to John Major when he was PM. He was a top-drawer civil servant. He went on to become head of the Joint Intelligence Committee, was the first permanent secretary at the newly created Ministry of Justice and had a stellar reputation. His report concluded that what Patel had done 'amounted to behaviour that can be described as bullying' – highlighting instances of her shouting and swearing at staff. Johnson chose to rip up the rule book, and backed her over the man whose job it was to advise on these things. On a Tory MPs' WhatsApp group, Johnson urged colleagues to 'form a square around the Prittster'.

With Johnson simply rejecting the findings, Sir Alex had little option but to resign. His statement was short and far from sweet:

> I recognise that it is for the Prime Minister to make a judgement on whether actions by a Minister amount to a breach of the Ministerial Code. But I feel that it is right that I should now resign from my position as the Prime Minister's independent adviser on the Code.

Allegations that Johnson had tried to alter the conclusions of Sir Alex's report weren't denied by Downing Street. Lord Evans, the chair of the Committee on Standards in Public Life, called Allan's resignation 'deeply concerning' and added: 'This episode raises serious questions about the effectiveness of the current arrangements for investigating and responding to breaches of the Ministerial Code.'

The Institute for Government was equally withering:

Incongruity between the prime minister's and Sir Alex's conclusions, the delay to publication, reports about attempts to change Sir Alex's conclusions, and his decision to resign suggest a process that has become very politicised. That is an impossible situation for a code of conduct that is highly dependent on principle.

None of this is normal. In the decade that I was at Westminster, sure there were scandals, but now we were seeing repeated, almost routinised lying as if it was just a standard operating procedure. It felt – from where I was watching, 3,000 miles away – that some of us in the media were just letting this behaviour go by, almost unchallenged. You report the first lie as something shocking, but by the time it's the fourth or fifth, you shrug. That is normalising – institutionalising, if you like – behaviour that is egregious.

The next Member of Parliament he scandalously tried to protect was nothing like as senior as Priti Patel – he was a former minister on the backbenches, but it was even more flagrant in its disregard for the rules.

Owen Paterson, keen Brexiteer and loyal Johnson supporter, had been lobbying on behalf of two companies that were paying him in excess of £100,000 per year in what the report found to be an 'egregious case of paid advocacy'. The former Northern Ireland secretary was found in October 2021 by the Parliamentary commissioner for standards, Kathryn

Stone, to have repeatedly breached lobbying rules on paid advocacy. Stone recommended a 30-day suspension from the Commons for Mr Paterson.

The commissioner said that the MP for North Shropshire had 'repeatedly used his privileged position' to make multiple approaches to government departments and ministers on behalf of the companies. He had also breached the rules on the use of rooms within the Palace of Westminster for personal gain. His Commons office was used 16 times for business meetings with clients between 2016 and 2020, and he also misused House of Commons headed notepaper.

It was a thorough report that had been endorsed unanimously by a cross-party committee of MPs. Ms Stone had done her work; MPs had reviewed it and approved. Now it was for Parliament as a whole to nod through the work of the committee. Except at this point, Johnson intervened in an unprecedented way.

The night before the vote, Johnson had been at one of London's most exclusive gentlemen's clubs, where he'd been dining with former colleagues from the *Daily Telegraph*. The columnist and former editor Charles Moore apparently bent Johnson's ear about his old university chum, Paterson. The next day, Johnson got in touch with his chief whip, Mark Harper, and issued an instruction that all Tory MPs should reject the committee's recommendation and instead set up an entirely new disciplinary regime where half the MPs would be Conservative under the chairmanship of a Johnson placeman.

This is parliamentary business and not government. There were howls of outrage, but by forcing the issue with a three-line whip, the measure squeaked through. Opposition parties made clear they would have nothing to do with a new disciplinary committee. The next morning, Lord Evans ripped up his long-planned speech to the Institute of Government to say instead that the Tory-led review into the disciplinary process for MPs was 'deeply at odds with the best traditions of British democracy'. The PM's own adviser on ethics publicly condemned the move as a 'very serious and damaging moment for Parliament'.

A totally unprincipled manoeuvre had been thwarted, and more support for Johnson, and the way he conducted himself, drained away. So what attracted the PM to try something so outrageous? Surely it couldn't be to get his revenge on Kathryn Stone after she found that Johnson had himself broken the Ministerial Code a year earlier over his holiday to Mustique, and the mystery over who had paid for it? Whatever the reason, it was a further erosion of independent and non-partisan regulation.

Johnson's personal conduct and his financial affairs were an endless source of mystery and controversy. George Osborne has told the story of how he tried to persuade Johnson to join David Cameron's government but the former London mayor, who had a large number of children to pay for, said he couldn't afford to give up his other lucrative sources of income to become a minister of the Crown. He was always professing to be close to penniless. As PM, he seemed to rely on benefactors, and none of these financial arrangements would be more controversial than the refurbishment of the Downing Street flat. Each PM is granted £30,000 from government funds to give the place a makeover. Theresa May had spruced the place up in 2016. But it was far too John Lewis for the tastes of Johnson and Carrie Symonds. They wanted something grander. The society interior designer Lulu Lytle was brought in … at a cost north of £110,000. If an MP has received a loan or donation, it must be declared to the Electoral Commission within 28 days. But no such disclosures about the financing of the refurbishment were submitted. At which point, enter once again the ousted and embittered Dominic Cummings. He alleged that the prime minister had arranged for donors to 'secretly pay' for the renovations on the private residence at 11 Downing Street, calling the plans 'unethical, foolish, possibly illegal' and adding that they 'almost certainly broke the rules on proper disclosure of political donations if conducted in the way he intended'.

The allegations were investigated by the PM's new ethics advisor, Lord Geidt, after the resignation of Sir Alex Allan. The report cleared Johnson of breaching the Ministerial Code and said that no conflict, or reasonably perceived conflict, of interest arose. However, Lord Geidt expressed that it was 'unwise' for Johnson to have proceeded with refurbishments without 'more rigorous regard for how this would be funded'.

A separate investigation by the Electoral Commission found that the money had come from a company belonging to Lord

Brownlow, who was made a peer in 2019 and had – I'm sure coincidentally – donated £3 million to the Conservative Party. Johnson professed ignorance about the source of the money. But it would later emerge that he had been less than candid. Text messages emerged in which Johnson asks Brownlow to approve the funds for the refurb to go ahead. Lord Geidt would say the failure to disclose these communications had shaken his confidence. Johnson offered 'humble and sincere' apologies in a letter to his ethics advisor. Labour's deputy leader, Angela Rayner, was scathing: 'Once again, by attempting to hide the truth, Boris Johnson undermines his own office. The prime minister's pathetic excuses will fool no one, and this is just the latest in a long line of sorry episodes.'

And it wouldn't be the last. Public appointments would be another area where Johnson – again – drove a coach and horses through normal practice. With the chairmanship of the BBC, Johnson reportedly wanted to appoint Charles Moore – yes, he of the failed bid to rescue Owen Paterson. Moore is a hyper-critic of the organisation and had been fined for refusing to pay the licence fee. But as the spotlight fell on his suitability and past views expressed on subjects like race and Islam, he withdrew. The person appointed was a former Goldman Sachs banker, Richard Sharp, who had been a big donor to the Conservative Party over the years.

What turned out to be murky – and ultimately fatal for Sharp's tenure at the BBC – was that he too became embroiled in

Johnson's personal finances, with the *Sunday Times* revealing that just before his appointment – which Johnson was recommending – he had helped secure Johnson an £800,000 personal loan. This was never declared. A cross-party parliamentary report found that Sharp had seriously undermined BBC impartiality by failing to divulge this. The report concluded that Sharp 'should consider the impact his omissions will have on trust in him, the BBC and the public appointments process'. Sharp quit, his reputation frayed, another casualty of flying too close to the Boris sun. And another area of public life where voters would lose confidence.

It seemed Johnson just wanted to put his pals, sycophants and cyphers into all the public positions of influence, whether they were suitable for the job or not. The longstanding *Daily Mail* editor Paul Dacre was put up for the chairmanship of the media regulator Ofcom, but an independent panel found that he was 'unappointable'. Friends at the Treasury told me of numerous attempts by Johnson's Number 10 to place wholly inappropriate people on key public bodies and quangos – and how they would resist wherever possible. He was flouting all democratic norms, and it took courage to push back.

But nothing was more shocking to the British public than the sorry saga of 'Partygate': the scandalous behaviour of some Downing Street staff during lockdown that would lead to Johnson becoming the first prime minister in British history to be convicted of committing a criminal offence while in office – an ignominious addition to his already sketchy CV.

The story broken by Pippa Crerar – now at the *Guardian*, but at the *Daily Mirror* at the time – and ITN TV correspondent Paul Brand provoked fury like I have never seen. It was visceral. Families who hadn't been able to attend the funerals of loved ones heard about the suitcases full of booze being wheeled into Downing Street, the cleaners having to wash the vomit off the carpets, the cavorting in the Georgian mansion house while everyone else sat at home obeying the rules the government had set for them. It was a truly shocking episode. But Johnson was determined – as ever – to brazen it out. The shamelessness was bottomless. Apologies fell easily from the prime minister's lips, but were any of them sincerely meant or felt?

The ill-disciplined, louche, libertine, 'I can do whatever the hell I like' aspect of Johnson is only one part of his personality. The other is his tendency to dissemble, obfuscate and lie when the finger is pointed at him. In June 2022, Lord Geidt finally quit over the Partygate scandal. He told friends according to multiple sources that he was sick of being lied to. He followed Sir Alex Allan in concluding that being the ethics advisor to Boris Johnson was an impossible job. To lose one ethics tsar may be considered unfortunate, to lose two …

Looking back on this whole period – and this is by no means an exhaustive list of scandals and untruths – perhaps the remarkable thing is how much Tory MPs were prepared to forgive and turn a blind eye to. The question I have mulled over throughout this shocking period is the extent to which Britain has undergone a structural change, and how much is it down to one or two bad actors. If Johnson had stuck to being a journalist in Brussels, would history have taken a different course? The forces that drove Brexit existed independently of Johnson, but the corrosion of standards in public life that got Brexit done? Well, that is on the prime minister. And the behaving with impunity? That is not structural; that is down to the man at the top.

It would be comforting to think that the end of the PM coincided with a sudden discovery of moral strength and purpose from Johnson's party – that they had a backbone after all. I suspect they would have continued to support him, but for one small thing. In politics there is always a tipping point – or an inflection point as they like to describe it in Washington. And it is a simple, self-interested binary: are my chances of political survival made better or worse by person X leading us into an election? As Partygate dragged on, and the anger of the public grew more intense, more and more MPs came to the conclusion that it was the latter.

The denouement had a slightly comic element to it. It concerned the deputy chief whip, a man called Chris Pincher – a case of nominative determinism if ever there was one. He had gone to the Carlton Club, the Tory establishment's watering hole, got drunk and started groping various men. A complaint was made about him. And Downing Street lied about what they knew. Again. The line was given to ministers who were sent out to do the morning round of broadcast interviews: this was all new to Johnson; he'd never heard any complaint about Pincher's behaviour etc. But it was untrue.

What Downing Street hadn't reckoned on was a recently retired civil servant calling it out. Simon McDonald, who had been the chief mandarin at the Foreign Office, sat in bed at his home in Winchester and decided enough was enough. At 7.30 on the morning of 4 July he tweeted this: 'This morning I have written to the Parliamentary Commissioner for Standards – because No 10 keep changing their story and are still not telling the truth.'

It was an Exocet. This seemed confirmation of a BBC story from the night before from one of their smartest young journalists, Ione Wells. In his letter to Kathryn Stone, Lord McDonald said Downing Street's claim that no formal complaints were ever made against the former deputy chief whip were 'not true'. He pointed out that in 2019 when he was permanent under-secretary at the Foreign Office – where Pincher was a junior minister – 'a group of officials' complained about his behaviour. 'An investigation upheld the complaint; Mr Pincher apologised and promised not to repeat the inappropriate behaviour,' he said.

McDonald then went on the *Today* programme to enlarge on his tweet and letter. The effect was devastating. Johnson seemed to be finally done. The cascade of ministerial resignations grew throughout the day. Power was slipping through his fingers. Rishi Sunak was the first out of the door, but others soon followed in a chaotic demarche. Nadhim Zahawi accepted

Johnson's offer to become the new Chancellor of the Exchequer, only to call on Johnson to stand down 24 hours later. Michelle Donelan became the shortest-serving Cabinet member in British history, when she resigned as Education Secretary 35 hours after being appointed.

It was over. As the walls started to close in on Johnson he threatened to call a general election. The word was put out that if Tories came after him, he would dissolve Parliament and go to the country in an election that might well have turned into a slaughter for the Conservative Party. It was Johnson's way of blackmailing his own party: give me more time otherwise I will blow us all up. But to have done that would have drawn the Queen directly into politics. Why, when the ruling party had such a commanding majority, was it necessary to grant a dissolution? If the general election was purely a device to save Johnson's skin, then it would be an entirely inappropriate thing to ask the sovereign to do. It was all unbelievable. Jaw dropping. It is my understanding from a senior Conservative Party manager that strong representations were made – and warnings issued by the Palace. It was then that Tory grandees decided enough was enough. There was, after all, a limit to what they would accept.

Lord McDonald wasn't even sure whether anyone would take any notice of his tweet when he posted it that morning on the Chris Pincher affair. He certainly never imagined it would be the straw that broke the camel's back. It had never been his intention to become a player. But he would later reflect on the wider significance of the Johnson government, one of many that he'd served in a lifelong career as a civil servant:

> Mr Johnson as prime minister was undermining the institutions that define the United Kingdom: Parliament, the Civil Service, the judiciary, the Union itself, and the UK's unwavering respect for international law. Everyone I know who worked for Boris Johnson enjoyed the rollercoaster ride for a time, but working for him damaged most of their reputations in the end.

I cannot think of another occasion when a civil servant has been so shocked and dismayed at the blatant gaslighting from Downing Street that he decides his only course of action is to go public. And of Johnson's disregard for the checks and balances that stop our democracy becoming a demagogues' playground: 'Most prime ministers are aware of the conventions. They don't undermine the system, they don't override other parts of the system. It felt to me as if Number 10 under Boris Johnson was doing all of that: undermining and overriding on any issue they wanted.'

Johnson's defenders – and Johnson himself – still protest that he got all the big calls right. He got Brexit done, even though perhaps the biggest lie he told was that the trade deal he'd negotiated with the European Union would not result in a border going down the Irish Sea, effectively leaving Northern Ireland still in the EU. It did. He was steadfast after Russia's invasion of Ukraine, and played a vital role in galvanising support in the West. True. His leadership then was notable. The vaccine rollout went well, though the Covid inquiry has again shone an unsparing light on the sheer dysfunction and hopelessness of so much of the Johnson government. He was optimistic and his 'boosterism' was appealing to so many. He is charismatic. And his premiership will go down as one of the most significant for the economic and political changes brought about by Brexit. But it is the corrosive effect he had on our politics that may well stand out even more clearly.

The postscript to Johnson's premiership came in multiple forms. The first was the cross-party report of the Privileges Committee. It was chaired by the veteran Labour MP Harriet Harman, but had a Conservative majority and it was to be the final word on whether Johnson had misled Parliament over Partygate. The committee was unanimous. He had. The MPs found his denials were 'so disingenuous that they were by their very nature deliberate attempts to mislead'. They were a 'contempt' of Parliament, because they stopped MPs from carrying out their 'essential task' of holding him to account. Over 106 pages they eviscerated Johnson. The committee concluded that Johnson's 'personal knowledge of breaches', combined with 'his repeated failures pro-actively to investigate' them, amounted to 'a deliberate closing of his mind' to what had gone on.

Johnson, having been briefed on what the report was going to say, resigned his seat in the Commons prior to publication. His reply to the committee was pure, unadulterated Trump: the committee had been a 'kangaroo court', their conclusions 'deranged'. The MPs on it had delivered 'what is intended to be the final knife-thrust in a protracted political assassination'. And on and on he went about the appalling injustice of it all. If there was a scintilla of reflection, of self-doubt, of remorse or of shame, it was not to be found here. There was self-righteous anger. There was flame-throwing fury mixed with a slightly whining self-pity: how can I possibly be treated like this?

The second postscript to the Johnson premiership came in his resignation honours list, where he sought to reward all the mates who had kept him afloat, and then went down with the sinking ship – the carousel of cronies, as one shadow minister called it. There was a knighthood for Jacob Rees-Mogg and a damehood for Priti Patel, and a young woman who had been a junior Downing Street assistant, Charlotte Owen was – bafflingly – made a life peer at the age of 29, meaning she will be able to vote on legislation for the rest of her life. There were howls that it destroyed what was left of his legacy; it was shameful; it was rewards for failure all round. But it was entirely true to Johnson. The manner of his departure was no different from his arrival – with all the collateral damage to Britain's democratic institutions that entailed, and the decline in public trust for our politicians that went with it.

But still he continued to cast a shadow. The final register of Members' Interests revealed that Johnson had trousered an eye-watering £4.8 million from speeches and the like in just a few months. He also signed a lucrative deal after he left the Commons to become a *Daily Mail* columnist. The Advisory Committee on Business Appointments (ACOBA) – the body that advises on what jobs former ministers can take for the two years after they leave office – found that he was in breach of their rules. And when Johnson went off to visit the president of Venezuela, Nicolás Maduro, at the behest of a hedge fund, ACOBA found that he had been 'evasive', 'avoided answering specific questions' and 'refused to be open'. *Plus ça change.*

And then came the 49 days of madness with Liz Truss at the helm – hardly the engine of trust restoration. The profiles when she arrived in Downing Street noted that throughout her career she had been completely underestimated by her colleagues. Just a few days into her premiership it struck me that it was the complete reverse: her abilities had been totally overestimated. There was a recklessness that is hard to fathom. In her zeal to drive change, there seemed not to be a single thought given to what the consequences of her policies might be. It was a slow-motion car crash that happened at quite a remarkable speed.

Her arrival into Downing Street more or less coincided with us launching *The News Agents*, and for that we will always owe her an enormous debt of gratitude. She is our patron saint; the woman who gave us a ratings boost for the technicolour shit-show she served up on a daily, sometimes hourly, basis. There is a serious question though about the talent pool in British politics and how it had been drained to a shallow puddle. How was it that the Conservative Party, this brutal winning machine, could reach the conclusion that the answer to their problems was Truss? A similar question that was rightly posed when Corbyn became Labour leader. I realise that I may have a very bad dose of 'old-fart syndrome', but the dominant figures of British politics when I came back from the US seemed decid-edly unimpressive. Where were the big beasts of yesteryear – the Blairs and Browns, the Heseltines and Thatchers – or even the Camerons and Osbornes? But for the rest of her life, Truss will be at the Cenotaph on Remembrance Sunday laying a wreath, as one of our former prime ministers.

It was the arrival of Rishi Sunak as her replacement that led many to believe – no, to hope – that after the most dangerous excursion into populist rule-breaking and crockery-smashing, Britain was back on a path towards 'normal' politics. Who could not be encouraged by Sunak's vow that he would bring 'integrity, professionalism and accountability at every level' of government? He didn't single out his predecessors for criticism over what had gone before; he didn't need to. It felt like a reset was going on. Sunak had come from a Goldman Sachs back-ground, and everything about him – from his narrow ties to his Prada shoes – smacked of Californian self-belief and the global elite but, for all that, with a surprising amount of brittleness when facing criticism. If there was a period when he was seen as a saviour, perhaps that was less to do with any extraordinary talents than the fact that he wasn't any of his most recent, inglorious predecessors.

Sunak is a technocrat. He likes a spreadsheet. The Windsor Framework to unlock the trade imbroglio with Northern Ireland brought about by Brexit was Sunak at his best. But a senior civil servant who worked closely with him painted a picture of him to me that was rather unusual. He said it felt as though there had been a complete role reversal: Sunak would brief the civil servants on the numbers in every column, but had no idea about the politics, while the civil servants found themselves talking him through the politics and more than once saying, 'Have you thought this through; are you sure it is wise to do this?' That – arguably – would take him down a path that would eventually lead to Rwanda.

It was Boris Johnson who first mooted the idea of sending asylum seekers to Rwanda. When it was announced, it felt like one of those half-baked schemes that is less of a policy announcement than a press release that you hope will get the *Daily Express* and *Daily Mail* writing headlines like 'Government gets tough with illegals'. A here today, gone tomorrow chunk of red meat thrown to keep the base happy.

But Sunak chose to run with it, even though it was absurdly expensive, highly controversial (maybe that was part of the appeal), and with absolutely no data to prove that it would have the desired effect: to deter the illegal immigrants, to kill off the evil trade of the people smugglers, to stop the small boats making their perilous journey across the Channel. One might argue that if you are prepared to gamble everything to get to the UK, board a flimsy, overloaded inflatable and risk your life drowning in the icy waters of the English Channel, the thousand-to-one chance that you might be forced to board a plane to Rwanda is not going to discourage you.

Soon after being appointed home secretary, James Cleverly made clear that he thought the Rwanda deal was not the 'be all and end all' of government plans to tackle illegal immigration. He also failed to deny that before his appointment he had described the policy as 'batshit'. But Downing Street was quick to contradict him. Rwanda *was* the be all and end all. If this were a roulette table, they were betting every last chip on it coming up black.

But after the UK Supreme Court ruled, everything had come up red. The five justices voted unanimously in November 2023 that there had not been a proper assessment of whether Rwanda was a safe country to send asylum seekers to. The court justices found there were 'substantial grounds' to believe people deported to Rwanda could then be sent by the government in Kigali to other countries where they would be unsafe. Rwanda was a country scarred by the inter-communal genocide of 1994, when over the course of a hundred days, 800,000 ethnic

Tutsis were killed by Hutu extremists. It has come on leaps and bounds since then, but a number of human rights concerns were still being raised about the rule of Paul Kagame, the country's powerful current president.

Nevertheless, Sunak was undeterred, and so his answer was to introduce legislation to Parliament to make it a matter of statute that Rwanda *was* a safe country. And because Parliament is sovereign, it would mean that even if – God forbid – another genocide took place, the courts would be powerless. Because the law says Rwanda is a safe place, *de jure*, it is a safe place. Opposition in the House of Lords was strong; from many Conservative peers there was an air of flabbergasted disbelief at what the government was doing.

None more so than that big beast of so many Tory administrations, Kenneth Clarke. The one-time home secretary, justice secretary and lord chancellor described it as a dangerous constitutional provision for a law to overturn something that was fact. It was a law, he said, that was like saying the colour black was white or that all dogs are cats. His argument was that there are limits to the sovereignty of Parliament. There had to be checks. And he warned that Rishi Sunak's legislation was in danger of moving Britain towards an elected dictatorship. No one had that on their bingo card when Sunak became prime minister, the self-billed restorer of standards to government and public life.

The parliament of 1992–97, when John Major was prime minister, had a fair amount of sleaze to deal with – a couple of MPs caught receiving brown paper bags full of cash for asking questions. There was the odd sexual peccadillo. But that parliament looks a model of sanctity, virginal virtue and self-abnegation compared to the one that came into being after the 2019 general election. We've had tractor porn, an MP locked up in a room and ringing his 78-year-old constituency secretary at 3.15am pleading for her to find £5,000 because he had fallen in with 'bad people'. We've had egregious lobbying, bullying, resignations, recall petitions. We've had security breaches and sexual assaults. It is without precedent. Out of 650 MPs, yes, a small minority, but enough wrong 'uns to sully further the reputation of politics and politicians. And that is bad for democracy. The moral vacuum of Boris Johnson may have passed, but the stench will take longer to clear. Where were the good chaps and chapesses when we needed them most?

CHAPTER 5

NEWS TRAVELS FAST (AND FURIOUS)

It was on a flight to Sydney at the end of 2021 – the hermit kingdom was finally opening up after its Covid lockdown, and there was a grandchild to meet – when I connected to the plane's Wi-Fi and saw there was a message from Emily Maitlis: 'Sopes, I've got an idea.'

For the previous two years, Emily and I had presented a podcast for the BBC called *Americast* all about the US presidential election. It was launched with no fanfare and zero marketing, but very quickly it seemed to become 'a thing' in a way that was totally unanticipated. There I was in Washington with the wonderfully geeky Anthony Zurcher, while Emily was in London. We would chew over the latest twists and turns of the election, get really stuck into some abstruse subjects – like how the filibuster works – but also have fun at the latest craziness of Trump v Biden. You could feel the audience engagement growing with each passing week. And it wasn't the typical BBC audience.

As North America editor I was told when I moved out there that my main job was to serve the prime bits of BBC News real estate: the *Six*, the *Ten*, the *Today* programme and the Radio 4 *Six O'Clock News*. And if I could knock out the odd blog, so much the better. These programmes still had big – if declining – audiences. But there was an unmistakable demographic tilt. Hardly anyone under the age of 60 was watching *BBC News at Ten* or listening to *Today*.

But *Americast* was an entirely different thing. Young people were coming up to me when I was back in London to say how much they loved the pod. Students doing their politics A levels or degrees were using us as source material. Teachers would ask us to cover certain subjects. I had to ring a law firm about something, and when asked to give my name, the young woman at the other end of the phone said, 'Not *the* Jon Sopel from *Americast*?' I had never been *the* anything before. Emily was finding something similar – although after her somewhat eye-catching Prince Andrew interview from a year earlier, she wasn't wanting for attention.

This all seemed to coincide with the BBC's increasing anxiety about why young people were turning away from their output. What could be done? If the licence fee was to be justified then it had to reach all age groups, all sectors of society. And suddenly, middle-aged correspondents were doing reports about hip-hop or the latest 'thang' among young people to try to lure them back. It all felt a bit patronising to be honest. Dad-dancing on the TV. There was earnest debate about whether young people had lost interest in news and current affairs, and whether there was now a lost generation to these venerated bits of the BBC output.

The former head of BBC News, James Harding, who appointed me to be North America editor, told me of the deep concern there was about the audience research, and how their efforts to deal with the issue had mixed results. The editor of the major evening TV bulletins decided he would commission a piece about the resurgence of vinyl, and whether young people even knew what it was or were interested. A reporter was tasked with going to Oxford Street to do *vox pops* – the bane of any journalist's life. With his film crew he stops a teenager, pulls out a record from a plastic carrier bag and says: 'I'm from the BBC *Six O'Clock News*, do you know what this is?' To which the teenager replies, totally deadpan: 'Yeah, it's an LP. But what's the *Six O'Clock News*?'

The problem was that the BBC was asking the wrong question. Young people may be lost to some of the old-fashioned, linear news bulletins and sequence programmes. But it is very wide of the mark to assume from that that they're not interested in news. How many young people are looking at the *Radio Times* to see what time and what evening their favourite programmes are on? They don't. There's catch-up. The corporation failed to pose a more fundamental question, which is why are habits changing, and how do people want – in the case of news – to consume it? The podcast seemed to be one obvious answer, but although our wonderful bosses at the BBC paid lip service to digital output like *Americast*, they never gave it the resources or the marketing that would really see it grow. Nor did they seize other opportunities that would turn the pod into a brand.

It's not my purpose to carp because I had the most wonderful time at the BBC and am eternally grateful for all the opportunities that I was given, working with people far brighter than myself – behind the camera lens and the microphone – who made me look and sound halfway intelligent. But when the comedy *W1A* was being screened I could barely bring myself to watch. It wasn't light entertainment; it was documentary. It was so unerringly spot-on that I could feel my toes curl within my shoes. Every new review with abstract nouns forming meaningless acronyms, every new job title which left you with no clue what the job was, every meeting at which, after much discussion, no decision was reached just felt too much like the real thing.

When *Americast* was riding high we were approached to turn the podcast into a live show and take it on tour. Not exactly a giant leap for mankind. But oh, what a voyage of discovery that turned out to be into the unfathomable bits of the BBC organogram. Oppenheimer may have found it easier to assemble the first atomic bomb.

We approached our editor about it, who said he would have to send it further up the BBC News tree. News then said they would need to talk to Sounds; Sounds copied in Radio 4; commissioners there wanted to consult Editorial Policy; Editorial Policy wanted to loop in the BBC's commercial arm, BBC Studios; Studios needed to speak to Marketing; Marketing wanted to get the views of the Press Office; and the PR people there wanted to speak to Legal about how the contracts would work, which of course necessitated bringing in Salaries and HR. The email chain had now amassed probably about 200 names, and you could almost hear the head-scratching and chin-stroking across the Atlantic in Washington. We were asked to stay patient. It's nearly there. We kept on being told what a splendid idea it was, and that everyone was right behind it as a concept. But it was just a bit complicated. There were a number of stakeholders to square. The seasons came and the seasons went.

The funny thing is, when you're in the BBC you are so inured to its quirks and idiosyncrasies – and what a hulking great bureaucracy it can be – that it seems totally unremarkable; normal even. It's only when you're out and you've taken stock that some of the absurdities of the place are brought home to you. After eating up a zillion man- and woman-hours, the BBC said we could do it but with so many complexities and strings attached that it became too preposterous to consider. They say a camel is really just a horse designed by a committee ...

So Emily's message came at an interesting time. When we eventually spoke it was to propose something that I hadn't considered – and that was leaving the BBC, where I had been for more than 35 years (and where she had been for around 20), and launching a daily news podcast with Global, the company that owns Heart FM, Capital Radio, Classic FM and LBC, among others. Along with our former editor from *Americast*, Dino Sofos, who had already left the BBC to set up his own company, we would launch this in the near future.

The first conversation I had to discuss this with the head of programming at Global, James Rea, was in mid-January while I was in Australia. The contract was negotiated and signed a month later. Rather fewer stakeholders, it struck me, than getting a live show off the ground at the BBC. *The News Agents* was born, although then it did not have a name, nor was there much of a blueprint of what we were going to do. There was only an idea that Global was prepared to back with enthusiasm and encouragement, as well as marketing heft that we never had for *Americast*.

We each had our reasons for jumping ship, both slightly aligned and slightly different. Emily spoke about hers when she delivered the MacTaggart Lecture at the Edinburgh Television Festival that summer.

She returned to her coverage of the whole Barnard Castle affair on *Newsnight*, and Dominic Cummings's behaviour. She told her audience in Edinburgh:

The intro stated bluntly and baldly that he had broken the rules. And it asked why the government – Boris Johnson – was standing by him … It was only the next morning that the wheels fell off. A phone call of complaint was made from Downing Street to the BBC News management. This – for context – is not unusual … What was not foreseen was the speed with which the BBC sought to pacify the complainant. Within hours, a very public apology was made, the programme was accused of a failure of impartiality, the recording disappeared from iPlayer and there were paparazzi outside my front door.

She would then go on to explain how during Brexit the audience was only being given a highly choreographed – and distorted – impartiality. 'We fell into what we might call "the Patrick Minford paradigm" [Minford being one of the few economists in Britain to speak about Brexit in a positive way]. In other words, it might take our producers five minutes to find 60 economists who feared Brexit and five hours to find a sole voice who espoused it. But by the time we went on air we simply had one of each. We presented this unequal effort to our audience as balance. It wasn't.'

This struck a chord with me. It was the same with business leaders – you could find any number of CEOs from FTSE 100 companies who would tell you of the damage they feared that Brexit would bring, but on the other side of the debate it felt as though the BBC had signed exclusive contracts with the bloke who owned the Wetherspoons pub chain, Tim Martin (knighted in 2023), and James Dyson, he of the eponymous household gadgets. There were endless voices against; there seemed just two for. I would add that nothing shouts confidence in resurgent post-Brexit Britain like moving your company headquarters to Singapore as Dyson did in 2019. While Wetherspoons in 2021 were complaining about labour shortages for their pubs. Where had all those Eastern European workers gone?

In 2016, I was accompanying President Obama when he flew from Saudi Arabia to London, and from London to Germany before heading back to the US. I was one of the small group of around a dozen journalists flying on *Air Force One* with him. He had come to London to offer support to David Cameron ahead of the Brexit referendum, and an unmistakable (possibly counterproductive) warning that Britain could expect no favours from America if it voted to leave. There would be no quick trade deal. I would file reports for TV and radio. Just as we were about to take off to fly to Germany for the last leg of the trip, I had filed a long piece for the radio bulletins on what Obama had been saying. I was told by the editor in the newsroom that it was fine in so far as it went. Then came the jaw-dropping 'but': it hasn't got any Nigel Farage in it, I was told. When I replied – I thought quite wittily – 'I don't think Nigel Farage is flying on *Air Force One* with us,' I was not very patiently told that every piece had to have internal balance. So I would have to add an additional paragraph including unrelated comments that Nigel Farage had made that day. It was preposterous, a cop-out. And there was a lot of it around, though for the most part I had been spared.

When I was in Washington, we had an early test of all this the day after Trump's inauguration as president. A special briefing was called at the White House on a Saturday evening. I just happened to have been doing a live hit for the evening bulletin, so was one of the few journalists around for it. Trump's newly minted spokesman, Sean Spicer, came barrelling into the briefing room to assert that the crowd for Trump's inauguration was the biggest in history. And it was just demonstrably untrue. As objective fact, it was a lie. Obama's first inauguration in 2009 had way more people at it. All you needed to do was look at the two identical photographs taken from the Washington monument looking towards the Capitol at the time of the speech.

So how do you report it? The 'both-sideism' way is to say, 'The president is claiming his inauguration was the biggest in history, but others disagree.' That evening, after a refreshingly brief editorial discussion, we said, 'The president is claiming his inauguration was the biggest in history, but that's not true.' It seemed a bold – controversial even – way to start coverage of the new president, but anything else would have been dishonest and misleading. And time and again, where necessary, we would call out untruths; we would call out when the president had been racist; we would say something was misogynistic; we would say he lost the election. And we would call out his big political successes too: the Abraham Accords (which saw the UAE, Bahrain and later Morocco normalise relations with Israel), the legislation passed to reduce taxes (and that is not me being political, it was a reflection that this was a political objective which he had achieved, despite fierce opposition). Impartiality is not weak. Impartiality is being bold enough to make calls and judgements on things when it is appropriate to do so. And as the North America editor, I felt it was my job to do that. Though often, of course, you are dealing in nuance. And then it is just as important to say to the audience why things may not be as simple as they seem. Rarely in journalism (or life) are things simply black and white.

But my ability to report the way I did has to be put in a broader political context. There was an infinitesimally small chance that at the end of one of my live reports on *BBC News at Ten*, the phone was going to ring in New Broadcasting House in London with a furious presidential press secretary on the other end of the line demanding to speak to the director general or the head of news. A call like that from Downing Street – as Emily pointed out – was not a rare occurrence at all. Because of the way the BBC is funded – and because of the way the UK media is regulated – politicians have always sought to influence what is being reported. And it goes without saying that if you are part of the governing party your words carry that much more weight and menace.

It is worth remembering that straight after Boris Johnson won the election in 2019, the order went out from Downing Street to all government departments that no ministers should appear on the *Today* programme. None. Ever again. Breakfast TV, fine, but if you're a producer from the *Today* programme, don't even bother ringing up to bid. It was an outrageous use of power to try to force the BBC's flagship news programme … well – to do what exactly? Bend the knee? Give ministers an easier ride? Or was it just the exercise of raw political power: we can, so we will. The Cummings-inspired diktat fell apart when Covid struck and political willy-waggling had to make way for what you do at a time of national emergency.

So when I received Emily's message about jumping with her, I thought it was both nuts and brilliant.

Often when I told people I worked for the BBC I would be asked 'Which bit?' – to which I would reply 'the B not the C'. Like some constitutions, which have a strict separation between church and state, the BBC should have had a strict separation between being a broadcaster, a B, and part of the corporation, the C. But as I readied to return to the UK there were sufficient stories that alarmed me over whether that was still the case. The best bosses that I worked for were the ones who acted as the shock absorbers to whatever it was the government was getting hot under the collar about. They would let you get on with the journalism – ferreting out the story, fact-checking, making sure you have all the angles covered – while they took the full impact of governmental ire.

But the post-Brexit environment meant that as a whole the newsroom was all too aware of the government's displeasure at the corporation, and Number 10 was far from restrained in making that clear. I don't say this as some naïf, shocked at what he was seeing. The BBC has historically had fraught relations with whoever is in government. Just read David Dimbleby's account of Harold Wilson blowing up at him over an issue he didn't want to be questioned about. Or Thatcher's fury over the BBC and the IRA. I remember going out on strike when I was in BBC local radio in the 1980s over government interference in the *Real Lives* documentary series and one particular episode called 'At the Edge of the Union', which featured an interview with Martin McGuinness – then one of the leaders of the provisional IRA. The government said he must not be given 'the oxygen of publicity'. The row would lead to Alasdair Milne becoming the first DG to be sacked from the post. There was a similarly fractious relationship between the Blair government and the BBC over the Iraq war, which would culminate in the then DG, Greg Dyke, and the chairman, Gavyn Davies, quitting. So, yes, it has always been an uneasy relationship – and rightly so.

But at the end of my tenure there it felt different. It wasn't just that the chairman of the BBC, Richard Sharp, had been a major Conservative Party donor – we had had the former Conservative Party chairman Chris Patten in that role, and excellent he was in it too. Nor was it that Tim Davie had been an office holder in his local Tory association in his much younger

days, and stood for election to Hammersmith and Fulham council as a Conservative candidate. If there was a problem with
Davie, it was that he was not from a journalistic background at
all. He came to prominence as a marketing man at PepsiCo. Yet
as director general he was also the editor-in-chief of the corporation. And there at times he seemed worryingly exposed. What
was new in the mix was that an active Tory hack, who had been
a former editor of political programmes – and had once been an
editor of mine – had been appointed by Boris Johnson to sit on
the board of the BBC.

Robbie Gibb had left the BBC to become director of communications for Theresa May in Downing Street, and in that role
he was chief cheerleader for a Tory prime minister. When he left
that post – and with a knighthood for his political service – Sir
Robbie Gibb was briefly involved in the establishment of GB
News. He was then put on the board of the BBC where, it seems,
he was all too willing to throw his weight around. If you are the
Conservative Party, he was the perfect appointment: someone
with a clear political agenda and pedigree, overseeing an organisation he had spent years working at, knowing how to get things
done and what levers to pull.

To understand how extraordinary an appointment this was,
just imagine if this had been the other way around. Say, after
leaving Blair's Downing Street, Alastair Campbell had been
appointed as a board member of the BBC, unleashed to settle a
few scores, and in a position to be instrumental in defining what

constituted impartiality over its reporting of the government. I think some of the Tory-supporting newspapers might have had a problem with that. (And even that's not a perfect analogy: Campbell had no experience of working at the BBC, whereas Robbie Gibb did; he knew how things worked there.)

One of the most controversial moments to become public was when Gibb contacted the then head of news, Fran Unsworth, to try to block the appointment of Jess Brammar – then at Huffington Post – to become head of the BBC news channels. According to the *Financial Times*, Gibb texted Unsworth to warn her off, and told her in no uncertain terms, 'You cannot make this appointment.' Otherwise, he cautioned, the government's 'fragile trust in the BBC will be shattered'. Gibb subsequently denied that he had sent such a message.

Later on, the *New Statesman* reported that Gibb brought journalists together to tell them to report Brexit in a more positive light and that he had concerns that people would think that over Brexit the 'BBC has an agenda'. And an investigation by the former *Guardian* editor Alan Rusbridger for *Prospect* magazine looked into the network of Gibb's contacts with the government and how he sought to affect the corporation's news coverage. (It was sent around delightedly by some BBC newsroom bosses in the hope that this might bring change.) It also revealed that Gibb was listed as the owner of the *Jewish Chronicle*, the main newspaper serving the British Jewish community. (Where the money came from to buy it remains a mystery.) So at a time following the 7 October 2023 terrorist attack by Hamas, when there was intense scrutiny of the BBC's Middle East coverage, one of the board members who concerns himself with impartiality matters was also the owner of the *JC*. In 2024 the government reappointed Gibb for another four years.

It is rare that an edict comes down from on high where a BBC boss says we mustn't say this or do that. Occasionally it does. After the Hamas attack, using the word 'terrorism' to describe what they did was ruled out (which seemed to me a contortion of the English language – if something causes terror and victims have been terrorised, what other word should you use to describe those who perpetrated the act?). More often though at the BBC you feel this weight on your shoulder telling you to be cautious. That is a good thing if it means you are going to tread carefully with what you say on air. The last thing you want is a reporter freewheeling. But when that caution becomes self-censorship, that is damaging.

This was particularly true when it came to Brexit. How many BBC reports and documentaries have there been on the difference it has made to the UK economy? When there were massive queues at the start of the summer holidays for people trying to cross the Channel, the reporter would mention that this was a result of every passport having to be checked – but never said that was down to Brexit. And nor did he mention that the British government hadn't followed up the recommendation to put in many more gates where passports could be checked.

And I'm not blaming the reporter at all, because everyone in the newsroom is painfully aware that the whole subject of Brexit is contentious and brings attacks on the BBC, so you self-censor to avoid touching a live rail that could fry you.

You see it in management too. Overwhelmingly – and I mean overwhelmingly – the editors I worked with were brilliant, creative, ballsy and questioning. But there is a class of person who sits in meetings and says, 'Well, we could do the story like that, but I think we should be aware of the risks if something goes wrong.' It's the perfect each-way bet. The story is a great success and the editor says, 'I'm so pleased we did it, and glad we considered the risks as well.' And if it goes to shit, he says, 'Well I did say, didn't I?'

A newsreader friend of mine was on a panel at an event organised by Tina Brown called 'Truth Tellers', in memory of her husband, the late, great Harold Evans – one of the towering figures in British investigative journalism. My former colleague argued it was right that the BBC didn't say that the 2024 Russian elections were rigged; instead, much better to say that critics accused Russia of rigging the election. But we know that Putin's critics and opponents are invariably dead, exiled or incarcerated. He received 87 per cent of the vote. It was not a free and fair election. It was rigged in the most brutal way possible. Not to make that clear is a cop-out. You don't need to add varnish to it. You just need to say that it is so. The corollary would have been to say in November 2020 that 'critics say Joe Biden won a rigged election'. How does it help viewers and listeners make sense of the world if you are not calling things when it is clearly so? It would be 'true' to have an introduction on the news that said: 'Some people are claiming that Joe Biden lost the election to Donald Trump, but others say he won.' True, but misleading. It is cowardice dressed up as impartiality.

The concern is that in this slightly cowed, 'don't stir the hornet's nest' environment, there is a tendency in the BBC to go for what might be called 'the symmetry of guilt' approach. Or put more simply, to say they're all as bad as each other. The millionaire Tory donor Frank Hester was reported in the *Guardian* to have said that every time he saw the Labour MP Diane Abbott, it made him hate Black women, and that she should be shot. He didn't deny it and apologised for being rude – as you might for belching at the dinner table – but claimed that his remarks were in no way racist or misogynistic. Downing Street initially said the comments were wrong, but denied they were racist. It was only when that position became so laughable and ludicrous that Downing Street said, yes, they were wrong and racist. But the big analysis piece from Westminster on the BBC website was how both Conservatives *and* Labour struggled awkwardly with the issue of race and identity. That's akin to saying both parties had a parallel problem in the Corbyn era with antisemitism. No: it was a Labour problem. Yes, Labour had had a problem with its candidate in the Rochdale by-election for expressing familiar tropes about

Jewish media power, and Abbott herself had been suspended from the Parliamentary Labour Party over comments deemed antisemitic. But following Hester's incendiary comments about hating Black women and wanting Diane Abbott shot – far and away in a league of their own in terms of outrageousness – the takeaway from the BBC's most senior person at Westminster was a version of 'a plague on both your houses'.

The BBC is possibly the most important cultural organisation in the UK, and wherever I travelled in the world over the course of my career, those three letters required no further explanation. I am proud to have worked for it for as long as I did. But it is the job of journalism to hold those in power to account. And, of course, you are going to give a much harder time to those wielding power than you are to those who merely issue press releases about what they would like to do – whether it be Democrat or Republican, Labour or Conservative. When you do that, you are going to offend and upset – and because of the BBC's unique funding model via the licence fee, ministers are going to breathe fire at you. Equally, when there is a Conservative government in power, you are going to get lambasted by Tory-supporting papers. It is astonishing how many senior editorial figures in the corporation are continually looking over their shoulders and worrying about what the *Daily Mail* might say. But the *Daily Mail* is never going to love the BBC, no matter how much you temper your journalism and flutter your eyes.

• • •

When Emily and I started *The News Agents* with the prodigiously talented, young and annoyingly well-read Lewis Goodall, our intention was to lift the curtain on how journalism gets made, and to have a more candid conversation about politics, and where it intersects with the media, economics and world affairs – but to be free of self-censorship and both-sideism concepts of impartiality. And yes, to have a laugh at some of the more ludicrous aspects of our politics and politicians. On a lot of issues we disagree, but the aim is to make politics engaging, interesting and fun for our audience.

If there is any mission statement it is to call out falsehood, and the populist rhetoric – from left and right – that has infected the bloodstream of so much political debate in the UK, the US and Europe. It is to resist starting culture wars, hold politicians to account for their words and deeds, explain that simple slogans rarely make good policy, and call out baseless conspiracy theories – a favoured tool of the populist.

For the moment, podcasts like ours are not regulated by the media regulator Ofcom, but I think we broadly stick to its guidelines – we cover all shades of opinion, we interview politicians of all stripes, we don't want the podcast to become an echo chamber for one set of views, and but for some occasional outbreaks of potty-mouth (mainly from Emily and me – Lewis is far too frightened of getting into trouble with his mum, Carmen) we are pretty much on the straight and narrow.

After so long in the US, seeing the toxic partisanship of cable TV, my sense of the importance of the work that Ofcom did grew. Of course there have been failures of impartiality in Britain by all the broadcasters. But as I was preparing to come back there were two new kids arriving on the block: TalkTV, launched by Rupert Murdoch via his British media company, News UK; and GB News, which would be backed by a hedge fund billionaire, Sir Paul Marshall. Marshall had been on a political journey: once a donor to the Liberal Democrats, he then threw his lot in with Vote Leave and became a supporter of Boris Johnson. The team recruited to get his news channel off the ground made it clear from the get-go that it was going to be unashamedly right-of-centre.

There was much talk of the 'Foxification' of British news, which at the time seemed to me significantly overstated. Competition is a good thing. And there is more than one way to tell a news story. Furthermore, Ofcom would surely intervene if things went too far.

So what does 'Foxification' look like? In America in the 1980s, the Federal Communications Commission (FCC) – the US equivalent of Ofcom – ripped up the rule book and said that broadcasters no longer had to follow the 'fairness doctrine' that had been in place since 1949 – the requirement that TV broad-casters present both sides of an argument if it wasn't a straight news report.

It's a definition of impartiality that a twenty-first-century regulator might find simplistic, even quaint – but for decades it kept US TV in pretty much the same space as the UK. The FCC would issue broadcast licences to television and radio stations on the basis that they would operate in the 'public interest, convenience and necessity'. Controversial subjects should be aired but with space given to competing opinions. There should be argument on the great issues of the day.

In 1959, a mandate of equal airtime for those seeking high office became federal law when Congress amended the Communications Act. But broadcasters were beginning to push back about being overburdened by regulation. By the mid-1980s – with technological change accelerating and the growth of cable and satellite giving competition to the three great behemoths of US television – CBS, NBC and ABC – the clamour for change, coupled with the impossibility of regulating so much output, became irresistible.

Whether Reagan was driven by ideology – he was famous for being profoundly opposed to big government and regulation – or whether it was a response to technological advances, the fairness doctrine was abolished in 1987. Two years earlier, the Australian media owner Rupert Murdoch had acquired US citizenship. Coincidentally, in order to own a TV network in the US, you had to have citizenship, too. A decade later he launched Fox News, a move that would have the most profound effect on the US media landscape and bring lasting change. His analysis was that although the conventional networks would say they were even-handed and fair, he believed there was an inherent left-leaning bias. And he wanted to offer something right-of-centre, for those who felt alienated from mainstream TV.

He had tapped into something. Fox turned out to be a massive disruptor. It was slick and well presented, with presenters chosen as much for their good looks as their journalistic prowess. And compared to CNN, the Ted Turner-owned news network, it was offering up a very different bill of fare. Its daytime programming was much like any other news network, albeit skewing a little bit right. But its breakfast and evening output was unashamedly right-wing, with anchors there to rabble-rouse. The currency they traded in was anger, and no culture-war subject – abortion, guns, gay marriage, immigration – was ever knowingly under-stoked.

Fox News was at its most raucous, most dangerous, most popular and – as it would turn out – its most vulnerable during the Trump years. Night after night, anchors like Sean Hannity and Tucker Carlson would cheerlead for Trump, lambasting Democrat weakness and amplifying the president's successes. They would present what they were saying as fact, when it was purely opinion. Trump would appear regularly on their shows – and on the breakfast show, *Fox and Friends* – where he would be allowed to opine at length without proper challenge. Those operating within the news division of Fox were uneasy about much of this, but Hannity, Carlson and other opinion leaders like Laura Ingraham and Judge Jeanine Pirro were the geese that were laying the golden eggs for Murdoch, so were therefore untouchable.

Their ratings were fabulous, and they had gobsmacking presenter salaries to match.

But the election of 2020 and its aftermath exposed the profound shortcomings of the Fox model. It's still enormously popular, and one of the most trusted news sources for a significant portion of American media consumers. But as the US population becomes increasingly polarised, what does that say about the news they consume? Does a news channel exist to tell people what is happening, or just to tell them what they want to hear? Is it news to inform, or news to affirm? These are fundamental questions of being a journalist. Our currency has to be the truth, whether uncomfortable or not. But at Fox it was exposed to be something different.

A foretaste of the coming storm came on election night itself. As it turns out Trump's praetorian guard was advising him to declare quite simply that he had won, regardless of voting results. On election nights in the US, the networks and news agencies – like the Associated Press – employ huge teams of experts to determine when it is safe to say who has won in this state or that. And there is a degree of competition to be the first to 'call' a victory. In November 2020, Fox became the first network to call Arizona for Joe Biden. AP would follow a little later. When this happened, Trumpland went berserk. His closest advisors were calling Fox executives demanding furiously and threateningly that they rescind the victory call. Fox anchors hadn't been told that the network was about to make this determination about Arizona, and they were apparently enraged. Likewise Fox viewers. They switched to an even more right-wing channel called Newsmax – because that was serving up what these people wanted to hear: that Trump was on course to win, and to suggest otherwise was a lie.

The call was right: Biden had won Arizona – but the executives and journalists who worked in the digital team on election night, whose job was to make the election call decisions, would soon find themselves restructured out of the company. One by one they were fired. In a conventional news organisation, you would be venerated for being first and for getting it right; at Fox you were out on the street.

But this was merely an hors d'oeuvre to the network's indulgence of Trump's conspiracy theories about the election having been stolen, which would lay bare the cynical values and hypocrisy that underpinned Fox News. It would cost the network a staggering $787 million to settle a legal case brought against it by Dominion Voting Systems.

Dominion manufactured the voting machines used in a number of states. An allegation was made – and then shamelessly amplified across parts of the Fox network – that the machines had been rigged to switch votes for Trump to votes for Biden. The mechanism by which this was supposed to happen was so outlandish as to be utterly absurd. The conspiracy theory could not explain why Trump won in certain counties but not in others; nor could it explain how the machines could be configured to do that. Nevertheless, the mere ventilation of this conspiracy theory in uber-polarised America meant that those who worked for Dominion were getting death threats. The company sued.

As part of the legal action, Fox had to disclose all emails and correspondence from within the organisation on the subject – and a trove of duplicity and dishonesty came tumbling out of this treasure chest. Privately, those at the top of Fox News and the big-name anchors snorted with derision at the claims, but worried that daring to fact-check Trumpworld's lies would hurt the Fox share price – of which many had substantial holdings.

For its sheer brazenness, this takes some beating. On 12 November, in a text chain with Laura Ingraham and Sean Hannity, Tucker Carlson points to a tweet in which a female Fox reporter fact-checked a tweet from Trump, saying there was no evidence that Dominion had altered votes in the election. In his reply, Carlson writes, 'Please get her fired,' adding, 'It needs to stop immediately, like tonight. It's measurably hurting the company. The stock price is down. Not a joke.'

Yet other missives from Carlson – who week in, week out had been the cheerleader-in-chief to the commander-in-chief – revealed that his love for Donald Trump was pretty skin deep. 'We are very, very close to being able to ignore Trump most nights. I truly can't wait,' he texted an unidentified person. 'I hate him passionately ... I can't handle much more of this.'

Other documents revealed that Carlson thought Trump's lawyer, Sidney Powell – at the forefront of pushing the Dominion voting machines conspiracy – was 'lying' – but still he wanted the reporter fired who dared to say it out loud. And the bosses knew it too. Rupert Murdoch referred to claims peddled by Powell, that Dominion voting machines 'flipped' votes from Trump to Biden, as 'terrible stuff damaging everybody'.

The texts and emails were part of a 200-page filing by Dominion ahead of a trial that had been scheduled in Delaware in 2023. 'Not a single Fox witness testified that they believe any of the allegations about Dominion are true,' Dominion argued in the filing. 'Indeed, Fox witness after Fox witness declined to assert the allegations' truth or actually stated they do not believe them, and Fox witnesses repeatedly testified that they have not seen credible evidence to support them.'

No wonder Fox lawyers recommended the executives to settle out of court before it came to trial. Better to cough up just shy of $800 million than have this exposed to brutal days of cross-examination under oath with the most senior figures in the company – both on air and behind the scenes – squirming as they sought to explain the yawning chasm between what was being reported on screen and what they knew to be true. It would have made for compelling TV, but wouldn't exactly have been brand enhancing.

The argument for Fox – or indeed GB News – is that there was a gap in the market for more 'liberal' journalism. It is a point to be taken seriously. There are issues where – and I hate the phrase – the mainstream media, or the MSM as its detractors would have it, have failed to be sufficiently attuned to the concerns of a good chunk of the population. That's why when GB News was set up and was saying it wanted to tap into the concerns of British people who felt marginalised, I thought it was a perfectly reasonable place to be.

But in the US, where Fox went, particularly during the Trump administration, had damaging side effects. If Fox was trying to monetise the pro-Trump sentiments of a section of the American public, then on the other side something similar happened. CNN and MSNBC became locked in competition to make money from being the most anti-Trump voice. The presenters with the most outspoken views did best. And though there was nothing to rival the lunacy of the Dominion Voting Machines saga, there was a profound sense you had stopped watching a news channel and this was opinion TV. If you loved Trump, you would never tune in to MSNBC or CNN; if you hated him, you would rather have root canal treatment than watch Tucker Carlson or Sean Hannity. The bifurcation of the US audience became almost complete.

What gets lost in this is any sense of public service; the very simple idea that you can present arguments, differing viewpoints and give space for opinion. And disagreement. In Britain we have – and always have had – highly opinionated newspapers, which have sought to influence the outcome of elections. The

US is totally different. Sure, the *New York Times* or *Washington Post* might tilt in a liberal direction; and the Murdoch-owned *New York Post* and *Wall Street Journal* the other way – but none of these papers has the clout nationally that its British counterparts have. The size of the US means that it is a misnomer to talk of 'the national press'.

The results of attempts to bring a US-style version of news to Britain have been mixed. TalkTV never really flew. Unusually for a Rupert Murdoch venture there seemed a certain indecision over what they wanted it to be, and how financially committed they were to it. Piers Morgan was the only stand-out hire, and but for him the rest of it felt a little limp. With his name, his contacts book (and a cheque book to help grease the wheels to get certain guests on), he managed to secure some huge interviews that really did make waves. The rest of it all felt a bit meh. And even Morgan, the genius self-publicist, quickly discovered that putting his interviews on YouTube was going to deliver far more eyeballs than TalkTV. A few months after launch, the BARB figures came out and they were unable to find a pulse.* The audience was so puny that it was measured as zero. In March 2024, to little fanfare, it folded.

The launch of GB News is remembered for the comedic aspects of it. There weren't enough microphones to go round for the number of guests on set. The lighting was so bad it

---

* The Broadcast Audience Research Board is the industry-accepted measure of viewers.

looked like someone had forgotten to put 50p in the electricity meter. Presenters fumbled and tumbled. Andrew Neil would be the front-of-house face of the new channel, and behind the camera its chairman. But it all went to hell. The confident talk from Neil was that it wouldn't 'slavishly follow the existing news agenda' and would report 'the stories that matter to you and those that have been neglected', delivering 'a huge range of voices that reflect the views and values of our United Kingdom'. The framing of the ambition couldn't have been clearer from these quotes. If Brexit had shown that a sizeable chunk of the UK population did not feel that mainstream politics or the mainstream media spoke to them, then this channel would be the safe haven for them.

Within a short time, Neil was gone, along with some other executives who had been recruited to deliver a different type of news channel. He said he had become a minority of one. A power battle was being fought and Neil had been vanquished. If you wanted to understand the direction of travel, his replacement as the main evening presenter was going to be Nigel Farage, he of UKIP, the Brexit Party, and any other party where copious amounts of booze and fags are on offer. Now whatever you may think of Andrew Neil – he had been editor of the *Sunday Times*, chairman of the *Spectator* and a fearless inquisitor on the BBC – he was a journalist through and through. Yes, his politics are to the right, but he has always been a hack first. Nigel Farage was always primarily a political activist and agitator – and to describe him as 'right-of-centre' doesn't quite cut it. He is way, way to the right of centre.

Reports of the imminent death of GB News turned out to be much exaggerated. The technical gremlins and snafus that had marked the launch were largely ironed out. It was finding its feet and was standing in a place that no one else had hitherto dared occupy in British television. It was – like its talismanic main anchor – cocking a snook at the mainstream, and more importantly the regulator, Ofcom.

A very different television news beast was emerging, and it was gaining traction and audience. Advertisers were taking a second look. It was clear its influence was growing on the right of British politics. And all sorts of darlings of the Conservative right were finding a lucrative way to supplement their meagre parliamentary earnings. Lee Anderson (who has since left the Tories to join Reform), Jacob Rees-Mogg, Esther McVey (weirdly appointed by Sunak as – literally – 'minister for common sense') and her husband and fellow MP, Philip Davies, were all given berths on the channel. No Labour or Liberal Democrat MP was offered the same. Money isn't everything, but a survey by the *Guardian* based on declarations in the MPs' register of interests found that while GB News had paid just £1,100 in contributor fees to Labour parliamentarians, it had paid a whopping £660,000 to Tories.

Not only that, when these people were presenting, there were repeated breaches of Ofcom rules: Conservative MPs interviewing the Conservative chancellor in a neither fearless nor impartial examination of the economic decision-making of the government. Rees-Mogg, the former business secretary and leader of the house, delivering breaking news as though he were some kind of latter-day Walter Cronkite. And though Ofcom has repeatedly ruled against GB News, it has had all the effectiveness of a supply teacher who's lost control of the class. The blurring of news and comment was becoming ever murkier.

Ofcom has ruled that shows hosted by Rees-Mogg, Esther McVey and Philip Davies broke rules which state that politicians should not usually front news coverage, and warned that the channel was 'on notice' about future breaches. The Ofcom code says a politician can't be a newsreader, interviewer or reporter in a news programme 'unless, exceptionally, it is editorially justified'. They can, however, front non-news programmes. OK. But isn't the channel called GB *News*?

Sir Paul Marshall, who has a 41 per cent stake in GB News, was in 2024 also reportedly trying to buy the *Daily Telegraph* group, which owns the Sunday imprint as well as the *Spectator* magazine. At *The News Agents*, in a joint investigation with the advocacy group HOPE not Hate, we discovered that Marshall had made his Twitter/X account private – but was using it to amplify the views of far-right commentators, predicting that immigration would lead to a hot civil war, claiming there were too many Muslims in the country. Calls for mass deportations of immigrants also seemed to find favour with him. He also either liked or retweeted homophobic views. When we contacted Marshall's representative for comment, the first thing that happened was that the hedge fund boss deleted all the tweets we had highlighted, as if that would make the problem go away. We had obviously taken screenshots of the most controversial likes and retweets. Marshall's spokesperson said in his defence that these were only a small proportion of the tweets that he had liked or commented upon.

When GB News was launched, the aim might have been to be right-of-centre, but as time has passed there has been a political drift in an unmistakable direction, which makes the question of 'Foxification' of British news real and urgent, particularly given the seeming reluctance of the regulator to intervene. Like the parakeets that now muscle and shriek all other birds out of the way in our London parks and gardens, a non-native invasive species is threatening to take over our longstanding way of doing broadcast news.

CHAPTER 6

A THEORY FOR EVERYTHING

On 17 January 2024, a statement was issued from Kensington Palace that Catherine, Princess of Wales, 42, had undergone abdominal surgery. The operation had been a success, and she would be in hospital for two weeks; based on medical advice, she was unlikely to return to public duties until after Easter. Kensington Palace said she wished to apologise for postponing planned engagements. Equally, William, the Prince of Wales, would not be carrying out any official duties while she was in hospital or immediately after being discharged. The palace was not going to specify the nature of the abdominal surgery and would not provide a running commentary on her recovery.

It was pretty shocking news. The fact that Kensington Palace said she was going to be in hospital for a couple of weeks clearly indicated that this was something very serious. And the tone from KP, as Kensington Palace is known in royal circles, was unmistakably earnest.

The shock only intensified when a separate statement came – this time from Buckingham Palace, or BP – saying that King Charles was being admitted to the same hospital in central London to undergo a corrective procedure on an enlarged prostate. It looked as though the two biggest stars of the post-Elizabethan, slimmed-down monarchy were going to be out of action for quite some time.

I had been at a dinner a few months earlier when the publisher of the *New York Times* had been in town and there was a former senior royal aide who gave a fascinating insight into the lack of coordination – and worse, competition – between the different, some might say rival, royal palaces. It was just a few days after Trooping the Colour, the great ceremonial occasion to mark the sovereign's official birthday. It would be King Charles's first since taking the throne. The expectation was that his photo would be on every front page the next morning. This may sound trivial, I know, but if you're a working royal your key performance indicator is how visible you are to the public, and that means how much publicity you get. The 2023 Trooping the Colour was the day before Father's Day, so quite independently, Kensington Palace had released a lovely photo of William and his three kids, Prince George, Princess Charlotte and Prince Louis, at Windsor Castle. Louis, the youngest, has his arms wrapped round his father's neck, while George and Charlotte on either side look up adoringly at their dad. That picture blew the King off the front pages. The royal aide at this dinner explained there would have been considerable consternation in Buckingham Palace at this upstaging.

This is worth noting because it was clear there was little or no coordination of messaging between BP and KP over the hospitalisation of Charles and Kate. The statement about the Princess of Wales was the epitome of vagueness, whereas BP was precise – it was an enlarged prostate that was being treated. And to the King's credit, that candour led to thousands of older men going onto the NHS website to find out about a condition which tends not to get spoken about.

True, KP had set parameters and tried to manage expectations, but why was one palace being more open than the other?

Very soon it all went completely bonkers. Initially it took the form of speculation about what it was that had kept the princess in hospital for two weeks, but throughout all this Kensington Palace held the line; it was not going to comment. But the pressure was growing. Why had there been no word? Why had Prince William pulled out at the last second of a memorial service for his godfather, leaving Prince Andrew – Prince Andrew, for goodness' sake! – to lead the royal procession into St George's Chapel for the service?

Social media abhors a vacuum, and so the space was filled with conspiracy theories about what might be behind it.

Then came Mother's Day, and Kensington Palace released a photo of Kate and the children that was almost as adorable as the one that had been released of William on Father's Day. It was the first public sighting of Kate since she went into hospital, and it was a slight bowing to pressure: an attempt to show that everything was all right. It had entirely the reverse effect. Social media sleuths started pointing out strange anomalies in the photo: a wrist not being properly aligned with an arm here; some fingers crossed in a weird way there – and Kate was not wearing a wedding ring. Then came the 'kill' notices from the main picture agencies used by the press and electronic media. They were telling their clients to not use the picture because it had been doctored. Of course, you can go back to Queen Elizabeth I to see the evidence of touched-up portraits to cast the sitter in a more flattering light, but never before had a picture released from one of the royal palaces been withdrawn. The release was cack-handed and clumsy, and Kate would be forced to fess up that it was she who had done the Photoshopping – and not very well. To get three young kids all facing the camera and looking good at the same time is not easy. So she composited a few different pics into one.

Conspiracy theories were now breeding faster than rabbits on IVF. Kate was in a coma. The photo of her in that picture was from a cover shoot she had done for *Vogue* a year earlier. She'd had an ectopic pregnancy, or been diagnosed with Crohn's, or she was suffering from a serious eating disorder.

The lack of a wedding ring meant that her marriage to William was over. She'd left him. On US TV one of the highly respected late-night comedians, Stephen Colbert, went down a most scurrilous route of speculation, which he has since (half) apologised for. And then, with an in-for-a-penny-in-for-a-pound attitude, the speculation ramped up a shrill notch further. Kate was dead. A royal announcement was imminent. Indeed, not just Kate, the King too. They had both died in an unprecedented crisis for the royal family.

The British press – in fairness – showed considerable restraint, certainly compared to the way they hounded and hunted Prince William's mother, Princess Diana. A paparazzi photo of Kate in a car with *her* mother was published in the US, but none of the British papers touched it. There was a photo that the *Sun* used, purportedly showing Kate and William at a farm shop in Windsor. The paper said it was publishing it 'in a bid to end weeks of online speculation which has seen wild conspiracy theories about Kate spread unchecked'. And one must presume with the implicit or explicit approval of the palace.

But the social media super-sleuths decided there was no way that was Kate Middleton. She was too thin; it must be a body double. It was a move to get us off the scent that she was dead. A company monitoring social media usage, BrandMentions, found that over the course of that week the hashtags #whereiskate #katebodydouble and #katemiddleton had been used on social media accounts and webpages reaching 400 million people.

It was all spinning wildly out of control. This in turn created what Paddy Harverson, former spokesman for Prince Charles and the boys – and still very much in touch with Prince William today – called a 'doom loop'. Newspapers felt the need to report how many conspiracy theories were out there on social media, and what people were saying. That in turn gave the theories a certain relevance – it's been in the papers, so it must be true. Which in turn led to more reposting on the social media platforms. And so the person who put the original totally baseless post out now has thousands of likes for it, and that leads others to quote it as reliable because so many people have seen it. At which point the social media company's algorithm kicks in and pushes it out to the millions of others who have been searching for that subject.

It was a feeding frenzy that was only brought to a brief halt when we heard from Kate herself. In a sad and moving video message, sitting alone on a bench in the grounds of Windsor Castle, she revealed that the abdominal operation had uncovered cancer and she was undergoing preventative chemotherapy. Quietly, cleverly and subtly, she tried to take the air out of some of the most pernicious rumours – she twice thanked William for being a rock, scotching the 'marriage is over' rumours. She asked for space while she underwent treatment.

It was hard to feel anything but pity and shame over the way we had all behaved. All the jokes and memes suddenly weren't so funny after all. A mother of three young children was sick and was being treated for cancer. The absence of William from his godfather's memorial service now had an explanation: it was the day his wife had been diagnosed. The reason they had wanted to say nothing was so that they could break the news to the children after they had broken up from school, so they wouldn't be hearing it from their classmates.

Then it all went a bit meta.

We started seeing conspiracy theories about the conspiracy theories. It had all been started by the Russians trying to sow discord and confusion (in fairness, it wouldn't have been the first time they had done that). No, it was the Chinese who were behind it. Social psychologists sought to explain the behaviour. Were the people posting this nonsense just feeling they were part of some entertainment show, almost as if they are starring in their own film, where they play the role of a digital-age Poirot or Sherlock Holmes? Was it born of alienation from society that they felt they could say whatever came into their heads without regard to real-life consequences? What happened to our ability to show empathy to other people's suffering?

Britain didn't used to be like this.

• • •

If you accept the premise that there is such a thing as 'national characteristic', the thing I love most about this country is our sense of humour: the ability to laugh at ourselves, the self-deprecating irony. We are a country that was made for the eye-roll emoji. How could you possibly believe in conspiracy when our leaders are capable of such fumbling, bumbling idiocy?

We've had our moments, of course. To say that Britain has no backstory of conspiracy theories would be overstating it. The death of Diana, Princess of Wales, in the Alma tunnel in Paris in 1997 did lead to a flurry of theories – many of them promoted by the grief-stricken former Harrods owner Mohammed al Fayed, whose son, Dodi, had died alongside Diana in the Mercedes limo. Was it a hit ordered by MI6? Had it all been organised by the Duke of Edinburgh? What happened to the mystery Fiat Panda that was seen coming out of the tunnel? What explained the high carbon monoxide levels in the blood of the chauffeur, Henri Paul? The truth was more prosaic: Henri Paul was going too fast entering a tunnel that has a bend while trying to shake off the paparazzi who were in pursuit – and the toxicology report revealed he'd been drinking heavily.

Then there was the death of the Ministry of Defence weapons expert David Kelly at the time of the invasion of Iraq. He took his own life after he'd been exposed as the source of a report on the *Today* programme questioning the reliability of the dossier about Saddam Hussein's weapons of mass destruction. His suicide was deeply shocking and rocked the Blair government. The prime minister himself looked haunted after learning of his death and being asked at a massively uncomfortable news conference in Tokyo whether he had blood on his hands. Just like the death of Diana in the Paris tunnel, the doubters saw more sinister forces at play.

Blair, to head off some of the fevered speculation, set up an inquiry under the former chief justice of Northern Ireland, Lord Hutton. The conclusion was that Kelly had taken his own life. But it is the law of conspiracy theories that if you believe in them you believe in them, and think that anything that provides evidence to the contrary is just further evidence of the depth of the deep state's willingness to lie to you, adding deception upon deception in a bid to cover its tracks. There was a Liberal Democrat MP, Norman Baker, who wouldn't let it go. He would write a book called *The Strange Death of David Kelly*, which insisted that he had not killed himself, but had been killed by the state because he had become such an embarrassment to the government. Kelly's family were furious with him.

But our fondness for conspiracy theories is nothing like as pervasive or historically significant as it is in the States. In my first book on the US, I had a chapter called 'Truth', which looked at how there was an American predisposition to believe in conspiracy theories, whereas in the UK we would always happily go for the cock-up theory of history. There's a lot in that book that I think stands the test of time; that chapter probably doesn't – because we are entertaining conspiracy theories now in Britain in a way that we simply didn't a few years ago. And it is a change in our country that is profound.

When Theresa May delivered a speech as prime minister at her annual party conference in 2017, her voice was hoarse and she coughed all the way through her address. A letter on the party slogan that is the backdrop on stage fell off, and a prankster was able to walk up to where she was speaking to deliver the PM a P45 notice. Armando Iannucci would have never dared dream up such a plotline for *The Thick of It*.

We remember the absurd. Like Neil Kinnock falling into the sea on Brighton beach as some well-intentioned photocall of him walking with wife, Glenys, goes horribly wrong. John Major with his shirt tucked inside his underpants, Blair sweating through a blue shirt in his party conference address – dubbed the 'things can only get wetter' speech. Prescott throwing a punch. Cameron riding a bike to work while his chauffeur drove behind him with a change of clothes. The MPs' expenses scandal with its attendant duck houses and moats. The entire Liz Truss premiership.

Even the way our politics is portrayed in popular culture is different: from *Beyond the Fringe* through to *Yes Minister*, on to *Spitting Image* and *The Thick of It*. The common thread? That for all politicians might plot and connive, what marks them out is their fumbling and bumbling. Less cunning wisdom, more Norman Wisdom. A political drama that originated in the UK but transferred to the United States, *House of Cards*, had a very different feel when Ian Richardson's Francis Urquhart became Kevin Spacey's Frank Underwood. Spacey's depiction was more menacing, darker. In Richardson's original there was whimsy as well as threat.*

US history is littered with conspiracy theories, many of which become industries in themselves. None more so than the assassination of John F. Kennedy in Dallas on 22 November 1963, an event which has generated countless books and films, worth billions of dollars.

Fall into enough rabbit holes, and what you realise quickly is that conspiracies really are Hydra-headed monsters: every time you take a scimitar to one theory, up pop another three to take its place. And obviously by trying to knock down a conspiracy or pick holes in the argument, you yourself become part of the conspiracy; you are part of the deceitful cover-up. You have something to hide and have your own Delphic reasons for wanting to bury the conspiracy theorists' 'truth'.

Reds under the bed, the McCarthy witch-hunts, J. Edgar Hoover, the invasion of the Bay of Pigs, the Vietnam War, Watergate, the Iran–Contra affair, Roswell: each and every one

---

* Perhaps one of the best American political dramas is *The West Wing*: the fictional portrayal of the travails of President Bartlet – and Josh and CJ and the rest of the gang. It showed a bunch of loveable, well-meaning politicos, trying to do their best against the odds in a Democrat White House. Now ask yourself: could you ever imagine such a feel-good programme being set in Downing Street with a prime minister and staff that we all adore, doing their best for Britain? OK, fleetingly, Hugh Grant gave us that in *Love Actually*. But that was a comedic cameo, not a whole TV series. We don't depict our politicians as heroes either. We're the land of Malcolm Tucker, not Toby Ziegler.

in their own way spoke to America's anxieties at the end of the buttoned-up 1950s and in the 1960s and 1970s – a generation who'd lived through World War Two, and were fearful of the changes that were coming to American society – from without and within. For a country that loved to talk endlessly about the American Dream, there were a lot of anxious and sweaty nightmares too.

By comparison, our cupboard for crackpot theories has historically been pretty bare.

I think there is a fundamental reason for this and that is in the different attitudes the two countries have towards what the scope of government should be. To make an obvious point: America is a lot bigger as a country than Britain, and that has a side effect that millions of Americans feel no connection with Washington, so are suspicious of it. There is also a profound wariness of government. The typical Brit, when something goes wrong, asks, 'What is the government going to do about it?' In the US, the question that citizens are more likely to pose is 'What the hell has this got to do with the government?' Ronald Reagan famously said that there is no more dread phrase in the English language than 'I am from the government, and I am here to help.'

For the Founding Fathers of the United States, one of the central concerns in drawing up a constitution was the fear that the nation might become overmighty and that the rights of individual states would be trampled upon. The 1791 Bill of

Rights is the clearest statement of the rights of the individual states. The Second Amendment, which absurdly gives all Americans the right to own as many guns as they want, had an intention very different from what it became. The right to bear arms and need for a 'well-regulated militia' was drawn up to stop a federal army from usurping power. Suspicion of federal government and the might of Washington is woven into the fabric of the US Constitution. This type of innate suspicion can be fertile ground for conspiracy theories.

There is one other aspect about so many of these conspiracies that have taken hold and captured the imagination. They are invariably advanced by people at the bottom of the pile in society who feel that the people at the top are plotting against them and working against their interests. Or to put it another way, those that are literally and metaphorically thousands of miles from power – and this goes back to my point about America being a big country – for them Washington, DC, is an alien land. And if you are at the margins, you – totally reasonably – want to find an explanation for why the doors to the most prestigious schools and the oldest universities and the swankiest clubs and the oak-panelled boardrooms aren't opening for you.

It's an anxiety that was ripe for exploitation – enter Donald Trump, a one-man conspiracy factory, knocking out plots and falsehoods faster than he could apply fake tan to his puffy face. There's nothing about him that fitted the classic conspiracy theorist. He went to the smartest schools, he bought and sold property – growing his fortune in the process. He also bought and sold politicians of all political stripes depending on whatever objective he was seeking at any given moment. He was the elite; he still is the elite. He's never been marginalised in his entire pampered, inherited-wealth existence. But here was a man who used the idea of plots and scheming as a cudgel to beat his opponents, as a way of shaping a narrative to suit his purpose.

It started at the time of 9/11, when he claimed to have seen Muslims in New Jersey celebrating the aftermath of the Twin Towers. He went on to start a hare running that Barack Obama had actually been born in Kenya; that his birth certificate had been falsified, and – therefore – America's first Black president was illegitimate on the grounds that to become the commander-in-chief you have to have been born in the United States. He even went after Britain's own intelligence listening post, GCHQ. He claimed the spooks there had been spying on his election campaign. GCHQ is known for having such tight lips they could have been sealed with superglue, but that comment from Trump brought a rare public intervention. 'Utterly ridiculous,' said a spokesman. Anything – everything – that could do him down was a conspiracy, invariably originating from subterranean, hitherto unknown, parts of the deep state. It perhaps culminated in his connections to QAnon, and the events of January 6th.

They say that imitation is the sincerest form of flattery –
and across the Atlantic it was starting to be imitated.

There were a few days in September 2023 when all of this
crystalised for me. And it concerned an unlikely duo – two
names you wouldn't immediately put together: Russell Brand
and Liz Truss.

In the aftermath of her disastrous premiership, Liz
Truss was seeking to relaunch her brand with a speech at the
Institute for Government. It had a strong Trumpian deep-
state vibe. In audacity that would make chutzpah blush, she
sought to argue that the 'reaction' from the 'political and
economic establishment' to her policies was the reason they
failed. She blamed us in the media and – well – just about
anyone: 'The anti-growth coalition is now a powerful force,
comprising the economic and political elite, corporatist
part of the media, and even a section of the Conservative
parliamentary party.'* And brazenly went on to argue that
her libertarian economic ideas were 'simply ... not fashionable on the London dinner party circuit'. It was the Bank of
England in cahoots with Whitehall; the media as the PR arm
of both. And I'm sure George Soros must be partly to blame
somewhere – he invariably is.

---

* In her one and only Conservative Party conference speech as prime minister, Truss identified key members of the coalition as people who live in north
London townhouses and make podcasts. We would later be told by one of
her staff that one of her biggest bugbears was *The News Agents*.

Truss, it turns out, is not one who listens to advice. On one of the first episodes of *The News Agents* – and just before she had been made PM – we interviewed her former tutor, Marc Stears, from when she was an undergraduate at Oxford. Despite the thousands of students he'd taught, she stood out. He remembered her as a young woman who, even when presented with empirical evidence that her ideas were unfounded, would press on with her argument regardless. She just didn't hear criticism. It would turn out to be an uncannily accurate portrait and descriptor of her brief sojourn in Downing Street (some whose mortgage interest rates skyrocketed would say not brief enough).

When Truss moved into Downing Street, she fired the experienced and respected permanent secretary at the Treasury, Tom Scholar. The new chancellor and chief secretary had never worked in the Treasury before. She refused to share her figures with the Office for Budget Responsibility. The Bank of England had been blindsided.

The chancellor she appointed was the somewhat arrogant Kwasi Kwarteng. He was an Eton scholar who had a world-weary air and spoke as if it was somehow too much effort to open his mouth properly to form proper vowel sounds. He bored easily, and could give the slight impression that you weren't really quite clever enough to be speaking to him. So there we had it: the British economy in the hands of a woman with a profound lack of emotional intelligence and a rhinoceros hide, and a chancellor with a *de haut en bas* manner. She was impervious. He was imperious. Not a great combo, as it turned out.

Together, they concocted a budget to slash taxes for the rich, but without saying how they were going to fund this giveaway for the wealthiest in society and the hard-pressed bankers whose bonuses would no longer be capped. No wonder that it was quickly dubbed the KamiKwasi budget. What scuppered this piece of economic tomfoolery was not the deep state, but the markets that Liz Truss had put all her faith in.

I mean, frankly, where was the bloody deep state when you needed it? Where were the puppet-masters, the grey-suited Sir Humphreys, the powerful forces of London's salons to say, 'Liz, are you sure you've thought this through?' Where were the grown-ups who might have said that if you introduce billions of tax cuts without saying where the money is going to come from to fund them you might get an adverse reaction from the money markets? But when in doubt nowadays, reach for a conspiracy theory, clutch at a plot. It is so much easier than facing an unpalatable reality that maybe this one is on you; maybe you've totally screwed up royally by believing in your own invincibility.

Liz Truss has since written a 100,000-word book on her 49 days in Downing Street – some might question what the length might have been if she had lasted a couple of years. *Ten Years to Save the West* is very long on those who let her down, who failed to tell her the consequences of what she might do, and extremely short on self-awareness or self-reproach or self-realisation. It is full of right-wing libertarianism – a small state, lower taxes and her argument that in Britain the civil servants have all the power with none of the responsibility, and the politicians have no real power, but all the accountability. For someone who so closely modelled herself on Margaret Thatcher – the clothes she wore, the photo-ops etc. – she was a million miles from Thatcher. It would be hard to imagine the Iron Lady engaging in this sort of stuff. I was with Thatcher when she went on a US tour just after she had stopped being prime minister. She appeared at the biggest venues and drew huge crowds. The Liz Truss show was like a rather substandard Beatles tribute act, years after the Fab Four had split up; stuck playing the smallest venues and travelling around in a beaten-up camper van. Her big outing was at a right-wing think-tank and conference just outside Washington, where the audience didn't seem quite sure who she was. The problem was underlined by the caption at the bottom of the screen on the right-wing cable channel that carried her speech. It said 'Liz Truss, British Prime Minister Sept–Oct 2022'. The blink-and-you-miss-it premiership.

Anyway, the same day that Truss was mounting her 'it was the deep state wot did for me' defence, Russell Brand was doing the exact same thing. Aspects of the entertainer/*enfant terrible*'s personal life had been put under the microscope in a series of disclosures from a joint investigation by the *Sunday Times* and Channel 4's *Dispatches* – detailed allegations of sexual assault and rape, which he denied.

It was a denial very much fitting Brand's new brand, and it was taken up by many of his supporters. It seemed that – encouraged by Brand – rather than addressing the question of whether he had done this, they asked and answered an entirely different one. What these conspiracy-minded citizens wanted to know was why was he being accused and what forces were at play.

Brand is a multimillionaire entertainer who has made fortunes from his books, TV and radio slots and one-man live shows. He was the naughty man from the noughties – bragging about his sexual exploits and his voracious appetite for sexual conquest. But in the words of a therapist, he has been on a journey. A journey that took him from conventional media to being a self-publisher. A journey that saw him talking less about shagging and more about wellness. It became a vehicle for him to entertain a variety of conspiracies about the war in Ukraine and vaccines, and anything else that took his fancy. In the States he was now known as a 'conservative influencer', with huge followings on YouTube (6.8 million subscribers), Twitter/X (11.3 million) and the uber-conservative Rumble (1.9 million).

The day before the story broke, Brand went in for a pre-emptive strike. Denying the allegations, he went on to ask: 'Is there another agenda at play?'– suggesting that the *real* motivation in the publication of the story was not to expose wrongdoing, but to bring down someone who had turned his back on, and posed a challenge to, 'conventional' media. The allegations of sexual assault and rape were all a smokescreen, they were just out to get him.

An almost allergic scepticism of the media is one of the foundational beliefs of the alt-right. No sooner had Brand put this out than you had the likes of Elon Musk and Tucker Carlson – the most powerful presenter at Fox News until his firing that April – rowing in behind Brand. Musk approved of his video, saying, 'Of course. They don't like competition.' And Carlson weighed in with: 'Criticise the drug companies, question the war in Ukraine, and you can be pretty sure this is going to happen.'

There was no shortage of voices in the UK saying similar things. But hold on, hold on. If it was just because he represented a threat – or competition – to other legacy media outlets, why did the *Sun* (which has the same owner as *The Times* and *Sunday Times*) go after my former colleague, Huw Edwards? He is the very epitome of the mainstream media and the establishment. Or Phillip Schofield at ITV? Maybe it's just that stories about celebrities in compromising positions sell newspapers, and always have done?

The two journalists at the *Sunday Times* who were behind the investigation I know well. The army of Brand supporters went after them with all the nastiness that antisocial media excels at. Rosamund Irwin – their media editor – and the reporter Charlotte Wace were chasing down a story of a very famous man who faced the most serious accusations. This was a serious investigation which the conspiracy theorist at the centre of it had sought to turn into something different. Look at the shiny object over there. Like the card sharks on London bridges with the three-card trick, he was trying to get us to look in the wrong direction.

If there were some like Brand who tried to hint at conspiracy, there were others, like former Cabinet minister and Boris Johnson fangirl Nadine Dorries, who went all in. Dorries had been the Conservative MP for Mid Bedfordshire and was very close to the prime minister: arguably his most strident defender. For her efforts she was brought into the Cabinet as culture secretary. She's a fascinating, perplexing woman with a backstory way more interesting than most Tory MPs'. She is outspoken, combative, sensitive, empathetic, and sometimes hard as nails. She doesn't fit into any conventional box.

And, as befitting a woman who was a prolific novelist as well as a politician, she released an absolute blockbuster of a book at the end of 2023, *The Plot*, which on the face of it is utterly devastating. A book about the conspiracy and dark forces at Westminster that brought down Boris Johnson, it moves at a breathless place. It is full of clandestine, cloak-and-dagger meetings where Nadine chases down her deep-throat sources in the unlit corners of Westminster's watering holes. And if true, the book is a devastating critique of politics, power and the Conservative Party. The trouble is that the word 'if' is doing an awful lot of heavy lifting in that last sentence.

There are many at Westminster who believe that the person responsible for bringing down Boris Johnson was – umm – Boris Johnson. The idea that it was a shadowy cabal of powerful string-pullers doesn't really withstand scrutiny. I mean, how is it that every one of us who has toiled in political journalism over the decades could have missed it? Missed this group of Tory men, blessed with an enduring omnipotence, who make or break Tory leaders at will. And what she has uncovered, she claims, is 'a damning trail of treachery and deceit by an obsessive pursuit of power, which threatens to topple the very fabric of our democracy'. This is big potatoes. The members of 'The Movement' – as she calls them – had been pulling the strings in the Conservative Party for 25 years. One of the central characters in *The Plot* is apparently so dangerous and feared that she cannot – dare not – name him for legal reasons. Or was it a fear that she would be bumped off for unmasking him? Or is it – and let me say this gently – that naming him (as many have done) would rob the book of its central character: the evil, he-who-cannot-be-named baddy, and with it the heady whiff of jeopardy?

The history of the Conservative Party is that it is a ruthless machine of government. If you look at the twentieth century, there are only three Tory leaders who never became prime minister;* compare that to all the Labour leaders who lost elections

---

* William Hague (1997–2001) and both Joseph Chamberlain (1906) and his son, Austen Chamberlain (1921–2).

and never won power. It's not that there's a deep and dark conspiracy, it's that the Tories will support their leader all the time they think they are going to win power with them, and will discard them once they think the head of the party has become a liability. The non-stop 24-7 shambles around Boris Johnson is what did for him.

The Johnson fan club – a declining band, but still not insignificant – would love to present his fall from grace as something other than what it was. Dorries's book has moments of genuine revelation. Her account of Robbie Gibb, a BBC non-executive director, lobbying the government over who should be the next chair of Ofcom, the body that regulates the BBC, is a fascinating detail. Totally inappropriate. Particularly so when Gibb was a former director of communications to Theresa May, with very close links to the Conservative Party.

And this is what makes the adoption of an all-embracing conspiracy theory to explain everything so maddening. There are details in the book that are factually accurate. But taken as a whole the book is fantastical. It's arguably a work of fiction masquerading as serious historical analysis.

Incidentally, my first contact with Dorries was when I was in Washington and she was the health minister in London dealing with patient safety during the pandemic. I had read an article she'd written about combining her public role with trying to keep her elderly mother – who had contracted polio as a girl – safe. This immediately struck a chord with me as my late mother had also suffered the terribly debilitating effects of polio when she was a youngster – something that might help explain my concern about vaccine sceptics. The fact that polio has virtually been eradicated from the planet should be the cause of the greatest celebration. It is a truly horrible disease. That it has been is down to the polio vaccine.

Nadine and I communicated quite a bit then, and she was appalled at the prospect of Trump winning a second term. She told me that she hoped his chaotic handling of Covid would be his undoing. There was a lot of friendly dialogue. So, when she wrote her book on the demise of Boris Johnson, she agreed to give her first interview to me at *The News Agents*.

A few days before the interview, when the book was being serialised by the *Mail*, I saw that none other than David Icke had tweeted approvingly of it. He wrote: 'What I have been writing for 30 years and this is only part of it. Former minister Nadine Dorries on the shadowy clique manipulating the Tory Party for 20 years (another clique owns the Labour Party and both cliques answer to a higher clique – the Cult).' Crazy stuff, huh? I quoted the tweet and said, 'The BIG endorsement Nadine Dorries has been waiting for.' And I included a lizard emoji. It was designed to point out the absurdity of Icke. But someone else took offence. On the day of our interview, when I was on the Eurostar coming back from Paris specially to do the interview, we heard from the publisher that she was cancelling. On further inquiry my producer, Laura, was told it was because of my Icke tweet. Seems some conspiracy theorists can be rather thin-skinned.

How did we get here? Why are we seduced into looking in the wrong direction?

When I became a journalist, my first job was at a local radio station in Southampton. We shared the building with the regional TV station South Today. The sports reporter was a former professional goalkeeper, David Icke. He had set the gold standard for conspiracy theories in the UK for decades. His Wikipedia entry notes soberly that he 'claims that there is an inter-dimensional race of reptilian beings, the Archons or Anunnaki, which have hijacked the Earth. Further, a genetically modified human–Archon hybrid race of reptilian shape-shifters ... manipulate events to keep humans in fear, so that the Archons can feed off the resulting "negative energy".' It's crackpottery of the highest order.

But with the Covid-19 global pandemic and the vaccination programme that followed he got a whole new audience. Forget lizard people, he had a new cause: the attempt by scientists and billionaires to take over our bodies through microchips, by altering our DNA through those evil Pfizer and AstraZeneca vaccines.

Just as the virus spread fast across the world, so too did the theories. And some were so outlandish they make reptilian shape-shifters sound like the sort of people you might see in the checkout line at Tesco on a Saturday morning. It felt like trust in our institutions and what we were being told was fraying. The overwhelming majority of us couldn't wait to get a notification from the NHS that we were now in the age cohort able to make an appointment to get the vaccine. But a vocal minority saw something much more sinister.

There was something of a wartime spirit as teams of doctors and volunteers set about vaccinating the population to give people vital protection against the ghastly ravages of Covid-19. We were the people who kept our distance, washed our hands until they were raw, and disinfected the food we bought in the supermarket. We scrubbed our tins of tomatoes and wouldn't let anyone in through the front door. I was in Washington at the time – a city that took the threat seriously, maybe with hindsight neurotically so.

One man even suggested that bleach should be put inside people's bodies because it did such a great job of killing the virus on hard surfaces. The disinfectant manufacturers had to then issue an urgent warning that people should not under any circumstances ingest bleach, and that the president of the United States should be ignored.

Some of it I look back on now and think we all went slightly mad – though maybe not so mad as to suggest we should be swigging from a Domestos bottle. And I fully acknowledge the deleterious effect that many of the Covid restrictions had on a lot of people's mental health – particularly young people with all that critical growing-up time deprived of social contact. But hindsight is a wonderful thing. Yes, some people thought there was massive state overreach at the time, but it was the precautionary principle. If by taking certain preventative measures you might keep yourself and vulnerable loved ones safe, why wouldn't you? It was the first global pandemic in a century – and the outcomes of the Spanish flu were horrific. Equally, though, this was the first pandemic where technological advances meant that brilliant scientists could offer us an escape route far more quickly than might have seemed possible.

That said, there was a small but significant minority who thought it was all a dastardly plot. In the US – always far more divided than the UK – whether you had been vaccinated was almost an indication of how you would vote in an election. There was a gubernatorial race in Virginia in 2021 in which the polls had the Democrat well ahead among all those who'd had the jab – about 75 per cent of the population. But he lost. It turns out the 25 per cent who had refused vaccinations had voted almost as a solid block for the Republican, Glenn Youngkin.

The vaccine didn't have that polarising, party-political effect in the UK, but there was a noisy minority who wanted to advance every conspiracy theory under the sun – and for the first time in Britain, they were getting an audience. Not only that, there was a militancy too that somehow seemed very un-British. There were groups with charming names like Alpha Men Assemble, who trained supporters in how to take direct action, how to break through police lines. Groups committed themselves to intimidating health workers and people queuing to get vaccines. Why? Because they said the programme of inoculating people was a form of genocide. There was even an attempt by some of these organisations to refer the UK government to the International Criminal Court. One of my former BBC colleagues, Jeremy Vine, had an angry mob turn up at his house, attempting to serve a writ on him for the crime of giving out public service information about the vaccination programme. It was pure intimidation.

The theories of what the vaccine did were wide, varied, and more than a bit bonkers. It was going to alter our DNA – presumably at some point we could all be plugged into the Matrix so our behaviour could be controlled. Then there was the Bill Gates theory. The former head of Microsoft has spent many of his billions in trying to find a cure for malaria and to make polio a thing of the past. On that he has been tireless and brilliant. But the accusation was made – and gained traction – that these new vaccines were actually implanting microchips into everyone. There were claims that huge numbers of people would die from taking the vaccine. There was even a thesis that 5G phone masts were designed to be used as a weapon against members of the public who had received the Covid vaccine. Fake news was spreading almost as fast as the virus itself, but without an antidote anything like as effective as the Covid vaccine.

I want to say there was a *modus operandi* of the conspiracy theorist, but that ascribes a cynicism that is unfair. Certainly, there were some who sought to profit from sowing doubt and confusion, but many just had a profound mistrust and dislike of authority. They were suspicious; they wanted to believe that what their doctors or ministers were telling them should be disbelieved. They couldn't accept that a vaccine could be developed so quickly and be safe. They distrusted the technology.

They would go in search of evidence to suit their instinctive narrative: again, news as affirmation, not information. And if you look hard, you will always find something lurking in the corner of the web that will justify your doubts. Go back to the end of the last century and the case of Andrew Wakefield. He was the physician who argued that the jab for measles, mumps and rubella caused childhood autism. His paper, published in the *Lancet*, caused a sensation – and led to millions of parents around the world havering about whether to have their children inoculated. Take-up rates plummeted and outbreaks of measles around the world shot up as a result.

What Wakefield didn't reveal was how much he stood to gain financially from his report. The *Sunday Times* would report he stood to make as much as $43 million a year from the sale of test kits. Others who had co-signed the paper withdrew their names. In 2010 Wakefield was struck off the medical register after the General Medical Council found that he'd been dishonest in his research, had acted against his patients' best interests and 'failed in his duties as a responsible consultant'. It was as damning a verdict as you could imagine and Wakefield did untold damage to millions of children's lives. But those whose instinct is to believe that vaccines are bad for you stuck by him. In their eyes, he was the victim.

With Covid, something similar happened – except with far more people willing to believe. A piece of scientific research would be wrenched out of context, and before you knew it, it would be the intellectual underpinning of a new theory – from the slimmest thimbleful of fact a swimming pool full of assumptions and speculation would be made. And these partial truths would ricochet around social media platforms, gaining velocity as they travelled, accumulating more likes and re-posts.

With GB News now on the rise, vaccine sceptics made their way onto TV screens too, able to advance their theories without contradiction to the channel's audience. Though doubts about vaccines can be found among all sorts, it is much more prevalent on the alt-right in the US – and that seemed to be finding an echo on GB News. One presenter, Mark Steyn – a Canadian author, not a doctor – was found by Ofcom to have breached rules on potentially harmful content when he misused official health data that 'materially misled' the audience. Ofcom said Steyn used UK Health Security Agency data to claim – falsely – that these figures provided evidence that a third booster against Covid was causing higher infection, hospitalisation and deaths. The author Naomi Wolf would also claim on his show that women were being harmed by Covid vaccines as part of an effort 'to destroy British civil society'.

Then at the beginning of 2024, another GB News host – former BBC presenter Neil Oliver (again not a doctor) – claimed that healthy, young people were dying of an aggressive form of cancer, and he linked it to the Covid vaccines. He spoke of a 'turbo cancer' on his show. This brought dozens of audience complaints – and another Ofcom investigation. This time though, the regulator said he had not broken any rules. It was free speech, even though medical experts have dismissed as 'misinformation' the existence of such aggressive tumours.

When I read this I tweeted out my slight disbelief, saying: 'Sorry. This is nuts. A presenter on a news channel uses platform to advance a conspiracy theory about a cancer in children linked to vaccines which is baseless, and OFCOM says it's fine. If facts don't matter on a news channel, then where are we?'

What happened next was instructive. The tweet was liked around 30,000 times – so it got a lot of pick-up. But the comments were almost uniformly hostile. A lot of it was the usual stuff: I was fake news; I was a liar and a loser. But a number of people pointed me in the direction of an oncologist who shared Neil Oliver's views. And this did interest me. They pointed me to Professor Angus Dalgleish.

Dalgleish, now in his mid-seventies, is by all accounts a distinguished physician, who has also had a political past. In 2015 he stood as the UKIP candidate in Sutton and Cheam, and is a firm Eurosceptic. Indeed, he warned that with Britain in the

EU, the NHS would collapse under the weight of having to treat European workers who were in the UK at the time.

But I couldn't find any other oncologist expressing those sorts of reservations about the Covid vaccine. The NHS employs around 500 oncologists across the country, and Professor Dalgleish's is a lone voice – but if you are a conspiracy theorist, you have a slightly counterintuitive approach to 'experts'. If 499 doctors tell me one thing and one tells me something completely different – call it the wisdom of crowds, if you like – I am going to go with the 499. However, if you believe that vaccinations are a terrible thing and will alter your body's DNA, and you are looking for a peg on which to hang your theory, you tend to reach for the one voice that will give your view an intellectual underpinning. Or the one piece of medical research that backs you up. It's confirmation bias of the highest order.

If you are a policymaker, a health professional or a politician, all of this should be deeply concerning. God forbid there is another pandemic or a different type of national health emergency, because surely you want there to be enough confidence in what you are saying that the populace will take seriously the advice you are giving. Social media has been an extraordinary accelerant to conspiracy theories of all shapes and sizes – but the behaviour of our politicians in the UK over these past few years has seen a deeply troubling erosion of that most precious commodity, trust. And it would be foolish not to think they are inter-related.

Maybe it was a side effect of all that time spent in isolation, and too much time in online chatrooms or scrolling through social media, that conspiracy theories have become so prevalent in Britain, where once they were absent. It is so easy to get noticed – say something outrageous but faintly believable and you will go viral. In TV we used to talk about the green-ink brigade. The people who, having seen you on TV, would send you long letters, invariably written in green ink – and block capitals – advancing theories about how they were being followed, how government-operated microwaves were telling them to do certain things. But in the days when people had to put pen to paper it was virtually impossible for these ideas to gain traction.

Years ago, when I presented a Sunday lunchtime political interview programme on BBC One called *The Politics Show*, a woman sent me a lovely card saying how much she liked my work. I wrote back thanking her. She wrote again, a little more effusively, and I replied warmly. Then the correspondence started drifting in a more personal direction: how attractive I was etc. So I thought it probably best to stop replying, which I did. After a while the correspondence stopped – to my relief. But then after a few months another card arrived – and there was quite a shift in tone: 'Hitler didn't build enough gas ovens for hook-nosed Jews like you.' The BBC had their investigations team look into it, and I was advised that the woman had – in effect – committed a hate crime. (The team also did a bit of digging and found out that she was an elderly church warden from Suffolk. Ah well,

I'm sure she does a lovely job on the church brasses.) I was told that I could: A. ignore her (not advised), B. put it in the hands of the police so that she would face prosecution, or C. warn her that my post is monitored and that if she made any further attempt to contact me then that is the path we would go down. I went for C.

My other job at this time was as one of the team of presenters on the BBC News Channel. And here a few of us would regularly receive – like every other week – a typed white A4 envelope with a Taunton postmark, inside of which there would be a neatly folded, small piece of kitchen roll on which had been carefully placed a little dollop of excrement. Nothing written inside it. Just shit. After tests it was established that it wasn't human faecal matter, but animal.

It's not new that people have crackpot, conspiracy-laden ideas. What is new is that there is now a highly advanced transmission mechanism for all of the shit.

CHAPTER 7

THE LAND OF UNCOMFORTABLE TRUTHS

Roosevelt Island is a ribbon of land on the East River in New York City – to the west is Manhattan with its dazzling array of skyscrapers, all steel and gleaming, reflective glass, and to the east is the borough of Queens. It was here in 2015 that Hillary Clinton launched her presidential campaign. At that stage – and it almost seems faintly charming now – one of the main attacks from Republicans who never believed that Donald Trump could be their candidate was that at 67 she was too old to be president.

I was there that day to hear Clinton deliver her speech to a flag-waving, enthusiastic, hip, liberal, right-on New York crowd. And the speech was – in some ways – perfectly tailored for this audience. It was a something-for-everyone speech. It leant into gay rights, it dealt with issues of race and discrimination, it was about breaking the glass ceiling for women, it was about immigration and pathways to citizenship for those who had entered the US. She wanted an Equality Act, a bill that would extend civil rights protections for transgender and other LGBTQ+ individuals. It was a speech that brought home to me how identity politics had taken a firm grip on the progressive wing in the US. This was America as a series of small patches of fabric on a giant quilt and she would say something nice and tailored for each.

It was a million miles from the analysis of her husband Bill when he ran for the presidency over 20 years earlier. Then, in the words of his brilliant plain-speaking strategist, James Carville, it was 'about the economy, stupid'. The analysis was that Bill couldn't win by just piling up the votes in the rust-belt states and the Atlantic and Pacific coasts, he needed to reach out beyond that. Hillary took the rust-belt states like Michigan and Wisconsin for granted. During the campaign she never once set foot in Wisconsin. Blue-collar America was firmly in the Democrat column, so no need to worry about that. Better to concentrate on those smaller segmented groups. She lost Wisconsin and Michigan – and with them the presidency.

Her speeches were the result of endless focus groups, message testing, qualitative and quantitative polling. Every word was stress tested by the marketing people, the whiz-kids. It was cautious, considered – and ultimately vanilla. Trump on the other hand was a man who worked much more on gut, tapping into the anti-identity identity politics that were just as potent in the US. He riffed freely, appealing to America's less better angels. He made illegal immigration his central message with downright abusive comments about Hispanics entering the country, and not-so-subtle dog-whistles to all sorts of prejudice that had become frowned upon during the Obama years. One woman echoed the views of many when she told me at a rally in Spartanburg, South Carolina, that Donald Trump said what she was thinking but she felt she was no longer allowed to say out loud. A lot of supporters loved that he was a one-man wrecking ball to what they saw as political correctness.

There was an exception to Clinton's heavily chlorinated messaging during the 2016 campaign. A recording, taken at a fundraiser in New York, was leaked just a few weeks out from polling day; in it, she talked about the core base of Trump supporters as a 'basket of deplorables'. Half of his supporters were racist, sexist, homophobic, xenophobic and Islamophobic, she charged, and Trump had amplified hateful views and voices. What she said may have had some truth to it, but it was politically crass.

It was a gift to the Trump campaign. Within days his supporters had put away their MAGA T-shirts and were wearing 'I'm a deplorable' ones instead. They were owning – revelling in – the identity Hillary had given them. Her remarks amplified the sense that she was the representative of the college-educated, bien-pensant, *New York Times*-reading, NPR-listening and CNN-watching metropolitan elite. While

– objectively ludicrously – Trump owned being the authentic, blue-collar voice of working-class America. Audacious, extraordinary, outrageous, sure. But surprising? Not really.

Identity politics alone may not have cost Hillary Clinton the 2016 election – there were other factors too: her private email server and the FBI investigation in the final days, the general perception that America was too interested in globalism and not enough in US workers. Trump proved to be the perfect antidote to Americans' weariness and wariness of professional politicians, of which Hillary Clinton – former First Lady, US senator, secretary of state – seemed to be the exemplar. But identity politics undoubtedly played a part. The Democratic Party was way ahead of where public opinion was, and never looked over its shoulder to see if the voters were following them.

When I came back from the US, it seemed to me there was a lot of this taking hold in British politics too, and a whole new language to accompany it that seemed distinctly unBritish – and I suppose when I say British, I mean tolerant. The progressive agenda of racial inclusion, concern about the environment, equality based on sexual orientation and gender seemed wholly unremarkable. Taking stock of Britain's past and the legacy of empire is absolutely right. Questioning the level of immigration in the country, and the need to control people entering the country illegally – again – needs to be addressed. But what I found remarkable was the way these debates were being conducted – and that may be less to do with the contentious policy area under discussion than it is the public square in which these things are now fought out. Twitter/X has become a scorched-earth, take-no-prisoners, kill-or-be-killed battleground where opposing views aren't debated, but lambasted and ridiculed.

There is a lot of academic research about how people have become 'radicalised' online. More and more time is spent on social media, which according to much of the academic research means you are prey to extremists who might want to influence or recruit you. Then there are the state actors who want to sow discord in the Western liberal democracies. We saw it in the 2016 US presidential election, in the Brexit campaign, and in any number of elections across Europe since. And let's face it, when you can open an account with a totally fictitious name and very little means of being traced, you can see how tempting it is to say whatever the hell you like without regard to fact, other people's feelings or the incendiary nature of what you post. Causing offence and transgressing all 'normal' lines is part of the game. You don't win Twitter by repeatedly saying 'but I respectfully disagree' or 'I'm not sure that is 100 per cent right'. British understatement, stiff upper lip, showing no emotion and a sort of genteel talking in code go out the window. Instead it's an arms race: if you hit me with a stick, I'm going to hit you with a club.

None of this was helped by Elon Musk's takeover of Twitter and its transformation into X. Partly driven by cost-cutting and recouping some of the fortune he paid for the microblogging site, and partly by a fervour for unfettered free speech (though Musk is strangely thin-skinned and litigious when he is the butt of criticism), a large number of the content moderators on the platform were fired. The Center for Countering Digital Hate published a report claiming that Twitter/X had failed to moderate 'extreme hate speech'. In reply, Musk sued them, alleging they had caused calculated harm with their 'baseless claims'. A new arena was being created, where the temperature was turned up and toxic discourse was the norm.

Nowhere is the toxicity higher than in the trans debate. It is the issue that on the podcast we know we are going to get most trouble if we go near it. It is also hard to think of an issue that affects – relative to the size of the population – such a small proportion of people (and I realise this is contested too) yet has attracted so much attention and controversy. It is a landmine for the unwary. And when you walk into a minefield, you have to tread warily.

Let's delicately pick through the statistics, such as they are. The 2021 census, which for the first time asked about this, found that 262,000 people in England and Wales identified as trans. But then controversy blew up over the phrasing of the question, and whether it could be misunderstood. Those doubts were reinforced when it was found that the areas with highest concentrations of trans people were where there were – similarly – the highest percentage of respondents for whom English was a second language; indeed, they were in areas that were culturally deeply conservative and where trans people were least likely to be accepted. It was another red flag. So now on the government UK website it says there are no robust figures for the number of trans people in the country.

Yet the place the issue has in public debate is large and the political impact of it in progressive politics outsized. The most obvious place to look at this is Scotland, where the ruling Scottish National Party (SNP) has done more to engage in this agenda than anywhere else. The SNP were the first in the UK to embrace gender self-identification. The Scottish Parliament passed legislation that decreed – in essence – if you were born a man but identified as a woman, then in legal terms you were a woman. The legislation made it easier for transgender people to obtain official gender recognition certificates. Gone would be the need to obtain a medical diagnosis of gender dysphoria from a doctor. Waiting times would also be reduced. And the minimum age to apply would come down from 18 to 16.

The legislation was passed by a coalition of SNP, Labour, Lib Dem and Green MSPs. But it was running way ahead of public opinion in Scotland. Opinion that hardened in the wake of the case of Isla Bryson, a trans woman who, in 2019, raped two women. Bryson was then living as a man named Adam Graham, but following arrest transitioned to Isla, and while awaiting trial was being held on remand in a women's prison. When that emerged, there was uproar. Isla Bryson was found guilty. But where do you send a trans woman convicted of sexual offences to serve her sentence? Does she go to a men's or women's prison? At first the SNP ministers tried to duck the question, saying it was purely a matter for the Scottish Prison Service. But as the backlash grew across the political spectrum, it emerged that the SNP leader, Nicola Sturgeon, had intervened to say that it must be a men's prison. In an ITV television interview, the normally eloquent and agile first minister tied herself in knots trying to answer the question 'Is a trans woman a woman?' When Sturgeon says she is, the interviewer demands to know whether the SNP leader can name a single woman who has ever been sent to a men's prison? It was a bullseye as a piece of questioning. Of course, she couldn't. So, despite this new law, the legislators themselves recognised it was only gender self-identification up to a point.

It drew into sharp focus the whole debate over 'safe spaces' for women and girls. If your daughter is at high school and the male PE teacher transitions to a trans woman, is it OK for her to be in the changing rooms with your child, any more than you would say it was acceptable for a male teacher to be in the girls' showers? What about a shelter for women who've suffered abuse – is it OK for a trans woman to go there? These were complicated questions, and questions to which polling gave the politicians a pretty clear answer. YouGov carried out a survey of 1,090 Scots for *The Times*. On the medical issue, 60 per cent said they disagreed with the proposal to do away with the need to see a doctor for a dysphoria diagnosis, with only 20 per cent in favour. When it came to lowering the age limit to 16, opposition rose to 66 per cent, with 21 per cent in favour.

It also drew unusual battle lines: this was not a debate that could be simply characterised as 'reactionaries' on one side and 'progressives' on the other, a conventional 'conservatives' v 'liberals' spat. This debate is often between those who would describe themselves as progressive women's rights campaigners – or as the trans lobby would have them, trans-exclusionary radical feminists (TERFs) – and LGBTQ+ activists. Both groups would say they are progressive in their outlook.

In the end, the government at Westminster used its reserve powers to block the Scottish self-identification legislation under section 35 of the 1998 Scotland Act – the first time this 'nuclear' option had ever been used. The SNP challenged this in the courts, but lost. There were signs that both proponents and opponents of the bill saw campaigning opportunities, regardless of whether it meant trans people found themselves in the middle of a culture war over it.

The most noteworthy, articulate – and probably most powerful – proponent of the need for 'safe spaces' for women – and opponent of the SNP agenda – is J.K. Rowling. The Harry Potter author is funny, sardonic, provocative, sarcastic and outspoken. But in the eyes of many in the trans community she is a bully, or worse. Rowling rarely takes her argument to the public prints or gives radio or television interviews. She has done one podcast on the subject. The forum where she chooses to express herself is Twitter/X. And with 14.2 million followers she's sure of a sizeable audience when she weighs in. During Covid, when a health body had tweeted about creating a more equal society for 'people who menstruate', Rowling replied '"People who menstruate." I'm sure there used to be a word for those people. Someone help me out. Wumben? Wimpund? Woomud?' She makes her point. But for saying these things she has received death threats.

Rowling has also been in the forefront of opposition to another, more recent piece of SNP-led legislation from the Scottish Parliament. The Hate Crime and Public Order (Scotland) Act, came into force – some said ironically – on 1 April 2024. The law creates a new crime of 'stirring up hatred' on the grounds of age, disability, sexual orientation, religion – or transgender identity. There is no doubting the noble ambition of the law (although it is rather strange that women qua women were left out of the scope of the bill). But 'stirring up hatred' can be a difficult thing to legislate against. How precise are the tools to measure it? If you have a speed gun and someone is travelling at 35mph in a 30mph zone, they're speeding. This is much more woolly.

The law states a person commits an offence if they communicate material, or behave in a manner 'that a reasonable person would consider to be threatening or abusive', with the intention of stirring up hatred. So with regard to the trans debate, is someone saying 'a trans woman is still a man' a hate crime?

It is certainly offensive to the person who defines herself as a trans woman. And the large and vocal trans lobby firmly believe in the idea that you are what you say you are. I think these people would regard comments like that as a denial of someone's identity. So, yes, a hate crime. But then there are many, who would describe themselves as eminently reasonable, who would say that just because someone self-identifies as a woman, doesn't make them a woman.* And you see the problems playing out in the arena of sport. Should a fully physically developed man who transitions be allowed to play women's sport?

It explains why the police in Scotland were extremely wary about this proposed law from the outset and now find themselves in such a difficult position working with it. Rightly, they have said they will investigate every complaint. In the first week there were nearly 4,000 calls made – 4,000 case files, presumably, having to be opened. One of those in the crosshairs from the get-go was J.K. Rowling.

She listed a number of trans women on Twitter/X who, like Isla Bryson, had been at the centre of controversy or criminal activity and said they were men. And she invited Police Scotland

---

* And then there is the reasonable view expressed by Professor Lord Robert Winston, one of the leading fertility experts in the world. Professor Winston said, 'There is no question that we can change our gender, we can do it by mutilating ourselves, we can remove bits of our body and therefore change our shape and so on. But you can't change your sex, because that is embedded actually in those genes in every cell in the body, that's the difference.' We could go into X and Y chromosomes here – but all I am seeking to do is make the point that legislating for this is bloody complicated.

to come and arrest her for misgendering them. The police said no crime had been committed. But a file will have been opened. And a number of prominent politicians who oppose the legislation will have found themselves in a similar position. If the police decide a complaint needs further investigation, they have been granted the power to confiscate your mobile phone and laptop to look for evidence that you harbour hateful views. And that simultaneously raised questions around free speech and state overreach.*

Not all SNP MSPs were behind the legislation. Joanna Cherry said: 'On the doorsteps, I hear real anger from constituents who think that too much time is spent on virtue signalling and not enough on the issues they care most about such as health, transport, housing and education.' She added that there was a sense of 'bewilderment' among many party members on the issues being focused on by her SNP Holyrood colleagues.

---

* The confusing and imprecise nature of the legislation is going to have another unintended consequence. Those who feel they might have been complained about – even if no prosecutorial action is taken – will then have the right to ask Police Scotland to reveal what information is held on them via subject access requests, which will bring in the information commissioner – and that will eat up more police time.

When asked whether misgendering would be an offence, one of the ministers responsible for the legislation initially said she didn't think it would be, but then added it would be for Police Scotland to decide. Hang on. Isn't that the same response that was given over the case of Isla Bryson and whether she would be in a men's or women's prison? Only that time it was for the Scottish Prison Service to decide. Bake the potato until it is really hot, and then hand over said hot potato to the police and prison service to deal with.

Meanwhile far-right groups sought to use the law against the then first minister in the Scottish Parliament and leader of the SNP, Humza Yousaf, alleging that he, a Muslim, had committed a hate crime by talking about the lack of non-white people in top jobs in Scotland. As I say, I don't doubt the honourable intentions behind the law, but legislation has to be easily enforceable and has to have public support. And if next to no prosecutions are brought because of the way the definitions have been drawn up, then aren't the groups that were hoping for some protection from this law going to feel betrayed, and even more angry? And if there are convictions that are perceived to be an infringement of free speech then those prosecuted could become martyrs. The clarion call that 'something must be done' is what politicians love to hear and what invariably makes bad legislation.

Trans people are rightly concerned about prejudice. The acts of hatred are well documented, most notably the murder of Brianna Ghey, the 16-year-old transgender girl stabbed to death in a Warrington park. The judge, in finding a teenage boy and girl guilty of the horrific crime, said that Brianna's transgender identity had been part of the motive for carrying out this vicious killing. Surely, if anything was going to lead to a reality check about where the whole trans debate had gone, it was this. Violent language often leads to violent outcomes. But on the day that Brianna's magnificently dignified mother, Esther, had been invited by MPs to listen to debate, Rishi Sunak – our prime minister – cracked a trans joke at the expense of the Labour leader, Sir Keir Starmer, mocking him for being unable to define what a woman was.

I'm not sure whether it was the insensitivity of it or the stupidity that got me most when I heard it. Sunak got a right old kicking, justifiably. But while Sunak was clumsy with the timing of his 'joke', don't think there wasn't strategy behind it. Conservative boffins believe that on this issue – if not many others in 2024 – they are where the public are, and this is a culture war well worth waging if it garners the Conservative Party votes. It's a wedge issue to be exploited.

Equally, though, on the other side of this, every time an academic is hounded out of a job by trans-activist students for daring to speak their mind on a university campus, it stokes the flames still further. Surely if we take anything from the tragedy of Ghey's murder it is that the debate needs to happen more calmly and more reasonably. If you want to carry public opinion, the goal should be winning an argument, not winning a fight.

The case of Kathleen Stock, a philosophy professor who taught at the University of Sussex, was a case in point. She had faced criticism for being a trustee of the LGB Alliance, a body which promoted 'the rights of lesbians, bisexuals & gay men, as recognised by biological sex'. Trans rights activists accused the group of being transphobic. A charge denied. But she quit her post at the university over what she described as a 'medieval experience' of campus ostracism and vilification. Stock said the central problem was the lack of support other academics gave her – and that fed through to student attitudes. In an interview for *Woman's Hour* on BBC Radio 4 she said:

> There's a small group of people who are absolutely opposed to the sorts of things I say and instead of getting involved in arguing with me, using reason, evidence, the traditional university methods, they tell their students in lectures that I pose a harm to trans students, or they go on to Twitter and say that I'm a bigot.

It seems particularly frightening that a university campus – a place that should be a wonderful furnace of ideas and viewpoints, of debate and argument – would want to create an orthodoxy where diversity of opinion is snuffed out.

Similar issues were being encountered in the world of journalism. Hannah Barnes, a former producer on *Newsnight*, working alongside Emily and Lewis, has done remarkable research into the Tavistock Centre in north London, and, in particular, its Gender Identity Development Service (GIDS). It was the only clinic in England and Wales dealing with gender identification issues in under-18s. A lot of the children that were being seen had multiple problems – they had suffered abuse, were autistic, had eating disorders. And yes, gender identification issues too. We've had Hannah on the podcast a couple of times, and what her research showed was that on the basis of no real data, doctors at the centre starting prescribing dramatic treatment to gender-questioning youngsters that would halt physiological development – puberty blockers, so the body stayed in a state of suspended animation while assessment was made of whether to perform gender-altering surgery. Because they were understaffed and over-stretched, these treatment decisions were often being made on the basis of appointments totalling maybe just a couple of hours. It was found that insufficient weight was given to other issues these youngsters were facing in their lives.

The view of Barnes and the team at *Newsnight* was not that this was about the rights and wrongs of gender identification; it was about whether life-altering medical treatments were being given, using drugs whose side effects were unknown, with too little consideration or evidence to justify the clinical decision. What she was investigating was a potential health scandal that would rank alongside Thalidomide, the haemophilia blood controversy, Mid Staffs and the like. Barnes wrote:

When people turn a blind eye and do not ask difficult questions, harm can be done. I have spoken with young people delighted with the care they received from GIDS, who have called it life-saving and who are living happy lives. But this is not true of everyone. And just as the voices of happy trans people should be heard and are valid, so are those of young people who have been let down and, yes, harmed.

The service being offered by GIDS was found to be 'inadequate' by inspectors from the healthcare regulator the Care Quality Commission, and its model of care was found to be wanting by an independent review of gender identity services. NHS England eventually closed the GIDS centre at the Tavistock altogether.

This was robust, even-handed, independent, evidence-based journalism, in the finest traditions of a BBC investigation. And the story has had consequences and brought change: exactly what you would hope for if a search for the truth has found wrongdoing.

Yet for all that this was ground-breaking journalism there seemed a terror from the rest of the BBC to go anywhere near it. If one outlet in the BBC gets a good story, it is invariably picked up by all other outlets, and celebrated as innovative and original BBC journalism. Not this report. Not this subject. It was as though the *Newsnight* team had created something radio-active, and the only safe thing to do was keep it in a lead-lined box in the *Newsnight* office. Don't touch it, they were told, no good will come of it. Barnes also wanted to turn her very detailed research into a book and engaged a literary agent. It was turned down 22 times before a small publisher picked it up

– and *Time to Think* became a bestseller. One publisher passed on it because the issue she was tackling was too controversial; others said they had authors on their 'list' who would be unhappy about the subject matter – while around half simply did not respond.

There is nothing polemical about the book. Barnes was asked why she hadn't called it a 'scandal', to which she replied that it is not for her to tell people what to think; it is for her to lay out the detailed evidence – fairly and impartially – and let others make up their own minds. Nevertheless, each time we have broadcast interviews with her, social media lights up with accusations that we have 'platformed' (a word I frankly hate) someone who is transphobic and hostile – and why aren't we interviewing a doctor instead of an 'ignorant' journalist.

In April 2024, an independent report into the working of GIDS by the respected paediatrician Dr Hilary Cass was published, and it reinforced everything that Barnes had found in the course of her *Newsnight* research. Cass doesn't call it a scandal either. But she comes mighty close. She found that children had been let down by 'remarkably weak' evidence on medical interventions in gender care. She also spoke about 'diagnostic overshadowing' – in other words, there had not been a holistic approach to the issues the child was presenting with. Invariably, she found, those who were being referred to the centre and being given powerful drugs affecting their hormones had a range of other mental health issues, of which gender uncertainty was only one. Far more attention should have been given to counselling than had been the case.

But it's her comments about the atmospherics around this issue that leap out from the pages of her report. She found that the 'toxicity of the debate' around gender has been 'exceptional', having a negative impact on the quality and availability of evidence. Young people had been 'caught in the middle of a stormy social discourse', Dr Cass says. 'There are few other areas of healthcare where professionals are so afraid to openly discuss their views, where people are vilified on social media, and where name-calling echoes the worst bullying behaviour.' If doctors were so intimidated by the aggression and threats on social media that they couldn't openly discuss their concerns and that, in turn, affected the life-changing treatments given to young people – then that *is* a scandal.

It feels that the land of uncomfortable truths is a place that few in modern-day Britain want to inhabit. Better to live in your own bubble, speak to like-minded people, howl down anyone who doesn't subscribe to your orthodoxy. It all feels so binary (and not, I hasten to add, referring to sex and sexuality). You are either for us or against us. There is no room for saying 'yes, but'. Social media, for all the huge advantages it brings, is not a place that is good for nuance. All of which is an absolute gift to the forces of conservatism who want to parody and ridicule progressive ideas. A whole new vocabulary has grown up to describe this: you are woke, a snowflake, a virtue signaller.

Or the tofu-eating wokerati, as one Conservative minister would have it.

Political parties have always been coalitions of differing views and differing issues. Just go to a party conference and see the range of stands, often with conflicting outlooks on policy. But with identity politics you can find yourself having an inward conversation that is not where the rest of the country is. How do issues that affect comparatively few people take up so much oxygen?

As we become more divided – and social media drives us into more extreme positions – is there a danger that politicians start to think that what is happening on the web is the real world? That they need to take up the cudgels to fight the social media fight? It is very easy, when social media generates so much noise and heat, for one to believe that that is where the centre of political gravity is. It's not.

· · ·

Once you leave the Twitter/X bubble and enter the 'real world' – once you move from social media pile-ons into the realm of in-person protest – debate and disagreement still exists, and things still get messy. But there seems to be a clearer path to consensus – though it's not without its challenges. In so much identity politics, activists think – maybe reasonably – that conventional politics has let them down, and that therefore the only rational and reasonable response is to take matters into their own hands. The 'Just Stop Oil' and 'Extinction Rebellion' protestors are the perfect example of that. They were inspired by Greta Thunberg, the Swedish student who took the world by storm with her one-woman protests – which spread like wildfire across a parched, globally warmed planet – as young people followed her example and walked out of their class-rooms in spontaneous shows of support for the environmental campaigner. Direct action had never seemed more popular. Or effective. Grown-ups couldn't ignore her, and suddenly she was being invited to the biggest forums where these issues were being debated. And this tiny figure would stand at the lectern, her head barely poking above it, looking barely old enough to be out on her own, and would rip into the world leaders gathered in the room with a gusto and unswerving moral force for their endless 'blah, blah, blah'. She accused them of using words that sounded great, but which had led to no action on achieving net zero in carbon emissions. 'Our hopes and dreams drown in their empty words and promises,' she told the audi-ence at one of the many UN conferences held on the subject, this one in Milan.

Non-violent civil disobedience grew. Extinction Rebellion blocked the Dartford river crossing by climbing high up onto the bridge's structures; Just Stop Oil – protesting about the contin-ued use of fossil fuels – would glue themselves to a section of the M25, bringing all traffic on the busiest orbital road in the country to a halt. If the objective was to gain attention, they certainly succeeded. But in the process of carrying out protests like this you can raise people's consciousness of the subject, and simultaneously turn people *against* your cause.*

The Just Stop Oil protestors justified what they were doing by saying they were saving the planet, and this was a far greater emergency to everyone than whether a few people were mildly inconvenienced on their commute. This was the only way to make their point, by scaring people out of their complacency. I am not doubting the urgency of their cause. I agree. The trajectory of climate change is deeply alarming. But I am sure there are many other pressure groups who could make their own case as to why they too should block a motorway. If every protest group engages in civil disorder, then eventually there's no social order.

Perhaps an example of more successful social protest is the Black Lives Matter movement. It started, of course, in the US with the shocking and callous killing of George Floyd by an appalling Minneapolis policeman, Derek Chauvin. For nine and a half minutes he knelt on Floyd's neck, starving him of oxygen until he died; all the time watched on by other

---

* As if commuting isn't frustrating enough, the prospect of a two-hour delay when you may have a hospital appointment, or your kid has an exam that you're driving them to, was tipping some over the edge. The protestors – as a sort of pseudo concession – said that if people had urgent appointments they would be let through. But when you have gridlocked the motorway, how does the person two miles back make known that she has a surgery appointment and is now going to miss it?

policemen who didn't lift a finger – and who were instead keeping at bay a crowd protesting at the slow, painful execution of Floyd by Chauvin. Floyd's crime was to have allegedly attempted to pay for something in a shop with a counterfeit $20 bill.

The protests fanned out across America. Yet the death of Floyd in Minneapolis arguably started to change things in the UK too. There were street protests that in character were not much different to what we saw in more or less every big and small city across the US. And there was one particular demonstration in the UK that is worth dwelling on.

On 7 June 2020, just a couple of weeks after Floyd had been so brutally killed, there was a march in Bristol that resulted in a statue of one of the city's most famous – and controversial – sons being ripped from its Portland stone plinth, covered in graffiti, and then dragged for a third of a mile before the half-tonne monument was lifted up over a barrier and dumped unceremoniously into Bristol Harbour – to huge cheers and whooping from those who had carried this out.

The bronze was of Edward Colston, a man who had made his fortune in the seventeenth century from the burgeoning slave trade. When I was a student, I would regularly visit my best friend at university in Bristol, and everything in the city seemed to be named after or connected to him. At the time I thought little about it – he was just some wealthy dude who was a benefactor and got buildings named after him as a result. But his fortune had come from that vilest of trades. Colston, as part of the Royal African Company, 'bought' about 80,000 men, women and children from Africa and then transported them in the most hideous conditions to the Americas where they were sold. Who knows how many perished en route.

There had been talk long before the removal of Colston's statue that there should be an additional plaque put on its plinth to contextualise better who he was and what he represented, but the city councillors could never agree on the wording. It never happened. So on Colston Avenue stood the Colston statue in a city whose wealth derived from Colston's slave-trading past. But on the imposing bronze statue to him, none of that was apparent.

Was it an act of vandalism to rip it down? By definition, yes. But was it vandalism with a purpose? Absolutely. Interestingly, four people went on trial – the Colston Four as they became known – for causing criminal damage. In the narrowest sense of the law it was a pretty open-and-shut case of causing criminal damage. They had torn down a statue that didn't belong to them and dumped it in the harbour. But the jury found them not guilty. Outside the court afterwards, one of the defendants, Sage Willoughby, told reporters, 'We didn't change history, we rectified it.' And he went on: 'This is a victory for Bristol, this is a victory for racial equality and it's a victory for anybody who wants to be on the right side of history.'

Eventually the statue was fished out of the harbour, and it now stands in a first-floor corner of the city's waterside museum M Shed, probably attracting more attention than it ever did before, and this time with much more historical context. No longer some patrician figure from yesteryear looking down from his elevated perch on the people below who knew the name but little of the backstory.

What's that theory about the fluttering wings of a butterfly in the Amazon being able to cause a chain reaction so significant as to create storms in Texas days later? The death of George Floyd on a Minneapolis street led to a statue being toppled thousands of miles away in Bristol, which in turn led to other cities in Britain to question their own pasts, and then to a wider, more searching examination of Britain's colonial past and its role in the slave trade.

There has been a wider cultural reappraisal and re-examination of historical narrative; other places looked again at the statues that were once proud municipal landmarks but which in the cold light of day seemed anachronistic. But what to do? Should these monuments to the past just be taken down like the Stalin statues were after the fall of the Soviet Union and melted down for their scrap metal value? Should we try to erase the bits of history that we now find ourselves uncomfortable with?

And you could see a similar debate being conducted on our football pitches around the country, where players started 'taking a knee' – a mark of solidarity recognising the need to stamp out racism in our national game. And again, something that started after the death of George Floyd. It is a journey. Racist chanting at football matches in England has reduced dramatically, indicating that perhaps attitudes are shifting. But when England lost to Italy on penalties in 2021 in the Euro final at Wembley after penalty misses by Marcus Rashford, Bukayo Saka and Jadon Sancho – three players with either Black or mixed-race backgrounds – the torrent of racial abuse was off the scale on social media. It was vile. Reprehensible. Nearly all of it was from anony-mous accounts, and a lot of it would have been generated by bot farms abroad wanting to stir up trouble. But it led to a number of prosecutions of fans who wanted to vent their racist views. When England had been riding high, these lads were England's finest; when we lost after their missed penal-ties, they were Black.

It seemed to me that that most genteel and loved organi-sation, quintessential in its Britishness, the National Trust, got it right. The Trust has been entrusted with some of the finest buildings and most glorious bits of architectural heritage that the country has, and its mission is a simple one: to make these great historical monuments accessible to everyone. They illu-minate our past. But when the National Trust decided it, too, needed to look at the historical context of some of its buildings, you would think from the reaction that it had come up with a plan to bulldoze these great edifices and turn them all into skateboard parks.*

The Trust produced a report four months after George Floyd's death that looked at connections between properties in the care of the National Trust, colonialism and historic slavery. It is an academic piece of work that focuses on 93 buildings which were found to have such a connection. The authors state in the introduction to their 115-page report that: 'We believe that only by honestly and openly acknowledging and sharing those stories can we do justice to the true complexity of past, present and future, and the sometimes-uncomfortable role that Britain, and Britons, have played in global history since the sixteenth century or even earlier.' The whole tone of the report is self-examination rather than self-flagellation. It notes that the practice of enslaving African people was a fundamental part of the British economy in the late seventeenth, eighteenth and early nineteenth centuries.

The response was swift. A new grouping of MPs and peers called the Common Sense Group (a misnomer if ever there was one) wrote to the *Daily Telegraph* to complain that the National

---

* Who had it on their bingo card that the National Trust – home of manicured gardens, Doric columns, stately homes and a nice cream tea – would find itself pitched into the front line of the latest raging culture war? In writing this I have just made the schoolboy error of googling the words 'National Trust woke', and the most recent article it points me to also has the word 'betrayal' attached to it. I wonder what heinous crime the wokerati at the Trust have committed now. It is that they have used a vegan recipe for their scones. Gosh.

Trust's leadership had been captured by 'elitist bourgeois liberals ... coloured by cultural Marxist dogma, colloquially known as the "woke agenda"'. The language was pure American alt-right. And the image it painted was of a condescending liberal elite that was betraying its decent, honest membership with all this 'white guilt'. Not only that, the authors had by this study 'tarnished' Britain's greatest son, Winston Churchill, by talking about Chartwell and the links it has to colonialism and slavery.

If it was just one mighty harrumphing letter to the *Telegraph* that would have had the retired colonels choking on their toast and marmalade (non-vegan), then fine. But the campaign grew ugly. An organisation called Restore Trust, backed by right-wing think-tanks, tried to mount a bit of a coup by placing its people on the board of the trust. There were death threats made to the Trust's director general, Hilary McGrady, who made light of it, saying it comes with the territory. But does it? Should it? And fundamentally, is it really that threatening to the sense of who we are to be able to contextualise our history? Is it distressing to know that these magnificent country houses might owe their sumptuous fabrics, manicured gardens and exquisite furniture to the enriching slave trade of 200-plus years ago? Surely it just gives a more textured picture of who we are and how we got here.

To those who think what the National Trust has done is unconscionable, I would urge them if they ever go to Washington, DC, to take a trip out to Mount Vernon. It is only about 15 miles from the centre, and it was the home of America's first president, George Washington. Built on a bluff overlooking the wide Potomac River, it is a comparatively modest house with a series of outbuildings, including the slaves' quarters. What I really commend you do is get the audio guide when you tour the place. There are two options. One is the straight audio tour, with a series of dates and timelines of when things were built, births, deaths and the like. The other is the slave's-eye view of what life was like. It is not larded with sentiment; it is purely a factual account of what was required to keep the place running. For example, the orangery, with its range of exotic plants, was the pride of George Washington – but in winter it required two slaves to work 24-7 to keep the fires burning and ensure the conservatory was warm enough for the sub-tropical flora and fauna to flourish. There is an explanation of the burial ground in the woods where the slaves were interred, their living quarters, how they were organised and what they ate. This is neither challenging nor 'woke'. It is illuminating; it is instructive.

Debates like these take us on a long voyage – one in which we are going to be buffeted by opposing forces. And there are some difficult issues – like the payment of reparations. The historian David Olusoga has acknowledged as much: 'Imperialism lasted centuries and we are only a few years into righting historical injustices – this process might last as long as imperialism or slavery.' But the journey has begun.

Societal change comes slowly, and that requires patience on the part of those campaigning for it. But populist politics,

with its promise of instant solutions to complex problems –
which invariably result in disappointment and disillusionment,
doesn't help.

A few years after Hillary Clinton's defeat to Trump in 2016,
Barack Obama decided to pitch in on the whole question of
campaigning and how to bring about social change. Obama
started his career as a community organiser in the South Side
of Chicago and devoted himself to doing just that. His message
was pretty blunt:

> I get a sense among certain young people – and this is
> accelerated on social media – that the way of me making
> change is to be as judgemental as possible about other
> people. If I tweet or hashtag about how you didn't do
> something right or used the wrong verb, then I can sit
> back and feel pretty good about myself because, 'Man,
> did you see how woke I was? I called you out!'

But he makes the argument that the world is messy; that
people with flaws are capable of doing great things; that political purity and never having to compromise or agreeing to
compromise is a chimera. He says this approach to grassroots
campaigning and politics is ultimately counterproductive.
'That's not activism. That's not bringing about change,' he
said. 'If all you're doing is casting stones, you're probably not
going to get that far.'

Yet the viciousness and vehemence with which so many of these debates are conducted have real life-and-death consequences. When I covered the 2016 presidential election, up the road from me was a pizza joint called Comet Ping Pong. For no fathomable reason it became the centre of a conspiracy theory. Far-right loons alleged on assorted message boards that it was the centre of a paedophile ring, run by Hillary Clinton's chief of staff. This nonsense migrated onto mainstream platforms, and before you knew it, a guy had driven up from North Carolina with a loaded AR15 assault rifle, walked in, fired a live round and announced he was there to free the children from the basement. There was no basement. There were no children. There was no sex ring.

During the time I was in Washington two members of parliament were murdered in Britain: the Labour MP, Jo Cox, and Conservative MP, David Amess. The killing of Cox was carried out by a far-right extremist Thomas Mair, who shouted 'This is for Britain' before shooting her three times and stabbing her repeatedly. David Amess, a hugely likeable Tory MP, was stabbed 19 times by a radical Islamist, Ali Harbi Ali – apparently over his support for airstrikes against Syria and for Conservative Friends of Israel. This is unconscionable.

Since then, Mike Freer, the Conservative MP for Finchley and Golders Green, an area with a high Jewish population, announced in 2024 that he would not be seeking re-election after his constituency office was fire-bombed and he faced a series of death threats. Before Ali Harbi Ali targeted Amess, he had considered attacking Freer. On our podcast, the head of counter terrorism at the Metropolitan Police told us that a record number of MPs now required police protection arising from threats from Islamists in the wake of the events in Gaza.

This is a challenge to all of us who believe in free speech and an open democracy. We want the brightest and best to stand for parliament – or for the local council. But who in their right mind is going to risk subjecting themselves to this level of vituperation? Of course, we must be free to criticise and lambast our elected representatives, but not to the point where they fear for their lives. Free speech must not become hate speech. There is a danger of extremism taking over our political discourse.

. . .

In the spring of 2024, as I was writing these final chapters, a row blew up. Arguably it should have been forgotten moments after it erupted. But it sort of grew, and the clouds thickened. A storm was brewing. And in its utter nothingness, it became – kind of – something.

It was about a football shirt.

To be precise, the England football shirt that the team would wear at Euro 2024 in Germany in the summer. And at £124.99, what the more gullible fans would wear once they have handed over that ridiculous sum of money to Nike, the shirt's manufacturers. The line from Nike was that the St George's flag on it was a 'playful update' of the red and white of the standard version. On the back of the shirt, around the neck, there is a small panel with the flag, now with shades of blue and purple.

I thought it was a bit daft. Attention seeking by Nike, who probably calculated that a bit of controversy wouldn't harm sales. But when it comes to the national sport and the England flag, everyone feels a need to weigh in. The Labour leader, Sir Keir Starmer, said the St George's Cross is 'unifying' and something 'to be proud of'. Prime Minister Rishi Sunak for his part said: 'Obviously I prefer the original, and my general view is that when it comes to our national flags, we shouldn't mess with them. Because they are a source of pride, identity, who we are, and they're perfect as they are.'

Fine. So no controversy. Everyone agrees that Nike should have left the flag just as it was. But it soon became a source of chest-beating with vicious attacks on progressives. A number of columnists found their blood simmering. Camilla Tominey in the *Telegraph* wrote of Shirtgate (and let's be generous and give it a meaningless 'gate' suffix): 'The English and their national symbols are treated with contempt by a liberal elite hellbent on mischaracterising any form of pride in England as bigotry.'

Umm. It was the Nike marketing department, not a liberal elite. It was a US corporation that is more hellbent on profit than worrying about the sensibilities in question. No one in her article is quoted as saying it is a good thing. I kept on looking for the liberal lefty who would justify it all with a 'We should be ashamed of that awful shirt with its connotations of skinheads, racism and the far right.' But it wasn't to be found; no one had said that. It was all imagined. The liberal elite agreed. Everyone saw this dwarf-sized 'playful' molehill for what it was: a dwarf-sized, playful molehill. But the Tominey tirade was only just getting started. It felt as though she was starting a fight in an empty room. There was no one to punch, but the jabs and left hooks were flying all the same.

No Scot, she argued, would allow the Saltire to be altered, or a Welshman the famous dragon. And she concluded: 'It speaks to a complete imbalance in how different nationalities are treated in the UK. Pride in being Scottish, Welsh or Irish is treated as entirely legitimate and benign, but being proud to be English – and celebrating England's emblems and national symbols – is deemed to almost be dangerous.'

From one man-made fabric football shirt with a small panel on the back can such man-made nonsense grow. But we end up with a lot of those on the right trying to turn it into a major row – a row about identity, about English nationalism and how it is England alone that faces this vilification.

And, of course, when that is the political direction you are coming from, no piece can be written without the accusation of wokeness. And Tominey doesn't disappoint: the shirt is 'embarrassingly woke'. Dumb, maybe. Misjudged, I'd give you that. But how is it possible to turn something that everyone agrees on into a source of division? The righteous anger is off the scale. If Tominey and her ilk can generate this much heat over the sale of a shirt, I wish she was put in charge of the national grid. The lights would never go out, and we would be free from the dependence on foreign oil and gas imports. But it is where we are. And it is the language that is used, fashioned as a cudgel, to divide.

It got me thinking about national characteristics: what is it about us and our society that, say, separates us from that big country on the other side of the Atlantic – or our neighbours across the Channel? More pertinently, can there be any such thing as a British characteristic? Does Tominey have any kind of point that Englishness is frowned upon? Look at the growth of the nationalist parties in Scotland, Wales and Northern Ireland. The Scottish referendum of 2014 was the explicit expression that a good chunk of the population no longer wanted to define themselves as British, but as Scottish; in Northern Ireland the fastest-growing party is the one that supports a united Ireland, Sinn Fein. In that context, would it be better to talk about Englishness, rather than Britishness?

Presumably those on the right who worry that Englishness is being trampled upon (by the jackboot of Nike?) would welcome the establishment of some kind of English assembly to mirror those that exist in Cardiff, Edinburgh and Stormont. Although this cohort are not normally overly keen advocates of additional layers of government. I am not sure I see this insecurity about our English identity (apart from in the columns of some Conservative-leaning newspapers). But how much demand is there for it? Where is the cry that the English are suffering a chronic democratic deficit by not having a parliament? Of course, it is asymmetric that the other nations have their own forms of assembly and England does not – but what is symmetric and ordered about any of Britain's constitutional arrangements?

Through the prism of sport, I find it quite easy to describe where I stand. In football I support Tottenham. When it's the World Cup I get behind England (and have travelled to various World Cups to cheer them on). If England have gone out, then I support one of the other home nations, if they're still in (I could add a whole sub-section here about our newfound greatness post-Brexit when, four days after that historic vote in June 2016, England lost to Iceland in the UEFA Euro Championships, with only Wales left waving the flag for Britain in the competition). If it's the Olympics, obviously I support Great Britain. And if it's golf's Ryder Cup, I am cheering for Europe.*

---

* Actually, I find the Ryder Cup fascinating. I don't know whether any polling was done on attitudes of golf club members towards Brexit (I haven't been able to find any), but if I was to speculate on the basis of having been a member at a couple of clubs and played at many more, I would guess the demographic of your average green-fee-paying member was by quite a sizable majority pro-Brexit. Yet every couple of years they are chanting for Europe. The blue flag with those gold stars is the one they're flying.

For me, the support remains as intense with each and every one of these tournaments. Each shows how multi-layered our identity can be. I am a Londoner, English, British, European. It doesn't feel that complicated. Also having been a regular attendee over the years at England football, cricket and rugby matches, I am not sure I have noticed any diminution of Englishness.

But what is it to be British and patriotic in this post-Brexit age? The way the whole Britishness thing got framed seemed needlessly divisive – that somehow the only real patriots were those who had voted to leave the EU – because how could you be a proud Brit and want to stay in the European Union? How could you want to sing 'Ode to Joy' when you could belt out 'Jerusalem' instead? It was as if they were mutually exclusive categories. Brexit was going to give us our blue passports back; we would have all the benefits of independence. No one would be pushing us around any more. Britain would stand tall in the world. The continent could do its own thing, and Brussels would no longer be part of our lives. But the 48 per cent who voted Remain are every bit as patriotic and British as the 52 per cent who voted to leave.

For some, the post-Brexit patriotism was a forward-looking thing: it would be about the UK becoming a Singapore-on-Thames, with a high-growth, low-tax, regulation-light economy – agile, nimble, highly educated and skilled, able to compete with the best in the world. It's a compelling vision, even if the reality has proved to be rather different. But a lot of it was rather backward-looking, to a nostalgia when a third of the surface of the globe was painted pink on maps to denote the reach of the British empire. And, yes, though don't say it too loudly, a wistfulness for when these islands were a good deal whiter than they are today.

The very odd thing about the Conservative Party is that in Rishi Sunak's government the Cabinet was nothing like as right wing as the parliamentary party at Westminster, who are in turn nothing like as right wing as the membership. And they are the people who elect who becomes the leader – so the gravitational pull is always to the right. So, yes, it is remarkable how Britain had its first prime minister of South Asian heritage – and there really was no kerfuffle about it – but he wasn't elected by the Conservative Party members – it was a deal stitched up at Westminster after the calamity of Liz Truss.

The post-Brexit years have also seen the principal anti-EU party, UKIP, morph into the Brexit Party and more recently into Reform – with Nigel Farage the constant driving force in all three. Its big-name recruit in 2024 was the former deputy chairman of the Conservative Party Lee Anderson, and his move sent shivers down the spines of Conservative MPs (at least of those who still had one) who feared that the former Nottinghamshire miner would do them real harm. Anderson's message was an alluringly simple one – and one that reeked of the nostalgia of yesterday – an *à la recherche du temps perdu*. He simply said: 'We want our country back.'

So when was this golden era? Was it pre-war when kids were running around with rickets? Was it post-war when we were still living with rationing? Was it the 1960s when those great, brutalist tower blocks went up around the country and there was the fear of nuclear Armageddon? Or the three million unemployed in the 1980s? It is very difficult to pin down a precise answer. But maybe if the question is framed slightly differently then it will be clearer. How about this then as the question: what is the appeal of Reform now that Brexit has happened? Its *raison d'être* is slashing immigration, both legal and illegal. It is the belief that there are too many foreigners in the country; the worry that as an island we are being 'overrun', that our values are being warped and subsumed by a foreign invasion. Is anyone going to Reform because of their policies on health service reform, penal policy, welfare benefits, housing, transport infrastructure or defence? I'm guessing not so much.

The columnist Allison Pearson wrote sympathetically about the 'we want our country' back mantra:

The feeling has been growing for quite some time. There is a sad, wistful kind of unspoken grief that our nation is being abducted by aliens who are hostile to its history and traditions, who pretty much despise everything we love about Britain and who work through any means possible (except democracy) to change and subvert it. Everything is bad about this country, or so they claim, apart from its ability to provide generous funds for their cruelly oppressed lives and rich material for their grievances.

Our country is changing; it always has. From the Huguenots fleeing the inquisition, the Jews escaping the pogroms (when my family came to the UK) then the Nazis, and more recently the Windrush generation coming to fill the jobs where Britain had skills shortages, there were those from Hong Kong, the Ugandan Asians getting out of harm's way when Idi Amin was in charge, the Indians, Pakistanis and Bangladeshis – and a lot of Poles have made their home here from when we were part of the EU. And sure, some communities have adapted better than others. Some have been more economically successful than others. There have undoubtedly been times when a high concentration of people moving into one area has led to seriously overloaded public services – whether schools, housing or healthcare – and that in turn has fostered resentment.

But 'an unspoken grief that our nation is being abducted by aliens'?

Challenges around immigration are many, but to generalise the effects of migration and claim that the country has become unrecognisable, that our Britishness is disappearing, feels very wide of the mark. The country is changing, evolving. Norman Tebbit, back in the Thatcherite days, was another politician who would like to give out the odd racist dog-whistle. His suspicion was that immigrant communities weren't properly integrating, and still owed their fealty to where they came from – so he came up with this idea of the cricket test – if you have Asian heritage and your country is playing England, who do you cheer for? But look at the England cricket team today, or the football team for that matter. Look at the fans wearing their England shirts on the terraces, or the supporters I see most weekends at Tottenham – they fully represent the diversity of the country: supporting their club, supporting their country.

I grew up in Stepney in the East End of London, just off the Commercial Road where I went to the local primary school – Harry Gosling – literally across the road from where we lived. Little did I know it at the time but there was a deep ideological underpinning to where I lived and the ethos of the place. My parents were social workers, and they ran this thing called a 'settlement'. We lived there too, along with a large number of students from the US who had come to spend a year working in one of the most deprived parts of the UK. It was a vast red-brick building over four or five floors, which had youth clubs, a kindergarten, through to a Darby and Joan Club. There was a net over the flat roof, which was where five-a-side football would be played. There were gymnasiums, a ballet rink, a squash court and a great hall where concerts would be put on. In the basement was a synagogue.

It had been opened in 1914 in the wake of the wave of Ashkenazi Jews coming into the country from places like Poland, Russia and Belarus. In large numbers they were fleeing the forced expulsions from their towns and villages – from their *shtetls*. Think the song 'Anatevka' from *Fiddler on the Roof*. But this surge in the Jewish population was causing alarm: alarm to the already well-established and well-to-do Sephardic Jewish community whose roots could be traced back to southern Europe, North Africa and the Middle East. They had been in Britain for centuries and these great families feared that this influx of largely poor, ill-educated, Yiddish-speaking Eastern Europeans was going to be seriously destabilising and would cause a massive uptick in antisemitism that would affect their lives too. With the backing of some of these wealthy Sephardic families, the decision was taken to create this 'settlement' – its mission to turn these newly arrived immigrants into upstanding British citizens and patriots. So what did they call the community centre? They alighted on the name the Oxford and St George's – the O-St-G: what could be more quintessentially English? The driving force behind its establishment was a man called Sir Basil Henriques – a Sephardic Jew who had been educated at Harrow and then Oxford.

The club focused on ideas of citizenship, the importance of education, family – and yes, maintaining Jewish religious traditions. But it was Britain that had been where these people had sought refuge and loyalty to king and country was a cornerstone, with all the young men and women in 1939 signing up to serve their nation, as indeed my father did. Your loyalty was to the country that had welcomed and taken you in. By the time my sister and I were growing up there in the 1960s, the club had largely served its purpose, it was mission accomplished. Just as I was unaware of the thinking behind the settlement when I was growing up, I didn't take much notice of the fact that quite a few of the adults seemed to have these small tattoos with a series of letters and numbers on their wrists and lower arms. These people had good reason to be thankful that they had been able to make their home here.

The last big wave of migration had happened either side of World War Two, and most of the Jewish community was making good its escape from the East End to the leafier suburbs of London. We moved to Maggie Thatcher's Finchley in 1970, swapping a place with a squash court, multiple gyms and an endless array of people wandering in and out for a three-bedroomed semi in a quiet crescent. It was quite a change. The Bernard Baron Settlement on the corner of Henriques Street and Fairclough Street is no more. It is now a block of flats.

For all that I had a Jewish upbringing, I am not practising. I married out, my children were brought up with no religion, and of all the ways I would define myself, Jewish would be way down the list. When my last book came out a kind woman from the *Jewish Chronicle* asked me to do an interview about how my Judaism had informed my writing. I declined because I couldn't see how in any way that it had.

And then 7 October happened. It felt shocking enough on the day, but as I learned more about what happened the worse it became. A pogrom had happened. This was the biggest attack on Jews since the Holocaust. Unspeakable and gruesome acts had been carried out by gloating Hamas terrorists. And – *ping* – a little Jewish identity light went off in my head and a visceral convulsion in my stomach. Why wasn't there greater condemnation from the international community? Why were there antisemitic slogans being daubed on the kosher butcher's shop in Golders Green? The little Jewish guy who ran it wasn't responsible for Israeli foreign policy. Attack Netanyahu, not him.

There came the realisation that buried deep in my DNA – and in a lot of other Jews I spoke to – was a fear of the catastrophic: that, like your ancestors, you might one day have to flee, make a run for it, pack a bag and see if anyone else will take you in. It is not rational. But it lurks.

The elision of anti-Zionism and antisemitism that has taken place since 7 October, though, is real. The surge in antisemitic attacks I find horrifying. Where I live there is an almost daily battle taking place, where members of the Jewish community post on a footbridge the pictures of those men, women and children kidnapped on 7 October. No sooner do they go up than they are ripped down. Calling for loved ones who have been kidnapped to be freed by a group deemed by the UK to be a terrorist organisation does not seem to me a controversial act. Yet everything is now seen in the most simplistic black and white. No need for any shading. For what it's worth, I believe that the only way towards peace in the Middle East is a two-state solution

– the policy of most Western governments. I think Netanyahu has been utterly reckless in supporting the building of illegal settlements in the West Bank – against international law. I think the people keeping his government afloat are reprehensible. And the sooner he faces justice for the corruption charges against him, the better. But what happened on 7 October was wrong. Hamas say they would repeat 7 October again and again until they destroy the state of Israel, and Israelis are going to want to defend themselves. But they will and must be held to account for the way they go about it.

Yet isn't it possible to feel the same anguish for those who've been kidnapped and the families in Israel who've lost loved ones as it is for Palestinian civilians who have been killed in their thousands as a result of the Israeli efforts to destroy Hamas? Can't we call for the release of the hostages as loudly as we call for a ceasefire? Are we incapable of holding two thoughts simultaneously?

It is the same sense of horror I felt at the Islamophobia that swept America after 9/11. The Muslims living in Minnesota or Michigan were no more responsible for Al Qaeda than Muslims are today for Hamas, or Jews are for Netanyahu's government. Yet some on the left appear to live in a nuance-free zone. Israel equals bad. Hamas equals – well, what exactly? Because you don't like the Israeli government (and sign me up here) are you going with an intolerant, Iranian-backed Islamist grouping that stones homosexuals to death and does not believe in women's equality and films on Go-Pro the rape and sexual mutilation of Israelis at a music festival?

Just as disturbing for me are the likes of Tommy Robinson, he of the extreme right English Defence League, turning up to support Israel and the Jewish community. Er, no thank you. In fairness, the bulk of the political class has sought to tread very carefully and thoughtfully on this, and that is to the credit of both Sunak and Starmer. So I don't think the siren voices in the Jewish community are right to catastrophise what might happen next in Britain. But I never thought I would ever see a row of police vans having to be parked outside a synagogue to protect worshippers going to *shul* on the Sabbath because of the potential flashpoint of a pro-Palestinian march passing nearby.

Here's an example of how crazily simplistic the debate has become. On the podcast we had an Israeli government spokesman, Eylon Levy. He and Lewis had been at Oxford together – they were not friends, but acquaintances. Lewis had interviewed him robustly and forensically on the podcast about why Israel wasn't doing more to get aid into Gaza and whether the Israeli Defence Force had committed war crimes. Levy is a smooth talker, if somewhat glib. When it was announced a few months later that Lewis was going to present a new Sunday programme on LBC, Levy tweeted a reply saying 'well done'. On that basis a whole load of people replied that they would and could no longer listen to *The News Agents*. Lewis was accused of being a 'Zionist shill' (an accusation that is absurd if you've ever listened to him) – because, unprompted and uninvited, Levy had commented on his new Sunday show. It's bonkers. And we can do better.

I thought of all this when I read Allison Pearson's column, and her suggestion that the 'aliens' who are taking over Britain think everything is bad about the place. Applying the smallest bit of scrutiny to her claim reveals it to be nonsense. I think Britain is the most wonderful country, and genuinely feel thankful to be living on these islands. And am sure anyone who has fled persecution and oppressive regimes where their lives were in danger would feel the same. Of course that doesn't mean it's nirvana here, but it is one of the great strengths of our liberal democracy that you can point that out, too, and say what you think.

It alarms me when it is suggested that patriotism must take this ostentatious form, and if you don't go along with that then you're not a proper patriot; if you mess with the flag of St George, you are messing with our identity. All of which, dare I say, displays rather a lack of confidence and fragility in what our identity is. Sometimes it feels as though to qualify as a proper 'Brit' you need to love the Last Night of the Proms. Just look at the furore there was when, at the height of Covid, the BBC announced it would play only orchestral versions of 'Rule Britannia' and 'Land of Hope and Glory' because of the health hazards of bringing a mass choir together. Some thought it a pernicious plot by 'woke' lefties at the corporation to deny British heritage because of colonialism and slavery. The right-wing press and government ministers went to town, and predictably the BBC backed down, with a compromise solution found.

The essay written by George Orwell on Englishness (although he readily acknowledges that much of it applies to the other nations within the UK as well) stands the test of time, even though when he was bashing away at his typewriter, German bombs were falling. Of course, the England of which he writes – it was 1941 – was ostensibly white, and had nothing like the number of immigrants that we have today. He asks:

> Are there really such things as nations? Are we not forty-six million individuals, all different? And the diversity of it, the chaos! The clatter of clogs in the Lancashire mill towns, the to-and-fro of the lorries on the Great North Road, the queues outside the Labour Exchanges, the rattle of pin-tables in the Soho pubs, the old maids biking to Holy Communion through the mists of the autumn morning.

Well, for 46 million 80 years ago, read 68 million today – and a much more ethnically and culturally diverse society. Today you don't hear many clogs clattering in Lancashire mill towns; there are some very trendy and expensive Birkenstock clogs in the bars around Shoreditch and Islington, but I don't think that is what Orwell had in mind. And frankly, there aren't a whole lot of Lancashire mills left any more. They've all gone to Vietnam, China and the Philippines. And maybe it's because I'm not an early riser, but I can't remember the last time I saw an old maid biking to Holy Communion. Maybe catching an Uber, but not biking.

Much of what Orwell describes may belong to a Pathé news-reel, with clipped RP accents and 'oh gawd blimey' cockneys, but his comments on nationalism and patriotism still resonate:

> The mass of the people are without military knowledge or tradition, and their attitude towards war is invariably defensive. No politician could rise to power by promising them conquests or military 'glory'... In England all the boasting and flag-wagging, the 'Rule Britannia' stuff, is done by small minorities. The patriotism of the common people is not vocal or even conscious.

It's a shrewd observation. *Telegraph* columnists aside, we are not chest-beating patriots like you find in America with their chants of 'U-S-A, U-S-A'. The national anthem (which doesn't get sung with anything like the regularity it does in the US) does not venerate military encounters, like 'The Star-Spangled Banner', with its celebration of fighting off the British at Baltimore harbour in 1812.

Nor does the British national anthem have anything like the bloodthirstiness of the French 'Marseillaise', which, in musical terms, is an absolute corker of stirring musicality. But look at the lyrics. The plotline is this: against France stands tyranny – and those tyrants have raised their bloody flag; what's more, those foreign soldiers are coming to slit the throats of your sons and your wives. So rally round and get ready to march, in order that you kill them, and once we've done that, well then we will water the fields with their impure blood. If it was a movie, it would get an 18 certificate. All we seem to want in 'God Save the King' is that our sovereign reign over us for a long time, with a tune that doesn't outdo the lyrics in its utter drabness.

This is the song we sing at international sporting fixtures – though obviously, north of the border it will be 'Flower of Scotland' and in Wales it's 'Hen Wlad Fy Nhadau' (The Land of My Fathers). And it's where both the best and the worst of our patriotic tendencies can be on display. In 2010, I was a presenter on the BBC News Channel during the World Cup finals in South Africa. The demarche of that tournament came in Bloemfontein: England v Germany. When I arrived at the fan zone it looked like the England fans were determined to drink the farming town dry. Before the game, the bars were overflowing. The three lions were roaring – drunk. The crowd – nearly all men – were lustily singing the 'Ten German Bombers' song – a couple of fans had brought along Airfix model Spitfires and Messerschmitts. And in the mode of 'Ten Green Bottles', they sang about how the RAF would shoot one down, and then there would be nine German bombers, and so on and so on. There were also chants of 'two world wars and one World Cup, doo dah, doo dah'. Some of the fans had come dressed as crusaders in a historical mash-up.

I don't know whether it is the worst of jingoism – you do find yourself laughing at some of it in all its puffed-up preposterousness. The song celebrating a previous victory over Germany with the refrain 'and even Heskey scored' is funny. But – overall – it is crowds of men, tummies full of beer and heads full of over-inflated ideas about the greatness of England and the England football team. It is Rule Britannia turned up to 11.

Then came 90 minutes of all too predictable pain (and yes, where was VAR when we needed it with the Frank Lampard goal that wasn't given?). Germany prevailed, and the England fans were going home, tails between their legs.

As we left the stadium the mood was desultory, depressed, deflated. The boisterous singing had been replaced by bitter muttering as clumps of fans wended their way back to assorted guest houses and camping sites: 'Why are we such shit?' 'Why do we always flatter to deceive?' 'Why does this always happen?' 'Why can we never rise to the occasion?' These weren't questions. These were statements that sounded like questions. That evening there came a dawning realisation that has stayed with me. Let's call it England football syndrome, but please forgive me if you're Welsh, Northern Irish or Scottish because I am going to generalise it. Why did it have to be so either/or? Why so black or white. It's possible that we are not the world's greatest, but neither are we the worst – nowhere near. Why do politicians persist with these vainglorious statements along the lines of 'the NHS is the envy of the world'. It really isn't any more. 'Our armed forces are the greatest in the world.' I am sure they're really good, but how do you measure that?

A famous line from a former US secretary of state, Dean Acheson, in the 1960s, was that Britain had lost an empire, but not yet found a role. Britain's answer to that identity crisis came when we joined the European Union (or the EEC as it was then) in the 1970s. But post-Brexit that question has returned. Britain has now lost an empire *and* the European Union. It feels there is still that sense of doubt about where we fit in the world.

The metaphor used by the British foreign secretary of the Thatcher and Major years, Douglas Hurd, to describe us came from the boxing ring. Britain punches above its weight, he said. We are a nuclear power, we have a permanent seat on the United Nations Security Council, we are a member of the so-called 'rich-man's club' of the world's wealthiest nations, the G7. We are still members of all those bodies today, but are we still punching above our weight? Undoubtedly, the US found us much more useful when we were inside the EU, so that Britain could act as the bridge – and the translator – of what Brussels is thinking and what the US will tolerate, and vice versa. And similarly, the EU thought it was a grievous loss when Britain left (though now that it has happened, it is hard to see any easy route back – even if that is what the British people decide they want). Maybe now we just punch our weight, or possibly, with our economic position having so deteriorated in the absence of new trade deals, a little below.

Yet politicians continue to mythologise Britain as a 'world-beating' country, the envy of everyone else. And I get it. The politician who is invariably creating the myth is the politician in power – and hoping to reap political reward for it. But why can't we just have a bit of a reality check on where we stand; a more balanced view of ourselves as a nation?

Some former senior mandarins, including a former head of the civil service, Lord Sedwill, wrote a report in 2024 – 'The World in 2040: Renewing the UK's Approach to International Affairs' – about the need not just to modernise how the Foreign Office works, but to reset how Britain sees itself. Their argument is that Britain needs to have a clearer sense of its 'purpose, history, interests and assets as an offshore, mid-sized power'. It 'will not be able to rely on just its traditional alliances with the US and Europe', rather it should form 'pragmatic' new partnerships with other 'middle powers' elsewhere in the world. And if you go to the Foreign Office in King Charles Street, the whole imperial grandeur of the place does seem slightly anachronistic. The charge that the identity of the place is 'elitist and rooted in the past', does not seem unfair.

Their description of Britain today seems accurate: a mid-powered, middleweight country. But that is not how our politicians talk about Britain, nor is it the language of the pompous and puffed-up Pooh-Bahs who write the leader columns in some of our national newspapers. Maybe a touch less hubris and a little more humility wouldn't go amiss. It is still a fantastic country and I wouldn't want to live anywhere else. But to reflect on these things doesn't make you a 'moaning minnie', you're not talking your country down, and it is not unpatriotic.

The undoubted king of performative patriotism is Nigel Farage. And after the disappointments of Brexit, he found he had a new role: to be chief critic of the version of Brexit the Conservative Party had enacted, and in particular the failure to tackle immigration into Britain – both legal and illegal. He even rounded on the Royal National Lifeboat Institution for becoming, in his view, little more than a taxi service for picking up illegal immigrants from sinking rubber inflatable boats in the Channel. As opposed to what? Sailing past them and letting them drown?

UKIP had become the Brexit Party in the run-up to the referendum, and by 2024 was Reform UK, with a determination to make the July general election the immigration election. After some havering and 'would he, wouldn't he', Farage announced that he was taking over the leadership of the party and would run in the Essex seaside town of Clacton, one of the most economically deprived areas of the country.

The day he launched was also the week of the 80th anniversary of D-Day, that remarkable day in June 1944 when British, US and Canadian forces landed on the Normandy beaches. I had gone to Clacton with Emily for the launch. And we watched as he stood on a picnic table, microphone in hand, while a few hundred elderly white men (mostly) cheered him on. He proclaimed that Reform was the only truly patriotic party. That only they could be trusted to stand up for the country. He wanted immigration cut to zero. No more foreigners. Some of the supporters we spoke to wanted to go a good deal further, and would invariably start their sentences with 'I'm not a racist, but ...'

The irony of the Farage pitch to have net migration at zero is that in Clacton it would have catastrophic effects. The health service in the area is heavily dependent on immigrant labour – ditto the care homes. Farmers say their crops would not be picked from the ground without foreign workers – and in the amusement arcades and fish and chip shops near where he was making his speech, what percentage of the workers were what he would call English? I'm going to say it was low. But that's not what his audience wanted to hear.

In his Union Jack-soaked, rabble-rousing address he accused Labour and the Conservatives of allowing D-Day to be forgotten, and said the reason so few young people knew about the sacrifice made by so many of our brave servicemen was down to the lack of patriotism of mainstream politicians.

Like Farage, I agree it is a crying shame when youngsters don't appreciate the sacrifice made by another generation so that we can enjoy the freedoms and liberties we do today. But as he stood on his table by Clacton pier, with the stall selling jellied eels and cockles and whelks next to him doing a brisk trade, he only told part of the story. Sure, those young men were absolute heroes. But why did those men die in their thousands storming the beaches of Normandy? It was to rid the continent of Nazism and its ideology of white supremacy. It was to make sure that there would not be another Holocaust, with its industrialised killing of millions of Jews, Romanies, gay people and communists. It was to destroy the forces of aggressive nationalism. It was to build a new Europe that would learn to live together peacefully after two world wars – through greater economic and political cooperation – an idea that would ultimately morph into the European Union. Funnily enough Farage didn't mention that bit.

The attempts by the far right to appropriate the flag and their self-serving definition of chest-beating patriotism is revolting. I confess, I don't have any Union Jack or St George's Cross socks. Sorry. But that doesn't make me – or you – any less of a patriot.

This book has sought to chart some of the factors that have corroded trust in our politicians and standards in public life, but there are also signs of hope. And perhaps oddly, in the tumultuous, mad political year that marked 2022, it was an occasion of celebration and then mourning: the Queen's Platinum Jubilee in February followed by her death in September. Both events in their deeply different ways seemed to answer the question I posed about the seeming inability of the US to unite on anything. With the death of Britain's longest serving monarch, it really did feel as though the nation came together, perhaps most vividly illustrated by those queues that stretched for mile after mile along the Thames with people prepared to stand out all night to wait to pay their respects at her lying-in-state in Westminster Hall – and they did so with solemnity. There was a glue that still bound us, and it was surprisingly strong – from the different nations and regions in the UK they came, from all ethnic groups and religions, but bound by a common sense of Britishness; and they were from all generations.

Here was a woman whose sense of service and duty had been an example over the decades, spanning the generations. When George Orwell wrote his essay on Englishness during the Blitz, Princess Elizabeth – as she was then – was getting ready to join the Auxiliary Territorial Service, and in so doing became the first female member of the royal family to serve full-time in the armed forces. The Britain of that era could not have been more different from the one she left in 2022. But the monarchy had adapted and changed with the times. Maybe not as fast as some would like, but the royal family gave Britain a soft diplomatic power around the world.

That sense of national unity after the Queen died may be down to the woman rather than the institution of monarchy. She had reigned over us for a very long time, and was a unifying force in the country. We may hate our prime ministers, but there was never that venom towards the non-elected head of state. Elected heads of state are a different matter. I was in Windsor on the day the Queen entertained Donald Trump on his state visit in June 2019. There they both stood on the dais as the anthems rang out. And it occurred to me that barely a second passed without me knowing exactly what Donald Trump thought, thanks to his incessant tweeting. I knew when he was angry, I knew when he was triumphant, I knew when he felt betrayed. For goodness' sake, I knew when I got a tweet at four in the morning what time he'd got up to go for a pee! But the Queen had been on the throne all my life, and I have never known what she thought about anything. What she felt was reserved for her weekly audiences with the 15 British prime ministers of her reign – and they never leaked anything – and her tightest inner circle, who never betrayed her confidence.

The day of King Charles's coronation was a Saturday in May 2023. Before the Queen's death there had been a lot of speculation that the nation might not accept him as the new king and that things might be a little rocky. The messy divorce from Diana, doubts about his suitability. Did we know too much about what he thought about architecture and the environment, in marked contrast to his mother? But on the morning he was crowned King I sat at home and watched the events unfold at Westminster Abbey. And then in the afternoon, I went from watching gold coaches on the Mall to the rather scruffier environs of the Tottenham High Road to watch Spurs play Crystal

Palace. Before kick-off, the 60,000 fans rose as one to sing 'God Save the King'. It was strangely and surprisingly (for me at least) moving. Perhaps the disunity of this nation is much exaggerated.

It is easy, tempting even, to transpose the polarisation so evident in the US onto the UK and think that we are all becoming much the same. Tempting, but it would be wrong. Just go back to the lockdowns over Covid. In the US, a lot of the Republican states were determined to go their own way by not closing schools – or shutting anything for that matter. But in Britain, focus-group work carried out during lockdown showed that far from thinking the government's actions were draconian and illiberal, a strong majority of the public was in favour of the government going further. In hindsight, I suspect many now think that ministers went too far, but it wasn't like that at the time.

In the US there was a clear partisan split on nearly everything to do with Covid – not just on lockdown, but on wearing masks, contact tracing, vaccine roll-out, even whether to take the vaccine. In 2020, the political historian, writer and podcaster Ezra Klein wrote a book called *Why We're Polarized*. Its focus is the US and it talks about the idea that polarisation has created what he calls 'stacked identities'. The pre-eminent research organisation in the US, Pew, puts it like this: 'Divisions between the two parties have intensified over time as various types of identities have become "stacked" on top of people's partisan identities. Race, religion and ideology now align with partisan identity in ways that they often didn't in eras when the two parties were relatively heterogenous coalitions.'

So, in the US, if you believe in relaxing gun laws still further and are anti-abortion and found Covid lockdown measures intolerable and think that climate change is a hoax, you are also likely to be white, rural and Christian – and of course Republican. If you are pro-gay rights, want a clampdown on guns, believe in a woman's right to choose, support widening access to healthcare and worry about global warming, you are likely to be more ethnically diverse, living in a city, you are more likely to be college educated – and a Democrat. The biggest religious grouping in the Democratic Party, according to research, is 'no particular religious affiliation'. Marketeers have found that these stacked identities will even indicate which stores you are likely to go to to do your grocery shopping. If you're a Whole Foods customer, you're a Dem. It didn't used to be like that.

Stacked identities, though, can also mean a more rigid and intolerant worldview, because by questioning one element of that identity you attack all of it. The result of this is that in the US it has made the process of governing almost impossible. The system of checks and balances, the rules on the filibuster and supermajorities mean that to get anything done requires compromise and consensus – and there is not much of that to be found.

There are some of these forces at play in Britain, and they were glaringly evident over Brexit, but as I settle in back home, I'm coming to realise that that was a particular moment in history, a single issue. Abortion rights is not a live rail in British politics in the way that it is in the US. Covid didn't divide Britain along party lines. No one wants guns in the UK, and there is a broad consensus on the need to tackle climate change. Religiosity is nothing like as important a badge of identity as it is in the States. Here if you talk about God and your relationship with the Bible, you're seen as a crank; in the US if you *don't* do that you're seen as unelectable.

There is a decency still in British politics that cuts across party lines and the whole idea of a stacked identity. Take the slightly odd proposal from Rishi Sunak on banning smoking. As a public health measure, it is highly significant and has been welcomed overwhelmingly by health professionals. The reason I say it is odd is the way it was drawn. If you were born on 31 December 2008, you will be able to buy as many cigarettes as you like for the rest of your life. If you were born a day later, you will never be able to buy a cigarette legally. Leave aside questions about implementation and how it will work practically. The point is that this was introduced into the Commons on a free vote, and although a sizeable chunk of the Conservative Party didn't back the move because it offended their libertarian beliefs, MPs from all parties supported the proposal by 383 votes to 67.

There is no way a Republican speaker of the House of Representatives would have ever dared introduce such a measure;

there would be a total mutiny from the party caucus. It would have brought condemnation from Fox News and conservative talk show hosts would have got very hot under the collar – and it would have enraged the Republican base. The organisation More in Common does polling to examine how divided different societies are around the world. On the phased smoking ban in the UK it found that around two-thirds of voters supported it, but that figure rose to 71 per cent among Tory supporters.

More in Common's UK director, Luke Tryl, says that in Britain there is still a deeply compassionate electorate and that those he brings together in focus groups are repulsed by some of the cruelty shown by attention-seeking politicians. On our podcast he drew attention to two comments in particular – first Suella Braverman – when she was still home secretary – saying that homelessness was a 'lifestyle choice', and then Lee Anderson – again when he was a Conservative MP – claiming that nurses had no need to go to food banks and should be able to cook a meal for 30 pence. 'It's not just that people say they disapprove of these comments,' says Tryl, 'it's that they react quite viscerally. It would be very hard to fake people's anger when, for instance, they hear comments that nurses shouldn't need to use food banks, or homelessness being a choice or criminalising people who give out tents to homeless people.'

There is another phrase that More in Common uses to describe British voters, and that is 'wonderfully inconsistent' – not only a guardrail against polarisation, but a description that heightens my pride to be British. It speaks of pragmatism, fair-mindedness and openness.

But those British guardrails against polarisation face endless new challenges, and laws are not keeping pace with technological change. Many will bring huge pluses to the way we live our lives, but there will be dangers too. In March 2024 I attended a conference in Montana with some of the most brilliant brains in AI, and while it is possible the new technology is going to lead to amazing breakthroughs in medical treatment with its ability to analyse big data, there are going to be some worrying consequences too – and the pace of change is both electric and terrifying. The ability to generate deep fakes in seconds and what that could do to the way elections are fought should concern everyone. If you are listening to this as an audio book, I promise this is my own voice, and it has taken three days to record. But in very few months, AI will listen to and learn all the idiosyncrasies of my voice, and be able to reproduce it exactly. In a second. So feed the words in, and instantly will be the Jon Sopel audio book. This is foothills stuff.

While this technology is galloping at a phenomenal pace, the moral debate about the rights and wrongs of generative AI and machine learning is becoming a small dot in the rear-view mirror. And the regulation is even further back down the road. Some of the most innovative minds in artificial intelligence, like Sam Altman from OpenAI, are considering the wider philosophical questions, but a lot of the investors who are piling into this space are – understandably – more interested in the return on investment than gnarly ethics questions. It really is the next frontier that is going to affect us all in different ways, some of which can be foreseen, others that can't even be imagined.

Listen to the military talk about the possibilities of AI, and it can get dark very quickly. We know now that China and Russia have developed hypersonic weapons. There will be no time to go up the human chain of command to get a decision on what to do, whether to shoot them down, because these weapons are moving so fast. So realistically, only AI will be able to decide what the military response should be. That raises profound questions of accountability. We are not there, but it is not that far away.

A more prosaic example of this new frontier, but one that is a taste of things to come, came with an audio recording, purportedly showing the mayor of London, Sadiq Khan, saying some pretty incendiary things about Remembrance Day, the most solemn day in Britain's calendar, and the rights of pro-Palestinians to march near the Cenotaph. The audio quality is not great, but it unmistakably sounds like his voice. It has the feel – deliberately I suspect – of a covert recording. And this came at a time of heightened emotion with the events in Gaza, post 7 October, stirring strong emotions and dividing opinion bitterly.

The clip used artificial intelligence to replicate Khan's voice uttering words scripted by the faker. He's heard to disparage Remembrance weekend – using an expletive – and says the pro-Palestinian marches planned for the same day should take precedence. And then you hear London's first Muslim mayor apparently saying: 'I control the Met Police, they will do as the mayor of London tells them.'

It was all baloney, and with the right AI tools would have taken seconds to confect. But the effects could have been devastating. It went hurtling round the internet, endlessly amplified by Khan's detractors – and he does attract a huge amount of venom on the far right – memorably and disgracefully encouraged by Donald Trump when he visited London while still president. Khan acknowledged that the clip really did sound like him, and the police were concerned that this could cause serious disorder. Khan said, 'The timing couldn't have been better if you're seeking to sow disharmony and cause problems.' It couldn't and it did.

The old-fashioned 'rebuttal units', which political parties used to rely on during general elections, seem almost quaintly anachronistic. 'The press release issued by the Labour Party is misleading because ...' That is not going to cut it today. Even the social media companies are struggling to keep up, despite employing tens of thousands of content moderators around the world to try – probably vainly – to monitor what is being uploaded. The velocity with which this stuff will travel will be like nothing we have seen before. And it is not clear to me how you erect safeguards to prevent it happening. There are authoritarian foreign states in whose interest it is to undermine the stability of the liberal democracies. And let's face it, it's much easier to upend an open society with free speech and few if any controls of the media than vice versa. Oh, to be a dictator and not have to worry about the inconvenience of election cycles. But there are activists and 'dark ops' people who work on the fringes of politics to stir trouble or do down an opponent. Keeping a track on this stuff is going to be nigh on impossible.

This is exactly where conventional media can step in to fill the void, but here too danger lurks. Simon Kuper in the *Financial Times* argues that we are coming to the end of the mass-media age, where news consumption is in steep, perhaps irreversible decline, with the internet's near destruction of conventional media – in other words newspapers, radio and television. He writes: 'The cliché used to be that people had moved to social media for news. Well, they have moved to social media, but increasingly not for news. After all, why let journalists you don't trust tell you about politicians you don't trust?'

But I am not buying that. It is undeniably true that newspaper sales are in steep decline, and there are challenges with radio and television audiences as they face competition from streaming services. The death of local newspapers is a real worry for our democracy. Who is going to scrutinise important planning decisions about where factories or incinerators get built? Where will the public pressure come from without a strong local media voice? Who's going to keep the local councillors on the straight and narrow? But big TV news bulletins still attract significant audiences, as do current affairs programmes on outlets like Radio 4. The newspapers, through a variety of means, have found ways to remain profitable and relevant online; the growth of new media – like our daily podcast – means we are attracting an audience very different – and much younger – in its demographic from conventional news programming. I was slightly taken aback when I went into a coffee shop in Covent Garden and the heavily tattooed young American barista said he recognised me from watching our video clips on TikTok. I just don't think it is true to say that the population has tuned out.

I've been in the business for 40 years as a hack, a scribbler, a newsman, a member of the fourth estate. When I went into the business, I did so because I thought it sounded like an interesting job. I was a bit of a gossip so liked being able to say to friends, 'You'll never guess what …' I liked the business of reporting a story in a hopefully engaging and catchy way. The first time I heard on the radio: 'Jon Sopel has the details', my little chest puffed out a bit. And then when I started to appear on TV, I thought I had made it. I liked politics and seeking to get under the skin of why decisions get made and the battles that needed to be fought to get these policies over the line.

But in all this I never thought to myself: I am play-ing an important part in upholding democracy. That would have seemed ludicrously self-important. When I started, the old-fashioned picture of the British hack was of the gin-soaked reporter, the acrid smell of cigarette smoke on their clothes, filing copy from a telephone box, slightly shabby and down at heel, working their contacts to get a scoop, in an endless battle with the bastards on the newsdesk over how long they can have for their piece. Nowadays there's less gin, fewer cigarettes and the race to the phone box after a court case or council meeting has gone – but the rest of it remains.

But maybe – after eight years in the US, and coming back to the strangeland UK that I am still familiarising myself with – I think that journalists should take themselves and their profession more seriously. I am not suggesting that we think of ourselves as the fourth emergency service. ('This is 999 – how can I direct your call?' 'Journalist! I need a journalist!') Of course we are not that. But in this new age of falsehood, disinformation, misinformation, deep fakes and lies, we have a herculean job ahead of us – and that is ensuring there is good, trustworthy information out there.

That means it is incumbent on the politicians not to trample over the rule book, as they have done. It means showing leadership and honesty about the scale of the problems we face, not spouting populist nonsense about how easy everything will be if only you give me your vote. It means not turning every difficult policy area into a wedge issue – there's been quite enough of that in the US. Too often it feels as though politicians aren't trying to convince people of the rightness of their argument, but looking at ways to vilify those who disagree with them – why try to unite people when it is so much easier to divide? Culture wars are corrosive.

That might in turn lead to voters feeling a bit more trust towards our elected politicians, with all their faults. Maybe we'll turn away from the far-fetched and outlandish conspiracy theories – and start to believe in the glories of the cock-up instead. Maybe we'll find ourselves able to listen to a variety of different arguments and not just live in our reassuringly echoey silo. Maybe we will come to realise that the battles fought out on social media with blood and guts spilling everywhere are not the real world, nor where most of the population lives.

If this sounds idealistic and naïve, sorry. But 6 January 2021 in Washington, DC, brought home to me just how high the stakes are. In Moscow and Beijing, they are rubbing their hands at what they see as the inevitable decline and what will be the ultimate fall of Western liberal democracy. Authoritarianism will prevail. Perhaps Britain's best political writer is the novelist Robert Harris. He started life like me at the BBC and working at Westminster – although he went on to much better things. His Cicero trilogy is instructive. Harris says:

> The thing that destroyed the Roman republic was the oligarchs whipping up the masses against an elite who had previously sat in control. You may say that's a good thing, but the lesson from the Roman republic is that you can destroy democracy and then it vanishes from the earth for 1,000 years or so.

My grandparents came to this country in the nineteenth century, fleeing for their lives. I feel part of a golden generation that has not known war, where I have had all the benefits of Britain's social contract – of decent schools, a health system free at the point of use for all. There are free and fair elections with power passing peacefully from one party to another, where there is a legal system with due process and the fair administration of justice. And a country where we can say what we think with a free press and impartial media. We mustn't take it for granted though. In the great sweep of history, liberal democracy is still an infant. It is not the norm. We need to nurture what we have so it can be passed on to the next generation. We might not be the greatest nation on earth, But Britain is still pretty damned good.

• • •

On 22 May 2024, just as I was finishing the edit of this book, Rishi Sunak called a general election. As it happens, I was in Prague that day celebrating my birthday with a lousy journalist's unerring sense of being in the wrong place at the wrong time. Prague is an inspirational sort of city though, and has endured many of its own Strangelands: the Prague Spring of 1968 before the tanks of the Soviet Red Army rolled in and suppressed the uprising, and then in 1989, the heady events that led up to the Velvet Revolution, which marked the end of communist rule in Czechoslovakia and the peaceful transformation to democracy. During the latter, the most popular pamphlet – or *samizdat* – from the dissidents was called 'The Eight Rules of Dialogue', which called for truth, fairness, understanding and empathy, informed and respectful discussion and an open mind. As I stood on the Charles Bridge looking at the stream of WhatsApp messages from my colleagues at *The News Agents* about the impending election announcement, I thought there would be little of that on show in the forthcoming weeks of campaigning. How weird that that style of dialogue helped bring a peaceful end to the Soviet Union, but just seems anachronistic and old-fashioned today.

There was another thought too. For all the shortcomings of Sir Keir Starmer (dull, socially a bit awkward, cautious) and Rishi Sunak (brittle, thin-skinned, unrelatable), neither man could be described as a danger to democracy; neither is an out-and-out populist wanting to take a wrecking ball to the pillars of our government, and both are institutionalists with respect for parliament and the rule of law. Both seem technocratic – one more comfortable with a spreadsheet, the other with a law book; in ideological terms both travel relatively light. Could a new Labour government under Starmer bring in a new era of relative stability?

Maybe so, but we have been here before, albeit not on this side of the Atlantic. After Joe Biden's inauguration, only weeks after the insurrection at the Capitol, the new president spoke optimistically about bringing the nation together, of binding the wounds, of reaching across the aisle, of governing in the interests of all the country. With Donald Trump licking his wounds in Mar-a-Lago, we thought politics would return to normal. After four years of heavy metal, power chords, crashing cymbals and a throbbing bassline at volume 10, the radio would be turned to easy listening, smooooooth FM at volume 4. Politics could become background noise in our lives again.

But it hasn't turned out like that, has it? The polarisation, the divisions, the name calling, the angry tribes yelling and shouting at each other have not subsided. The culture warriors are still at each other's throats. This is not because Biden didn't try; he did. But it takes more than one man. There are structural drivers to this – some economic, some social.

Those forces of division in the US are now to be found here too. The Foxification of the UK media looks set to persist, conspiracy theories continue to be the go-to explanation for anything and everything, the culture wars are not dying down. Social media and the growth of AI is only intensifying these tendencies. If anything, everyone seems angrier. Now even genteel book festivals are held to ransom by anonymous activists who say they will disrupt and go after authors unless they denounce this or that. There seems no willingness to engage in debate, or to say that the person you are talking to might have a point. Russia and China – the axis of autocracy – are revelling in the West's discord and disharmony. And certain sections of the left and the right in British politics have become the useful idiots of dictators who want our democratic foundations to crumble.

The general election delivered a landslide victory to Sir Keir Starmer. For the Conservatives it was their worst election performance ever. The campaign was rough, but in marked contrast to what happened in the US in 2020, there was a peaceful transfer of power with a gracious Rishi Sunak accepting defeat, apologising for his shortcomings, taking responsibility and wishing Starmer the best. His farewell comments in Downing Street were pitch perfect and spirit-lifting after the 14 years that had passed. It was in the finest traditions of Britain's parliamentary democracy. Starmer was similarly serious-minded about his victory. It was time to put country first, not party. It was about rebuilding trust and confidence in our institutions. So far so good.

But this was an election that also underlined the extreme volatility and instability in Britain. Yes, Labour won big – but on a very low share of the vote. In constituencies with large Muslim populations it haemorrhaged support and lost seats to independent candidates, furious over Labour's support for Israel. The Greens were also beneficiaries of antipathy to Labour. What happened on 4 July was a loveless landslide, born more of fury felt towards the Conservatives than affectionate embrace of the Starmer project. And Reform, the political party owned (and I use the word in its literal sense) by Nigel Farage, now has five members of parliament, including Farage himself. Right-wing anti-immigrant English nationalism now has a voice in Westminster. The party picked up 4 million votes, came second in scores of constituencies and, but for the vagaries of our first-past-the-post voting system, could legitimately argue it should have far, far more. In 2024, these votes helped destroy the Conservatives in the so-called 'red wall' seats. But Starmer will be all too keenly aware that in five years' time it could be Labour constituencies that are vulnerable to the populist insurgency. Tackling illegal immigration, and making the argument for managed, highly controlled legal migration, has never been more urgent.

British political stability has since universal suffrage rested on a two-party system buttressed by a voting system that makes it difficult for others to make progress. But in 2024 the two main parties of Labour and the Conservatives scored their lowest share of the popular vote ever. The Liberal Democrats won 72 constituencies, the highest for a third party since 1923. Voter turnout was the lowest in 20 years. None of this speaks of huge voter satisfaction with the two-party status quo. None of this speaks of solidity going forward.

While the British general election was unfolding, the French president, Emmanuel Macron, shocked his country – and the rest of Europe – by calling a snap parliamentary election, after France's anti-immigrant, right-wing populist grouping, the Rassemblement National (RN), had dominated in the recent European Parliament elections. The party is the son of the Front National and is run by Marine le Pen, the daughter of its founder Jean-Marie, whose first electoral success I covered back in 2002 as Paris correspondent. At the end of June 2024, I was back in Paris, taking a break from our election campaign, to report again on the relentless rise of the far right in France, this time on the cusp of taking power for the first time since the Nazi-supporting Vichy government of World War Two. The unthinkable in French politics has become very much thinkable. The RN may not have achieved control of the National Assembly, but it is already planning for the 2027 presidential election. This has all happened in a little over two decades; two decades where the parties of the political mainstream have failed to tackle the drivers of this populism – immigration, crime, the cost of living – and that profound sense of alienation from the elites who run the country. Who is to say the same couldn't happen in Britain? You can be sure of one thing: Nigel Farage has been watching closely what's been happening in France and using it as a template of how Reform can grow to be a similar force in Britain.

It would be lovely to posit that, with a new government in place, our strange land is set to become normal again; that the past few years would be merely an aberrant blip in our national story of moderation. But the populist right is alive and well in Britain, with the threat that it poses to the very existence of the Conservative Party – and, who knows, maybe in a few years to Labour too. With Sir Keir Starmer installed in Downing Street, all may look reassuringly dull, but the volatility across the entire political landscape is real. I dream of a 'normal land'. But we're not there. Not even close.

ACKNOWLEDGEMENTS

I had been trying to write another book, and felt – well – rather constipated. Maybe writer's block is a more elegant way of phrasing it. We were with the grandchildren in Australia, and I had set myself some targets for writing the tome that I was struggling with – and every time I sat down and opened my laptop, I found an excuse to do something else. Anything else, in fact.

That led me to call my literary agent, Rory Scarfe, to alert him and the publisher that I was never going to meet the publication deadline. Rory and I fell into conversation, and he was asking about how I had adjusted to being back from America, and I think I might have started ranting. It was one of those 'and another thing …' conversations. At which point, he cut me short and said, 'That's your next book.'

He then called my brilliant (and long-suffering) publisher Albert DePetrillo who was wonderfully encouraging. He probably calculated that one book is probably better than no book. But as an American who has lived for a long time in the UK, he has been a perfect sounding board in this project. And I have had nothing but professionalism, encouragement and infective enthusiasm from the team at Ebury – yes, Laura, Anna, Molly, Shammah, I'm talking about you.

I also want to thank the small, perfectly formed team at *The News Agents*, who are brilliant even though they are appallingly rude to me with their malicious falsehood that I spend all my time on holiday. I've been writing a book, for the record. Maitlis, you are brilliant. Lewis Goodall, thank you for reading the manuscript and making me feel like you were the teacher and I was a slightly wayward pupil. Your insights – as always – were brilliant. Thank you. And thank you to all the team at *The News Agents* for this amazing, harum-scarum ride.

The judgements that I reach, though, in this book are my own. And unlike my previous books from when I was in the US, I have not had to have the BBC rat-catcher check the manuscript for anything that might cause problems – whether that is a good thing, I will leave for you to judge.

And finally, I want to thank Linda, Max and Anna for their unflagging love and support – and, yes, occasional criticism, designed to keep feet firmly on the ground. I couldn't do any of this without you.

Jon

Braemar, Scotland

INDEX

ABOUT THE AUTHOR

Jon Sopel was the BBC's North America Editor for eight years, before launching *The News Agents* podcast with Emily Maitlis and Lewis Goodall in August 2022. During his time at the BBC, he covered the 2016 and 2020 elections and Trump's White House first-hand, reporting for the BBC across TV, radio and online.

He is the author of *If Only They Didn't Speak English: Notes from Trump's America*, *A Year at the Circus: Inside Trump's White House* and *UnPresidented: Politics, Pandemics and the Race that Trumped All Others*.